Battles
In Britain
and their political background
Volume 1
1066-1547

Battles In Britain

and their political background

Volume 1

1066-1547

William Seymour

Drawings and Battle Plans by W. F. N. Watson

HIPPOCRENE
BOOKS, INC.

By the same author
ORDEAL BY AMBITION
An English family
in the shadow
of
the Tudors

Endpapers: Assault on a castle in 15th century, source unknown

Illustration on page 2: Bayeux Tapestry, William is told that Harold is near

To Jenny
Whose map-reading passeth all understanding

Copyright © 1975 William Seymour and Sidgwick & Jackson Limited

ALL RIGHTS RESERVED

HIPPOCRENE BOOKS, INC.
171, Madison Avenue   New York, N.Y. 10016

ISBN 0-88254-370-9

Library of Congress Catalogue
Card Number 75-34555

Printed in Belgium

Contents

TABLE OF BATTLES BY COUNTIES

England			*Chapter*
Gloucestershire	Tewkesbury	1471	*11*
Hertfordshire	Second Battle of St Albans	1461	*8*
	Barnet	1471	*10*
Leicestershire	Bosworth	1485	*12*
Northumberland	Flodden	1513	*13*
Sussex	Hastings	1066	*2*
	Lewes	1264	*3*
Herefordshire and Worcestershire	Evesham	1265	*4*
North Yorkshire	Fulford	1066	*1*
	Stamford Bridge	1066	*1*
	Towton	1461	*9*
Scotland			
Midlothian	Pinkie Cleuch	1547	*14*
Stirlingshire	Stirling Bridge	1297	*5*
	Falkirk	1298	*5*
	Bannockburn	1314	*6*

Preface

To cover adequately the more important British battles in one volume requires a book that would be too large for convenience, and so it has been decided to produce this work in two volumes. The division falls conveniently after the battle of Pinkie Cleuch (1547), for there was a gap of almost 100 years before any further major fighting took place in Britain, and by that time there had been considerable weapon development. The second volume will cover battles from the Civil War to Culloden.

Several useful books have been written about British battles, but very few of them attempt to give the reader in any detail the reasons why the battles were fought, what motivated the principal protagonists and what right, if any, they had in taking up arms. I have devoted a good deal of space in trying to present the background to the battles without, I hope, obscuring the main purpose of the book, which is the reconstruction of the actual fights. Similarly, although any book on battles must inevitably be chiefly concerned with a description of the fighting and some account of strategy, tactics and military principles, whenever possible I have endeavoured to bring out the human side and give thumb-nail character sketches of the commanders.

No apology is made for the frequent reminder that our knowledge of many of the battles is far from precise. Half the enjoyment of visiting the battlefields and walking the actual site of conflict is to decide for ourselves, with what information is available, just how it happened, and in some cases exactly where. It would be very wrong to be dogmatic about events that took place up to a thousand years ago; even where we have reliable eye-witness accounts we cannot be certain that facts and information that have not come down to us over the centuries may have made decisions we now think should have been taken appear hazardous, if not impossible, to the commanders at the time. It is all too easy to pass judgement in the certain knowledge of what subsequently occurred, but a more difficult task, although an intriguing one, is to try to understand the problems as they presented themselves to the commanders at the time.

In the 700 years of military history covered by the two volumes of this book there were many changes in weapons and tactics, but all the battles were fought by men like ourselves, who experienced the same emotions of fear, boredom, weariness, despair (and sometimes defiance) in defeat and exhilaration in victory, for basically the deep springs of human action have remained fairly constant down the ages. There are few, if any, new facts to be found in these chapters; the ground has been well covered before and the contemporary and near-contemporary accounts of each battle carefully sifted and narrated. My object has been to retell them in a straightforward and I hope easily understandable manner, and wherever the facts are open to more than one interpretation, or the exact site of any battle cannot be certainly determined, I have tried to piece together the mosaic of these long-forgotten fights in a way that may stimulate the reader to further personal investigation. I have also avoided the temptation to forecast the possible outcome of any battle had the losing side been the victors; it is a fascinating, but usually fruitless, undertaking for which—perhaps fortunately—there was no space.

It only remains for me to offer my thanks to those who have helped me with advice, encouragement, hospitality and, in some cases, hard work in the preparation of this book. It is not possible to mention all of these kind people individually, but to some I owe a special debt of gratitude. First to my secretary, Miss M. H. L. Taylor, who has not only typed and re-typed the manuscript many times, but has undertaken part of the research and made many useful suggestions. Colonel W. F. N. Watson has embellished the book with his superb illustrations, helped me in the annotation of the photographs and master-minded the weapons development table; the battle maps that he has drawn were based on the appropriate Ordnance Survey sheets, by permission of the Director of Ordnance Survey.

Many people have read through parts of the manuscript and given me the benefit of their advice, and of these I should particularly mention Mr Ivan Roe, Doctor David Cox, Mr G. C. Baugh, Mr Alan Young and Mr Michael Lynch. The staffs of the London Library and the Dorset County Library have taken enormous trouble to produce books and information.

During my visit to St Albans Miss Muriel Wilson and Miss Wells, of the City of St Albans Public Library, gave me great assistance. To all of these I am most grateful. Finally, I am indebted to William Armstrong of Sidgwick & Jackson for his patience, understanding and advice.

William Seymour
Falconer's House
Crichel
Wimborne
Dorset.

CHAPTER 1

Norsemen

Fulford and Stamford Bridge

20 September 1066 and 25 September 1066

Stamford Bridge is eight miles east of York on the A 166. In 1066 the actual bridge was some 400 yards upstream from the present one and about twenty yards below the modern cut in the river. Part of the site is now occupied by caravans, and on the left (or eastern) bank the ground rises fairly steeply to Danes Well garage. The main fight took place just south of the A 166 on what is now private property. The farm is called Battle Flats Farm.

King Edward the Confessor died on 5 January 1066, and almost immediately the Witan, or Great Council, elected Harold God-winson, Earl of Wessex, to be their king. Harold ascended the throne uneasily: he had scarcely a drop of royal blood in his veins; the Earls of Mercia and Northumbria, Edwin and Morcar, had no love for him; and there were two foreign claimants to the throne who had been anxiously watching and waiting. Earls Edwin and Morcar, who were brothers, do not appear to have opposed Harold's election, but he had to make a journey north before Northumbria would give him her allegiance. By marrying the Earl's sister Aldyth Harold gained the acceptance of these powerful men and their thanes, but on account of the long enmity between his house and theirs he could never be entirely confident of their loyalty.

When the Anglo-Danish King Hardicanute died in 1042 the Danish male line came to an end, and Magnus King of Norway laid claim to the English and Danish thrones under an agreement made between him and Hardicanute. He invaded Denmark, and had he not died in 1047 would almost certainly have attempted to wrest the English crown by force from Edward the Confessor. Magnus's successor, King Harald Hardrada, was a man in every way built upon a scale larger than the usual run; six feet six inches tall with a massive frame, he was reckoned the greatest captain of his day; he had pursued glory and risked every hazard from his own shores to the gates of Constantinople. In 1066 this fearsome Norseman was ready to revive Magnus's claim to the English throne. The fact that

9

that claim was flimsy in the extreme mattered little, for he saw the possibility of England once more entering upon a period of profound decline, such as had many times before opened the floodgates to a Viking invasion. He was confident that as in the past the islanders would be unable to withstand the foray.

Duke William of Normandy's claim to the English throne had slightly more substance than Hardrada's. Through his great-aunt Emma, who married first the disastrous Ethelred the Redeless and then the truly splendid Canute, he was first cousin once removed to Edward the Confessor. There is also good reason to believe that Edward, who had spent some years in exile in Normandy and was very pro-Norman, had, as long ago as 1051, promised William the succession – although he had no right to promise the crown of England to anyone. Moreover, quite recently, when Harold had been shipwrecked on the French coast, William had rescued him from the unscrupulous clutches of the Count of Ponthieu who held him captive, and, after treating him with the utmost respect and favour as an honoured guest and comrade in arms, had induced him to swear an oath that he would not oppose William's accession to the English throne. In those days an oath was a much more binding affair than it later became, and for good measure William concealed some holy relics beneath the cloth covering the table when William's half-brother, Bishop Odo of Bayeux, administered the oath.

This artifice was to strengthen William's cause in Rome, for, the sanctity of the oath apart, Harold was already at a grave disadvantage with the papacy. Ever since Robert of Jumièges had been unlawfully replaced in the see of Canterbury by Archbishop Stigand, the Roman curia had regarded the church in England with considerable displeasure if not hostility. Furthermore, the new pope, Alexander II, had been elected with Norman support, and so William had little difficulty in ensuring that when he marched he did so with the Holy Father's blessing and under the papal banner.

So much then for the two iron-willed foreign princes who were making ready with ruthless determination to fight for England. What of the Saxon earl, recently elected king, who was preparing to defend his kingdom against this two-pronged threat?

In the time of Edward the Confessor there were three great earldoms, Wessex, Mercia and Northumbria. Godwin Earl of Wessex had risen to prominence through the favour of Canute, whose cousin he had married, and during Edward's reign he became the most powerful man in the land – not excluding the king who under pressure had married his daughter. Godwin's eldest son Sweyn, an unpleasant man, died on a pilgrimage to the Holy

Coins: 1: Edward the Confessor,
2: Harold II, 3: William I, at the
British Museum. Below: Canute
and Edmund Ironside in equal
combat, from Chronica Majora I
by Matthew Paris, at Corpus
Christi College, Cambridge

Land, and so when the Earl died in 1053 he was succeeded in the earldom by his second son Harold – a golden youth of much promise and in high favour with the King.

Edward the Confessor was a good and pious man, but a weak, vacillating king; he would have been better suited to a monastery than a palace. Shortly after promising the throne to William he was forced to dismiss many of the Norman faction from his court, and in 1054 he seems to have had a change of heart. He sent for Edmund Ironside's son, Edward the Atheling, who had been in exile in Hungary and had married the King of Hungary's daughter. Edward arrived in England, but died before he reached the court – some said in mysterious circumstances – leaving a young boy, his son Edgar, as the only surviving member of the ancient royal house. Earl Harold was the most powerful man at court, and probably persuaded the dying King Edward to promise him the crown. In any event the Witan was not prepared to entrust the kingdom at this time to a boy, and Harold met with little opposition. He was certainly the best man England could have found. Nevertheless, it was a coup d'état; he had seized the throne with speed and resolution not only from the two foreigners who thought it belonged to them but also from the legitimate royal line of England. This was an added burden amongst the immense difficulties and pressures that beset the newly elected warrior king.

Harold's troublesome younger brother Tostig had been banished from the earldom of Northumbria, and it was he who opened the fight against Harold. He had taken refuge with his wife's half-brother, Count Baldwin of Flanders (whose daughter Matilda married William), and in May 1066 he set sail from the French coast, certainly with William's blessing if not with Norman aid. His attempt at invasion was a hopeless failure: having raided the Isle of Wight and briefly occupied Sandwich, his force was cut to pieces in Lincolnshire by Edwin of Mercia and he sailed on with his few remaining ships to join the King of Scotland, and from Scotland he promptly got in touch with Harald Hardrada.

Harold did not need his brother's traitorous actions to realize that he would soon be called upon to face sterner opposition; but he realized the vulnerability of the southern coast and accordingly moved down to the Isle of Wight to supervise defence preparations. He was not unaware of Harald Hardrada's ambitions, but he may have thought that the threat from Normandy was greater, or perhaps more imminent; he therefore mustered all his ships and concentrated his military strength in the south. Harold's corps d'élite were known as house-carls; they were of Danish origin, having been raised by Canute as a royal bodyguard. Armed principally with shields and long double-handed battle-axes they were perhaps the finest infantry in Europe at that time; they were in fact mounted infantry capable of covering great distances quickly on their shaggy ponies, but they invariably dismounted to fight.

The house-carls were the kernel of Harold's army, but they were a comparatively small force of around 3,000 men, and for weight of numbers he depended on the fyrd. This was a levy of free men raised from each hundred* and liable to serve for a period of two months annually. During that time they were paid and provisioned by the shires, but if their period of service had to be extended (and this was seldom practicable) they became a charge on the state. It was possible to assemble about 12,000 of these irregulars at any one time, and although they are sometimes described as nothing better than an ill disciplined rabble this is not true. Certainly they carried a curious assortment of weapons, ranging from spears, axes, stone slings and javelins to scythes and even pitchforks, but many of them were well led by their thanes and capable of giving an excellent account of themselves. A part of this force could be transported on ponies. The English army was without cavalry, and virtually without archers.

Harold must have called out the southern fyrd immediately after Tostig's attempted invasion, and retained them and his fleet under arms for most of the summer; but by the first week in September their rations and pay were running out and being mostly subsistence farmers they were sorely needed on their own holdings. And so on about 8 September Harold was forced to disband his levies and sail his fleet back to London. It was an unavoidable but desperate situation, for he knew very well that William was by now ready and only awaiting a favourable wind.

However, the first camp fires of an invading army were to be seen not in the south, as Harold had expected, but in Yorkshire. The King had not been back in his capital more than a few days when he learned that Harald Hardrada and the egregious Tostig had sailed up the Ouse and disembarked at Riccall. Harald Hardrada, taking advantage of the north wind that had kept William in harbour, had sailed via the Orkneys – then a part of the Norseman's dominion – where his liegemen the Orkney earls had ships and men to join him. Tostig may have sailed with Hardrada from Norway, or more likely met him at some point off the Northumbrian coast,

*At this time the English shire was divided into districts known as hundreds (varying in size) for fiscal and administrative purposes.

and together they proceeded south sacking Scarborough and penetrating Yorkshire from the mouth of the Humber. Accounts vary as to the numbers of the combined fleet, but certainly no fewer than 200 longships sailed up the Ouse. These open boats, averaging about seventy-five feet in length and seventeen feet in beam, were rowed by thirty men. They could sail far up rivers on account of their shallow draught, and their usual complement was around sixty men. It seems reasonable to suppose, therefore, that this armada brought rather more than 10,000 fighting Norsemen to plunder and pillage the northern part of the kingdom. Even with William only waiting for a wind, Harold could scarcely afford to disregard so formidable a host.

Northumbria and Mercia between them comprised the whole of the north and Midlands; their earls, Morcar and Edwin respectively, were able to command a very considerable force. They had prudently anchored their small fleet at Tadcaster, which probably determined the Norsemen to disembark at Riccall: if they had sailed beyond the junction of the rivers Ouse and Wharfe the English fleet might have been able to come between them and the sea. Leaving perhaps as much as a third of his men with the longships, Harald Hardrada advanced on York, some ten miles to the north. This is a part of Yorkshire that is very flat, and although the

Norse longships

fields are now well drained and neatly cultivated 900 years ago this whole area was wet and swampy, even after a dry summer. There was also at this time a large water-filled ditch to the east of the road.

The Earls could not have known whether Harold would march to their aid; indeed, they may have considered this unlikely in view of the Norman threat. They decided not to wait behind the inadequate defences of York, and on 20 September they advanced and gave battle. The two armies met at Fulford, now a suburb of York but then an open and very wet field. The battle, which lasted for most of the day, was a hard slogging match. At first the English gained considerable success on their left flank, but Harald Hardrada was an experienced commander quite capable of delivering a decisive blow at the right moment. When the English army in the centre and left were most hotly engaged he swung his left away from the river and before long had rolled his enemy into the ditch, slaughtering many and drowning even more. The Earls' army was cut to pieces, and the conqueror's standard, the famous *Landwaster*, fluttered triumphant over a field strewn with the bodies of fighting men that England could ill afford to lose.

Fulford is often dismissed as a minor affair, but it was a battle of great importance. Had Harold been able to communicate with the Earls in time, and instruct them to remain upon the defensive until he could arrive, this large northern army would not have been decimated and the combined force available to oppose William might quite likely have thrust the Norman invasion back into the sea. Neither Edwin nor Morcar took any part in the Battle of Hastings, and there is no evidence that this was for any reason other than that they could not assemble fresh levies and reach the rendezvous in time.

For some reason, perhaps because Tostig wished to preserve the city, the victorious Norsemen did not march on York. Instead they fell back on their ships and entered into negotiations with the vanquished for the surrender of the city and delivery of hostages. We do not know for certain what occurred, but it seems that the people of York, and even the Earls, may have agreed to terms that were both humiliating and treacherous. No satisfactory reason has been put forward for the selection of the site for the reception of the hostages. Stamford Bridge is eight miles east of York and all of twelve miles from the Norsemen's base camp at Riccall; it is a place where four Roman roads met at a crossing of the Derwent, and one of these led direct to the coast. The royal palace of Aldby was nearby, which may have appealed to Tostig, but the choice of venue cannot be explained on these grounds.

Additional supplies of food, negotiations for the hostages and the movement of the main army from Riccall to Stamford Bridge would have occupied a little time, and it is unlikely that the Norsemen would have arrived on the Derwent before 24 September. The next day they must have received an unpleasant shock. Incredibly, as they were relaxing in the meadows, they suddenly saw, a mile or so to the west, the glint of sunshine off many helmets, and as they looked more closely through the clearing dust the standard of Wessex and the banner of the Fighting Man (see p. 29) told them that Harold of England was upon them. The King had been faced with an agonizing decision, but he did not hesitate and, with the same rapidity of movement with which a few years earlier he had broken the power of the Welsh prince Griffith ap Llywelyn, he raced his house-carls up the straight Roman road – long since grassed over – to the north, calling out the shire levies as he went. The men of England responded to their king's valour and vigour, and by the time he reached Tadcaster on 24 September his army must have been quite considerable, and may have been further enlarged by some of the survivors of Fulford.

In the space of four days Harold and his army had covered 180 miles: it was one of the great marches of history. We can be fairly sure that the night of 24 September was spent in Tadcaster. The men and ponies must have been incredibly weary, and Harold himself had risen from his sick-bed only a few days earlier, but before dawn they were under way again and into York. Here Harold may have intended to pause a while to allow his troops time to regain their strength, but hearing that the enemy were only eight miles off and blissfully unaware of their peril he ordered the march to continue. We may imagine that there was much grumbling, and it is a measure of the greatness of the man, and the excellence of his troops, that he was able to infuse such discipline into a rapidly assembled and ill assorted force as to bring them to the point of battle in such a condition that they were able to defeat an army reckoned by many to be the best in Europe, and led by a legendary, unconquerable giant.

The allied army – for such it must be called, as it consisted of Norwegians, Flemings, Scots and even some English – was caught completely unprepared for battle. The two leaders, King Harald Hardrada and Earl Tostig, probably thought the English king was fully occupied in the south, and certainly unable to be anywhere near York. It is true that Hardrada, as a normal routine measure, had outposts on the west bank of the river Derwent, but the main body of troops were taking their ease on the east bank in the fields around the present site of Danes Well garage and Battle Flats Farm. So warm was the weather and so unsuspecting were these warriors that many had discarded their mail tunics. A mile to the west of Stamford Bridge the ground rises at a village called Gate Helmsley and Harold's army could not have been visible to the enemy outposts until they had topped the ridge, so there could not have been much time to organize the defence. The outposts were ordered to stand firm on the west bank for at least sufficient time to allow the main body to don their mail and take up the best position available, and a messenger was urgently despatched to Eyestein Orre, commanding the troops at Riccall, to march with all speed to the battle.

The ground slopes fairly gently to the river, and those few Norsemen fighting with their backs to the water were in an unenviable position. Nowadays the banks are not steep at this place (although they are just below the present bridge), but it is fairly safe to assume that they were before the river course was altered, and there is no doubt that only strong swimmers lightly equipped could have escaped other than by the narrow wooden bridge. Tired though they must have been the house-carls and fyrd men showed few signs of it during the battle, and the sheer weight of their attack was altogether too much for the small body of men holding the river; they were swept aside like autumn leaves, and many who were not killed by Saxon weapons perished in the Derwent.

However, one Viking hero, unknown in name but glorious in repute, held the bridge alone, steadfast in the face of every Saxon assault. He stood at the west end of the bridge taunting the house-carls to hazard themselves and match his skill; and as they fell beneath his powerfully plied axe his comrades on the east bank raised a mighty cheer. For a little while this great berserk held the bridge, and many a Saxon body was despatched downstream by his bloodstained axe, but the end came quite suddenly, and rather ingloriously. A short way upstream a house-carl found a swill-tub which he managed to paddle, under cover of overhanging willows, to beneath the bridge. Here he was able to manoeuvre his craft to immediately below the spot where the Viking stood, and through one of the chinks in the planks of the bridge he thrust his spear into a particularly vital and unprotected part of the Norseman's body. With a piercing scream the Norseman fell, and the Saxon army was soon across the bridge.*

*The *Heimskringla Saga* of Snorri Sturluson (an unreliable guide for the actual battle) curiously makes no mention of this magnificent feat of one of its own compatriots; but English chroniclers, who do mention it, are unlikely to have invented an enemy hero.

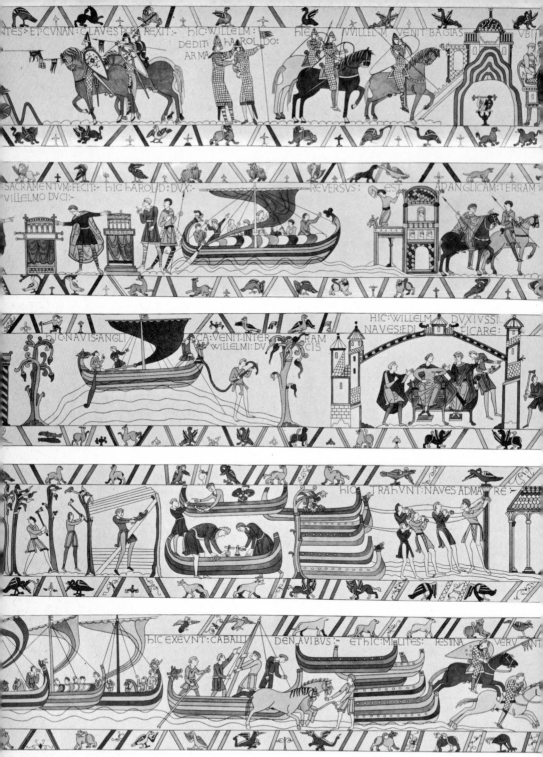

Left to right: Row 1: Harold knighted by William, William arrives at Bayeux. 2: Harold's oath before William, Harold returns to England and arrives at Westminster. 3: An English ship goes to Normandy, William holds a council. 4: Trees felled to build ships, the fleet built and dragged to the sea. 5: Fleet nears England, horses landed at Pevensey, invaders gallop to Hastings

Unlike the Battle of Hastings, about which we know quite a lot, thanks to the Bayeux Tapestry and certain French chroniclers, accurate details of the fight at Stamford Bridge, if they were ever written down, have not survived the centuries. We know that the Vikings in defence adopted the shield wall, a formation later to be used, with certain modifications, by the Saxon army at Hastings. The allied commanders probably had their men drawn up shoulder to shoulder in the shape of a hollow triangle with its apex presenting a comparatively narrow front. Once across the river and formed up the English would have had but one objective, to smash the shield wall, for there could be no retreat except into the dark and swirling waters of the Derwent.

At some time during the day – it may have been before the fight began, or more probably not until the river had been crossed – we are told that Harold offered his brother peace and the restitution of his earldom if he and his men would return to their allegiance; but rascal though Tostig was it is to his credit that he had sufficient honour not to turn traitor twice.

As to how well matched for numbers the two armies were we cannot tell. Probably the English had the advantage initially because the day was far gone before Eyestein Orre and the Riccall contingent joined the fight. It was to be a trial of strength between the house-carls and the Vikings, each vying with the other for

Battle of Stamford Bridge

pride of place as Europe's foremost infantrymen. Both knew that the clash would be savage and the slaughter great.

The Saxon army could not have arrived at the Derwent much before 11 a.m., and it would have been well past midday before the first assault against the shield wall. Those accounts, therefore, that say the fighting lasted until dusk are very probably right, because the Norsemen stood their ground magnificently, and only inch by inch could the Saxon axes, slings and javelins perform their remorseless task. As men fell others took their places, and every time a wedge was made it was quickly closed. But when the day was nearly over the Norwegian king, a heroic figure who had dominated the battle, was felled by a well aimed English missile. Earl Tostig tried to rally what was left of the polyglot army, but those were the days when the loss of their king struck a chill into the hearts of soldiers who so long as he lived would bravely withstand the most murderous onslaughts. The shield wall began to crumble, and the men from Riccall found they had arrived only to die. Soon Tostig and Eyestein Orre had joined the fallen, and there was no one left to rally the survivors round the *Landwaster*.

Briefly, and for the last time in history, that proud raven surveyed the carnage of a British battlefield; and then the dreaded emblem was trodden underfoot as the Norsemen fled the field, pursued all the way to Riccall by the utterly exhausted but triumphant Saxons. In victory Harold proved magnanimous; he allowed Harald Hardrada's young son Olaf and the equally young Orkney earls who had remained with the longships throughout to leave without ransom – but under oath not to invade England again. The defeated enemy required only twenty-four ships in which to return to their homes. As they sailed away down the Ouse it was the end of an era, for they were the remnants of the last Scandinavian army ever to harass the shores of England. Harold, never a vindictive man, buried his brother in York, which is where he would have wished to lie. The bones of King Harald Hardrada may still rest beneath Battle Flats Farm, for his namesake kept the promise he is said to have made, that all he would get was seven foot of English soil.

It was a decisive victory, but not won without cost. The housecarls and the levies had been sadly depleted. Harold retired on York, but although the fickle inhabitants of that city greeted him as a conquering hero the King's mind was sombre. He knew that an even sterner task lay ahead, and that somehow he must fill his thinning ranks and once again be prepared to stake his crown, his reputation, and indeed his very life upon the terrible hazards of war.

CHAPTER 2

Normans

Hastings

14 October 1066

The site of some of the fiercest fighting in the Battle of Hastings is in the grounds of Battle Abbey and Battle Abbey Park, which lie just to the south of the town of Battle on the A 2100 road to Hastings. Battle is some six miles north-west of Hastings and sixty miles from the centre of London. Most of the battle took place on what is now private property, but every point of importance can be viewed from the public grounds of Battle Abbey, or from the roads and public footpaths surrounding the area.

Points of interest outside the grounds of Battle Abbey are the primary school, which was approximately the left of the Saxon line, and from where the visitor can appreciate the steepness of the neck of land on its east side; the hedge bordering Powdermill Lane from where the site of the fighting round the hillock is best seen; the grounds of Glengorse School (if permission can be obtained) from where the Senlac position first became visible to William; and the windmill on Caldbec Hill, which offers the best viewpoint for Harold's approach march and the line of pursuit after the battle.

Duke William of Normandy was about to set out on a day's hunting in his park at Quevilly, near Rouen, when a messenger from England arrived to tell him that Edward the Confessor was dead and that Harold had been proclaimed King of England by the Witan. William was exceedingly angry, and for some time only William FitzOsbern, perhaps his closest friend, dared reason with him. The Duke was a fiery man not likely to be serene in disappointment, but once his anger had cooled he was capable of comprehensive judgment. He knew that if he was to get the English throne he would almost certainly have to fight for it, but though his prime bent was military he was also something of a diplomat, and he was well aware that his case as well as his army would need strengthening before the venture could take place. Messages were therefore exchanged between William and Harold, in which the Norman reminded the English king of his oath and called upon him to honour it. Predictably Harold refused; William made ready for war.

At a meeting of his innermost council William received much encouragement, but when the larger gathering of his barons was assembled at Lillebonne and asked to ratify the inner council's resolve that William should right the wrong done to him by Harold through force of arms, he met with considerable opposition. For a time it looked as though the necessary support would not be forthcoming, but once again it was William FitzOsbern who gave the lead. As the barons' elected spokesman he compromised them to such an extent that it was difficult for any of them to avoid the commitment, and their loyal support was finally achieved through the personal approach of William to each of them individually with words of high resolve, reward and reassurance. Soon news spread throughout western Europe that William of Normandy was about to undertake a holy mission against England blessed by the Pope, and that in the event of success those who offered their services would be assured of rich rewards. Volunteers flocked to Normandy from all parts of France and even Italy.

The system of military service in Normandy was entirely different from that prevailing in Saxon England; the Norman army was a feudal army. Each baron, or bishop, held his land on the understanding that he raised and equipped a prescribed number of mounted knights for the ducal service, and on this occasion William and his friend FitzOsbern had prevailed upon the barons to bring twice the number of men prescribed for their particular holdings, and to assist with materials and money for the building of the fleet. Most of the men now being conscripted by their feudal overlords would fight as infantry, for problems of transport would restrict the number of horses that could be brought across the Channel. The mounted knights probably did not exceed 2,000.

Although this was before the days of armour for horses the knights themselves wore long coats of mail slit at the bottom to fall over the saddle, cone-shaped helmets fitted with nose-pieces, and neck-guards of fine mail which were usually attached to the hauberk. Their weapon was a lance or sword – occasionally a mace – and they carried kite-shaped shields. The infantrymen wore leather hauberks covered with flat iron rings and quilted; their helmets were similar to those of the knights and their stockinged legs were bound with leather thongs. They carried shields large enough to protect most of the body and fought with swords, spears or short axes. The archers wore no mail, and their headgear was a cap; they used the short bow which had a maximum range of 150 yards.

The question that has never been satisfactorily answered is how large was the force that William transported across the Channel. Some of the chroniclers mention the staggering figure of 50–60,000, but most modern writers consider this to be a gross exaggeration.* There is not space to discuss the various known factors that have to be considered when trying to arrive at a reasonably accurate figure for the total force, but it seems most likely that it would have been around 8,000 and certainly not more than 10,000. While this host was being assembled on the hills above the small town of Dives, the ring of the woodcutter's axe could be heard throughout the surrounding forests, for there was no Norman fleet of any consequence and most of the transports (open single-masted boats) had to be hewn from the round log and put together in an incredibly short time. It is unlikely that these small craft could have held more than twenty men, so William would have needed about 1,000 to carry the army and necessary non-combatants, 2,000 or so horses and a certain quantity of provisions and war materials.

All through the summer the work proceeded, and gradually the small harbour at the mouth of the river Dives filled up with newly made craft. By August sufficient ships had been assembled. Throughout this long period of waiting only William's iron discipline and inspired leadership had kept his large army from deserting or looting. Harold, as we have seen, was unable to keep his men together, and when at the beginning of September news reached William that the fyrd had been disbanded he sailed his fleet – not without loss – to St Valery, at the mouth of the Somme, where he would get fresh provisions and have a shorter voyage to the now unguarded south coast of England. Here then at St Valery the destiny of two men – and indeed of two peoples – waited upon the veering of the wind.

At last, on 27 September, two days after Harold's victory at Stamford Bridge (see pp. 16-20), the wind moved into the south. Embarkation lasted for most of the day and towards evening William, in the *Mora*, a ship presented to him by his wife, led the fleet out of harbour. On the morning of the 28th the invaders were off Beachy Head and William steered for the old Roman castle at Pevensey, whose landlocked harbour has long since been reclaimed from the sea. Here the army disembarked completely unopposed, and on the next day William removed both men and ships to Hastings. At that time Hastings, situated on a narrow peninsula and protected by the Brede and Bulverhythe estuaries, was an ideal

*However, Piers Compton in his *Harold the King* supports the high figure of the early chroniclers.

place for a covering action in the event of a withdrawal on the fleet becoming necessary; it also had an excellent harbour. The road to London was barred by no soldiers, but William dared not move too far from his base. Instead he erected a wooden fortress with materials brought over for the purpose, and waited – with increasing uneasiness – upon events.

It is usually accepted that Harold received news of William's landing while at a banquet in York on the evening of 1 October; only Guy of Amiens states that the news reached him while on the march south, but this account may well be correct. Even allowing for the fact that there were problems requiring attention in the north and that the soldiers badly needed a rest, it would have been a grave dereliction of duty on the part of the English king – and a most uncharacteristic action – had he dallied in York for four whole days after he must have known that at last William had got the wind he wanted. He returned as he had come, down Ermine Street, and may himself have ridden ahead of his army, for there was much to be done: fresh levies had to be hastily assembled, and either on his way to London, or while there, we know that he paid a visit to Waltham. Here, in the beautiful abbey that he had founded, and which was dedicated to the Holy Cross that worked such miracles and had become the battle-cry of the Saxon army, the attendant monks echoed the prayers of a suppliant monarch.

By the time Harold reached London, if not before, he would have learned of the devastation of the countryside around Hastings. William deliberately set his men to scourge and pillage and burn. He knew Harold's impetuous nature, and guessed rightly that the proud dynamism of the English king would never allow him to play a waiting game while part of his kingdom was burning. It would have been better had Harold done so, for the further William marched from his ships (and he certainly couldn't play a waiting game) the greater became his perils and his problems; while Harold needed time for the fresh levies to rally and the valiant veterans of Stamford Bridge to recover from the rigours of their forced march. While the King was in London his brother Gyrth tried to persuade him not to march against William, but to leave the fighting to him and his other brother Leofwine, who were bound by no oath; but Harold, conscious of his kingship and aware of the magical aura of the crown, would not hear of it. Besides, he looked upon a fight with zest and thrill.

We do not know for certain the day that Harold left London, nor the number of troops that marched with him. It seems most likely that he delayed his departure until 12 October, and there may

Bayeux Tapestry: Harold is shown to the people after his coronation at Westminster

25

W·F·N·WATSON·

Above: The Fyrd 1066. Saxon armies usually fought on foot but house-carls and many of the fyrd rode on ponies.
Below: Norman knights 1066

W·F·N·WATSON

have been no more than 5,000 men with him, for some contingents would have met him en route and others would have been ordered to march direct to the appointed rendezvous. Harold was marching into his home county and would be fighting on ground he knew well. We know that the selected rendezvous was a hoar apple tree and that it stood just beyond the southern boundary of that massive forest called the Andredsweald. Such trees were often prominent land and boundary marks; this one may have been situated on Caldbec Hill (three-quarters of a mile north of Battle), then the junction of two or three local roads, or it may have been on the actual ridge where Harold took up his defensive position. It is yet another detail of which we cannot be sure, but in either case the distance from London was some sixty miles.

Harold would have reached the rendezvous on the evening of the 13th, and much of his army, well strung out and utterly exhausted from trudging miles over rough and rutted tracks, would trickle in throughout the night, finding their way by the light of a waning moon – it was twenty-two days old. There would be no roistering; instead, as each party arrived they would throw themselves upon the dew-soaked ground and, with the stolid indifference of the soldier to what the morrow might bring, quickly fall asleep.

The writings of French chroniclers are almost our only window on this long forgotten past, and they are an unreliable guide to any interpretation of Harold's intentions. There has been much argument over the years as to whether Harold always intended to fight a defensive battle, or whether this was forced upon him by the rapid advance of the Norman army from its base camp at Hastings. The present writer is of the opinion that the English king, with foreknowledge of the ground, said to himself, 'This is the place where I shall defeat the French.' A purely defensive battle hardly fits with what we know of Harold's character, and his previous campaigns had been the embodiment of the offensive spirit. But if occasionally hasty in judgement he was a competent and experienced general. At Hastings Harold was facing for the first time in England a body of determined and well armed cavalry; he had had the opportunity of seeing cavalry in operation while campaigning with Duke William a short while back, and he must have realized that before he could achieve a decisive victory he would have to blunt the cavalry weapon. What better way of doing this than to invite them to attack a difficult position, and at the appropriate time to counter-attack with part or all of his force and roll back a tired and dispirited enemy.

That Harold intended to go over to the offensive, and was con-

27

fident of victory, is borne out by the fact that he ordered what few ships could be manned in time to leave London and sail round the North Foreland to ensure that William's fleet, now beached under the protection of Hastings Castle, would not put to sea without a fight. But first there would have to be a battle of attrition. The alternative would have been to catch the Normans off balance, as he had done the Norsemen, but here there could have been little hope of surprise and he might well have given William the chance to make use of ground of his own choosing and more suitable for his cavalry.

A general faced with the necessity of taking up a strong defensive position could not have selected a better site than that chosen by Harold. From Caldbec Hill there runs a narrow neck of land (now largely occupied by Battle High Street) and from this isthmus the ground drops away steeply on both sides – particularly to the east. At the point where this narrow ridge begins to dip into the marshy area, called in medieval days Sandlake, or Santlache, and known to history as Senlac through the French pronunciation of 'Sand-lake', there is a fairly level cross ridge stretching for approximately half a mile east and west. The slopes down from this Senlac ridge were not nearly so steep as those from the neck of land connecting it with Caldbec Hill – indeed the slope at the west end is only one in thirty-three* – but troops attacking the centre and east end of the ridge would be severely handicapped by the climb. On the other side of the slightly undulating valley the ground rises gradually to Telham Hill, the summit of which is a mile from the Senlac ridge and nearly 200 feet higher. The ground between these two high points, especially that on the west, must have been very wet and marshy even in October, for it was intersected by a number of streams – one of them now dammed to make a chain of fishponds – and by the Asten brook. The southern slopes of the Senlac position may have been cultivated, but it is more likely that the whole ridge was rough, open ground covered by gorse, bracken and bramble. The Bayeux Tapestry depicts a few trees, as was to be expected in a well timbered area.

In addition to its being a natural defensive position, across the ridge and the land behind it there ran not actually the Roman road but the ancient trackway from the coast which eventually joined the Lewes–London Roman road; Harold, therefore, effectively barred William's direct advance upon London. Even if the rendez-vous, as seems likely, was a little way back at Caldbec Hill, Harold

*C. H. Lemmon, *The Field of Hastings*, p.37.

28

would have been on the Senlac ridge soon after first light (approximately 5.30 a.m.) and here he would have received word of William's advance. The *Anglo-Saxon Chronicle*, although of no assistance with the battle, assures us that Harold was taken by surprise, and it seems, therefore, that he would have had little time to erect any effective defence works. We can be fairly certain that reinforcements for the English army would continue to come in at any rate during the early hours of the battle, so the line when first drawn up may have been comparatively thin. Almost all accounts agree as to the site of Harold's command post and the fact that the English fought in a very dense formation. The flanks may have been extended as the levies came in, but more likely these were sent to strengthen the existing front.

The Saxon left extended to the area of the present primary school, and the line cut diagonally across the east-west abbey ruin with the right flank close to the wire fence now dividing the abbey grounds from the park. It was thus a little over 600 yards long and although at an angle to the present Hastings road was almost square to the ancient trackway which left the metal road at the abbey lodge gates and continued straight up the hill to the spot near the Norman stone where Harold had his headquarters. Here, close-guarded by devoted house-carls, stood the standard of Wessex – a golden dragon on a red or purple background, which was certainly carried by Edmund Ironside at the Battle of Assingdon in 1016, and was probably the royal standard of all Alfred's line. Harold had a personal banner that was also carried in battle, and known as the Fighting Man. Legend had it that it had been woven by his mother Gytha, and that the helmet, mail and weapons were sewn with sparkling gems. Harold himself chose the design and it is not impossible that the Cerne giant, or the larger figure of a fighting man on the Sussex downs above Wilmington, both of which are probably pre-Saxon, inspired his choice.

The most reliable accounts of the battle are those written by William of Poitiers and William of Jumièges; both were living at the time and wrote their story in the early 1070s. William of Poitiers, who was chaplain to Duke William, was not present at the battle but in earlier life he had been a soldier, and although he, like most of the other earlier writers, greatly exaggerated the numbers of soldiers taking part on both sides, his account of the fighting is, together with the Bayeux Tapestry, our best guide to the battle.

We know from these sources that in the first phase of the battle the Norman infantry were overwhelmed by the weight of missiles hurled at them by the Saxons. Now most authorities place the house-carls in the forefront of the Saxon line, but it was the fyrd who were armed with missiles and javelins. Even if the house-carls were placed slightly lower down the slope these tall hand-picked men would have felt distinctly uneasy at having to stand with their backs to a bunch of over-excited shire levies hurling stones and javelins just above their heads. It seems reasonable to assume, therefore, that some of the levies were placed in front of the house-carls with orders to withdraw through the ranks after they had discharged their missiles – in the early stages their place may even have been taken by a second line of 'slingers'.

Thus by nine in the morning the English army was drawn up on this famous ridge under command of its king, who had with him his two able and courageous brothers. But what of the Normans? William had staked everything on being able to put all to the test in an early battle, and it must have been with considerable relief that he learned on 13 October that his formidable adversary was about to oblige him. The Norman leader had been agitated, morose and unsure of himself in the days since the landing at Pevensey, but now we see him with all doubts and fears vanished and in their place determination and resolution. He gave orders for the army to be ready to leave the Hastings camp at dawn the next day – Saturday 14 October.

The head of the column (which stretched for about three miles) would have been on the march by 5.30 a.m., and we are told that William himself had reached Telham Hill by the time news was brought to him of the Saxon position. Telham Hill was some six miles from the Norman camp and the rear of the column could scarcely have reached it much before 8.30. While the army closed up and prepared for battle the Duke would have ridden forward to the point, now occupied by Glengorse School, from where the Senlac position first became visible, and decided upon his plan of attack. Nevertheless, the army still had to descend into the valley and deploy across difficult ground before battle could begin. It is generally stated that the first Norman assault went in at nine o'clock, but it is difficult to see how a long column could form line in less than an hour, so it would appear doutbful that any attack could have been made before 9.30 at the earliest.

The Norman army, which may have numbered very slightly less than Harold's when his was fully assembled, was to attack in line on a three-division front. The right was given to the Franco-Flemish mercenary contingent under the command of Roger of Montgomery, with Robert of Beaumont, William FitzOsbern and Eustace of Boulogne. Their section of the Saxon line lay in the area

30

House-carl. The blade of his axe was as much as a foot across, with a 5-foot helve. It was held in a left-handed grip to strike a foe's unshielded right side

WFN WATSON

now covered by the Chequers Hotel and the primary school. On the left were the Bretons and men from Maine and Poitou who were commanded by Alan of Britanny. Originally their left probably rested on the small hillock* which was to be the scene of much heavy fighting, but during the battle they appear to have extended their line to the west somewhat in order to allow more room for the Norman centre, which was larger than both the two wings put together, and perhaps to enable them to deliver a flank attack. The Bretons had the easiest part of the slope up which to attack, but the wettest part of the field on which to deploy and manoeuvre. The Norman centre was under the personal command of William, who rode into battle carrying a mace, and from his neck hung some of the relics upon which Harold had sworn his famous oath. He was supported by his two half-brothers, Robert of Mortain and Odo Bishop of Bayeux, and they were faced with a fairly steep ascent to the centre of the Saxon line, now a part of Battle Abbey garden. Each division was drawn up in three echelons: archers, heavy infantry and cavalry.

The battle lasted all day, and we can safely assume that there were certain definite pauses – possibly between each of the distinct phases into which the battle fell – for no troops wearing chain mail and attacking uphill could keep up a sustained effort over a period of almost nine hours. William opened the fight with his archers. These troops made little impression on the Saxon phalanx, and when they came in range proved very vulnerable to the shower of well aimed missiles, which accounted for many of them. Moreover, as Harold was virtually without archers, the Normans were soon left with no arrows. This first phase in the battle could not have lasted much more than an hour.

It was now the turn of the infantry, and as is so often the case it was they who bore the brunt of the fighting throughout the day. The whole line advanced to the attack, and although they suffered grievously before they reached the English these were tough men, most of them schooled by many seasons of campaigning in their native lands. Their struggle with the house-carls was a bloody one and both sides fought bravely. The footsoldiers made a dent here and there, but the Saxons remained steadfast, shouting 'Out, out' and 'Holy Cross' as they laid about them with their huge axes. Thus the second phase.

The heavy infantry now fell back in a perfectly orderly manoeuvre to allow the cavalry, the corps d'élite of William's army, to

*Clearly recognizable from the hedge bordering the road called Powdermill Lane.

pass through into the attack, with the infantry keeping close behind ready to exploit the expected success. But the cavalry were at a disadvantage: the boggy ground on the left of the Norman line was by no means ideal for forming up, and in the centre and on the right they were faced almost immediately with a steep slope which greatly lessened the impetus of the attack. It was not possible for the unprotected horses to be ridden at any speed against the still intact Saxon line, and losses were suffered in the attack. But it was about now that a vitally important incident took place.

The Breton knights on the left may have been less courageous than their allies, or perhaps they faced opposition even fiercer than that which assailed the other cavalry. In any event they gave way, and in their retreat not only rolled back their own infantry, but by exposing the Norman left flank forced that division to retire precipitately. It was a crisis moment for both sides. Before the battle Harold had given strict instructions that on no account was any man to quit his position without orders; yet a number of men on the Saxon right charged down the slope after the fleeing Bretons. We must suspect that these were a body of ill disciplined shire levies who thought they had stood their ground long enough and could not resist the chance to chase and chastise the hated invader. But it is just possible that they left the Senlac ridge as part of a prepared counter-attack under the orders of Gyrth or Leofwine. Whatever the cause the result was the same. For a moment the whole Norman line was in confusion, and to make matters worse William was unhorsed and a shout went up that he was dead.

There are those ready to condemn Harold for not advancing his whole force at this critical moment, but at this distance of time we should not attempt to criticize a man who was undoubtedly a great general, and to whom the field of battle on that autumn day in 1066 must have appeared quite different from what it does to us who stroll around the pleasant abbey grounds 900 years later. At any rate the chance, if it ever was there, was fleeting: William rose to the occasion by removing his helmet so that all could see him, and exhorting his men to greater efforts. Not only that, but he immediately rallied the cavalry and swung them onto the now hopelessly vulnerable English. Much slaughter took place around the hillock and where the fishpond now is, and although the Norman cavalry floundered in the mud and many riders were unseated, not a single Englishman regained the Senlac ridge. But by the time all this had taken place Harold's army would have reached its full strength and he would have had men to fill the gap. William of Poitiers assures us that when the next Norman attack went in they

London Road

recreation ground

Manser's Shaw (Malfosse?)

playing field

Long Plantation

new pond

Bretons

new pond

Powdermill Lane

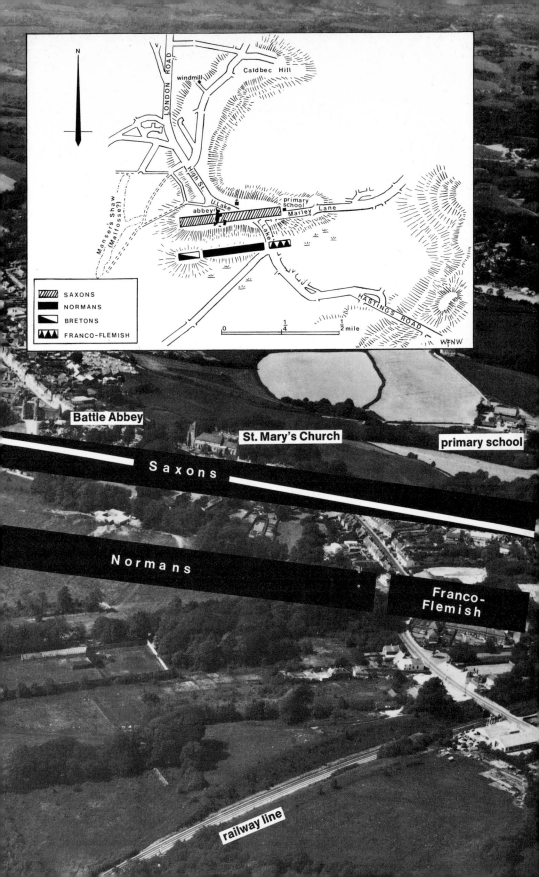

N

LONDON ROAD

windmill

Caldbec Hill

High St.

Manser's Shaw (Malfosse?)

U. Lake

abbey

primary school

Marley Lane

Lake

HASTINGS ROAD

SAXONS

NORMANS

BRETONS

FRANCO-FLEMISH

0   1/4   1/2 mile

WFNW

Battle Abbey

St. Mary's Church

primary school

Saxons

Normans

Franco-Flemish

railway line

CECI DE RVNT AQVIERAN

Pages 34–5: Town of Battle from south-east showing battle of Hastings. Inset shows modern town of Battle and estimated position of armies at 9.30 a.m.

found the Saxon line almost intact.

At this stage it is almost certain that there was a considerable pause in the fighting; both sides had taken a severe battering and there was much reorganizing and replenishing of weapons to be carried out. The day would have been more than half spent by the time William sent his knights once more into the breach. Again they could make little impression on the valiant house-carls, supported by the sturdy men from the shires, and again men and horses floundered in vain among the dead and dying. Undoubtedly they weakened the phalanx, but the greatest damage to the English was caused by a repetition of the Breton incident, this time on the French right. William of Poitiers says that there were two feigned retreats inspired by the excellent – albeit fortuitous – results of the Breton rout. He may be reporting correctly, for during the pauses in the battle there would have been an opportunity for William to coordinate such a manoeuvre. But it has to be remembered that a feigned retreat is a very difficult operation of war to control, and it can have dangerous consequences. It is more likely that the retreats were genuine, but that William, profiting from the first one, was quick to swing in reserve cavalry which, aided by a downhill charge, dealt swift destruction to the pursuing Saxons.

Somewhere around four o'clock in the afternoon the last, most crucial and bloodiest phase of the battle began. Time was running short, not much more than two hours of daylight remained, and Harold's army still stood rocklike upon the ridge, defiant and full

36

Above: Bayeux Tapestry: Harold is wounded by an arrow and his men slain

of fight. William risked all on this last attempt. Each of the three arms were to combine in one final push. The archers were ordered to increase the trajectory of their arrows, which might not cause many casualties but would have the effect of raising the shield wall; under cover of this fire what was left of the cavalry (some would have been held in reserve) and the still numerous infantry were to join with the enemy. Once more the house-carls fought valiantly under an avalanche of iron and steel, but the solid phalanx of Saxon soldiers had started to crack. The gaps made by those who had left their posts and died on the slopes below could no longer be filled; the Normans were able to gain a footing on the plateau, and once upon level ground the few remaining knights, closely supported by the heavy infantry, began to drive wedges into troops now assailed even from the sky.

The Bayeux Tapestry depicts Harold's brothers as being slain at a comparatively early stage in the battle, while some chroniclers say that they were still fighting in the last assault and that William, by now always in the thick of the battle, actually slew Gyrth himself. We do not know the hour of their death, but we can be fairly certain that Harold died a little after sunset on that memorable day. At a time when the chaos and confusion of the close hand-to-hand fighting were at their height, and the Normans were putting in all that they had to force an issue while there was still light, the English king was seen to stagger and clutch an arrow that had pierced his eye. As he leant upon his shield in fearful agony, a body of four Norman knights charged home and cut him down before the house-carls could close around the standard and drive them back.

It was very nearly the end. The house-carls fought on devotedly as yard by yard the Normans strengthened their foothold upon the ridge. The English king and his equally brave brothers lay dead; the position could no longer be defended and the levies had had enough. They broke and fled, hoping that night and the great forest would cast a concealing cloak upon them. William let loose what cavalry he had kept in reserve. The light was almost gone and the country difficult to ride over with steep, treacherous slopes on either side of the neck of land over which the beaten English were hurrying. What exactly occurred will never be known – four chroniclers writing at various times in the hundred years after the battle give differing accounts – but somewhere between the Senlac ridge and the Andredsweald the last act in the tragedy was played out. It seems as though, in the failing light, a number of horsemen overrode a steep ravine, or covered ditch, and those who survived the tumble found themselves confronted by a party of retreating Saxons. In the ensuing mêlée some of the French were killed and Count Eustace of Boulogne was wounded. It was no more than a delaying action, for William soon got the pursuit under way again, but the French were sufficiently impressed by the magnitude of the disaster to call the place Malfosse.

William the Bastard, Duke of Normandy, had won the battle, and the Norman dynasty was born. But there was great glory for England that day as the few remaining house-carls closed their ranks and died with their king under the golden dragon of Wessex and the banner of the Fighting Man. Legend has it that Harold's body had been so mutilated that it could not be found for some time, and that it was eventually recognized by his devoted mistress Edith Swan-neck. This may or may not be true, but the body was certainly found, and was – at first – denied a Christian burial. William had staked his claim to the throne principally on a perjured oath; he could not therefore accede to Gytha's request that she might be given her son's body for burial in hallowed ground.

However, the Conqueror paid due honour to a courageous foe; he gave the English king a soldier's farewell upon the cliffs of the coast that he had striven so valiantly to defend. Later, when William was secure upon the throne, the body of King Harold II, accompanied by Normans and Saxons alike, went in solemn procession to Waltham to be buried beneath the high altar of the church that he had founded and loved so well.

CHAPTER 3

The Barons'War

Lewes

14 May 1264

Simon de Montfort's army at Lewes took up a position before the battle that extended approximately from the present derelict grandstand of Lewes racecourse eastwards to the edge of the chalk pits on Offham Hill. This position can be reached by walking up the sunken track (almost certainly the same one over which Simon led his army) which leads immediately off the A 275 road at the village of Offham, a mile north of Lewes, and runs due south-west up to the extensive plateau where the army was deployed. The main fighting probably took place in the vicinity of the Offham chalk pits and towards the end of the two spurs which run south-east from the plateau towards the castle and the prison respectively. There was also some mopping up in the town itself.

The visitor wishing to study the battle, and perhaps draw his own conclusions as to how it was fought, should view the field from Simon de Montfort's position on the downs above Offham; from the keep of Lewes Castle, where Prince Edward would have had his first view of the baronial army, and from the remains of the Priory of St Pancras (marked on the one-inch Ordnance Survey map, sheet 183, just to the south of the town), from where he can appreciate the difficult position in which King Henry found himself at the outset of the battle.

By 1258 it had become clear to almost everyone that Henry III was a disaster as a king. He had come to the throne in 1216 as a boy of nine, but not until 1232 (five years after he had officially declared himself of an age to rule the kingdom) did he feel himself strong enough to challenge the prestige of his great justiciar, Hubert de Burgh. From then on he had moved from one crisis to another: conflicts with his prelates and barons (not with all of them, for much of the time not even with most of them, but with a powerful minority) who were determined that he should rule without the help of his foreign friends and in accordance with the terms of the Great Charter forced upon his father King John; a disastrous

Above: Seal of Simon de Montfort at the British Museum. Left: Effigy of Henry III in Westminster Abbey. Below: Seal of Henry III

campaign in France to regain the French possessions his father had lost; punitive expeditions against the Welsh princes; and in 1254, worst of all follies, an entanglement with the Pope over an offer (with exorbitant financial liabilities attached) of the Sicilian crown for his second son Edmund.

Henry's appearance is known to us from the superb effigy in Westminster Abbey and the description left by William de Rishanger. He was a man of medium height and strong build with delicate hands and a handsome head, enhanced by a prominent nose; his otherwise fine features were spoilt by a drooping eyelid – a defect that he passed on to his eldest son. He was capable of great charm, although his affection was chiefly reserved for those who flattered him; his piety was absolutely genuine and because of his love of art and architecture we are indebted to Henry for the rebuilding of Westminster Abbey. But there was much to dislike about him. He was weak, and like so many weak men he was obstinate; he was quick-tempered, vainglorious and a decided sybarite. At a time when the country needed a strong hand and dominant personality he was too easily influenced by bad advice and too inclined to surround himself with his wife's Savoyard and Provençal relations, as well as his obnoxious French half-brothers. Frequently forced to bow to the passions of the hour, he was incapable of honouring any pledge.

Quite different was the man soon to raise the standard of revolt against him. Simon de Montfort, Earl of Leicester, was perhaps a year or so younger than the King, and through his marriage to Henry's sister Eleanor in 1238 had become his brother-in-law. When Simon arrived in England in 1231 to claim his inheritance of the honour of the earldom of Leicester and stewardship of England he and Henry were the greatest friends, but although the de Montforts were a most devoted couple Simon's marriage to the King's sister soon became the cause of many petty acerbities between him and the King.

There is no contemporary effigy of Simon that can be trusted, but his deeds have been recorded, and his praises sung or his actions condemned, down the ages. He was a man uplifted above the crowd, and in a generation that was not short of great men he was perhaps the greatest of them all. He was not as saintly as Louis IX, he may not even have been as pious as Henry, although he was a consistent and conscientious Christian, but far outstripping his faults and peccadilloes there were many qualities that make for nobility in a man.

Simon de Montfort has been accused of arrogance, ambition,

spite and ill-temper. He certainly had a quick temper, and perhaps like many great men he possessed some ambition and displayed some hubris; but he did not champion the baronial cause on account of his enmity for the King; nor can he be accused of responsibility for the civil war, or for the destruction of the baronial plan of reform. It was Henry, not Simon, who brought civil war to the country, and having once agreed to the plan of reform Simon's only fault was that he was one of the few determined to stick to it. At a time when the English and French nobility were beginning to draw apart it must be remembered that Simon de Montfort was born and bred a Frenchman, and although a highly intelligent man who numbered among his friends some of the leading English clerics of the time he probably never spoke English. But he was in the forefront of those who recognized a nascent nationalism and he genuinely wished to bring England to a juster and better way of life.

The crisis of 1258 orginated as a financial one, brought about by the absolute refusal of the Great Council to advance any money for the ridiculous Sicilian venture in which Henry had become involved. The King had always maintained the closest relationship with Rome, much to the annoyance of his own clergy, who greatly resented the papal place-men and extortions. He must therefore have been deeply distressed when his ally the Pope, weary of his weakness and vacillation, threatened to excommunicate him and bring the whole land under an interdict unless the money for the expedition was quickly forthcoming. Clearly something had to be done; but the barons had had enough of foreign interlopers and illusory empires and demanded certain safeguards as the price of rescuing their king from his stubborn ineptitude. About the end of April a small cabal of the more powerful of their number, which included the Earls of Gloucester, Norfolk and Leicester, headed a party of knights who arrived armed at the Palace of Westminster and so frightened the King that he agreed that a committee of twenty-four (half to be nominated by his council and half by the barons) should meet at Oxford on 11 June to draw up terms for what was to become a constitutional revolution.

The barons had at last realized that the trouble went deeper than the presence of incompetent foreign favourites and exorbitant extravagance; the foreigners would have to go, but there would also have to be total administrative reform. Government in future could not be conducted by the king alone, but by the king in council. The Provisions of Oxford provided for conciliar government that was cumbersome and complex, but in that summer of 1258 England took

42

an important step forward along the road to constitutional monarchy; and through the Provisions of Westminster, which came into force a year later, important changes were affected in land tenure and a much needed curb was put on ecclesiastical and baronial jurisdiction. Magna Carta was a lengthy document of some sixty-three clauses most of which dealt with points of dispute between the king and his barons; the Provisions of Oxford were a form of written constitution which laid down the method whereby the clergy and the barons were to play their part in the running of the country. The magnates, as well as the king, were called upon to fulfil certain obligations towards their tenants, and all took an oath in 1258 to uphold the terms of the Provisions.

It was never intended that the Provisions should be permanent, but in providing for them to last twelve years the barons hoped that their king would be held in leash for the rest of his life. Henry chewed the thongs of thraldom sourly, took the oath and bided his time; but Prince Edward reacted strongly against the new arrangements and was with difficulty persuaded to swear, perhaps by his father, who never could understand why anyone regarded an oath as binding. Simon de Montfort does not appear to have been over-enthusiastic about the terms hammered out at Oxford, and was certainly not the leader of the barons at this time. Only when many of them began to weaken and Henry set about undermining the Provisions did he stand out as the most steadfast and determined of them all. He had not long to wait, for events marched forward remorselessly and in anger and bitterness the country fell into anarchy.

There was a cleavage in the baronial ranks in 1260. The powerful Earl of Gloucester had quarrelled with Simon, and Henry, an adept at dividing his enemies, quickly made capital out of this split. By May 1261 he had obtained a bull from the Pope absolving him from his oath on the grounds that it had been taken under duress, and by May 1262 – when Simon de Montfort was in voluntary exile in France – he felt strong enough to formally revoke the Provisions and revert to personal government with the aid of his foreign friends. But a force had been set in motion that could be arrested only by wise and conciliatory government on the part of the king, and of this Henry was incapable. The county knights had been given responsibilities under the Provisions which they were loath to surrender, and even the common people had been stirred by the promises of reform which now seemed about to elude them. Moreover, the barons may have been temporarily divided by a conflict of interests, but they were not unmindful of their former triumph, nor disposed to surrender the fruits of that long, wearisome struggle.

Left: Infantry. Left: chain mail hauberk with long sleeves ending in bag-mittens, kettle-hat. Right cervellière over leather coif, quilted gambeson. Below: 13th-century knights or mounted men-at-arms. 12th and 13th-century innovations included closed helms, calf-length surcoat, sometimes reinforced with plates on the inside, gamboised cuisses to protect the thigh and plate jamberis or schynbalds on the lower leg, and the flat-topped shield

WFNWATSON

W·F·N·WATSON

In that July, while Henry was on a prolonged visit to France, Simon's rival the Earl of Gloucester died; his young heir, Gilbert de Clare, threw in his lot with the barons. During the King's absence his newly appointed ministers proved totally unable to cope with a deteriorating situation, and by December, when Henry at last arrived home, the whole of the Welsh border was aflame. Llywelyn ap Gruffydd was rampaging along the northern and middle march and his Welshmen had threatened Chester and Shrewsbury, while the marcher lords were far too busy squabbling among themselves, and alternatively laying waste estates belonging to the King's friends, to interfere with Llywelyn.

In April 1263 Simon returned from France, either on his own initiative or more probably at the invitation of the barons. The country was crumbling into civil war and from now on Simon assumed the leadership of the diminishing band of magnates who were still prepared to honour their binding pledge. Having won over the principal towns and castles in the west and gained the support of Llywelyn, he marched eastward along the Thames valley carefully avoiding any clash with Prince Edward, now at Windsor, and reached Kent. The Queen (with the crown jewels) and her Savoyard uncle the Archbishop of Canterbury made their escape to France, but as Simon had secured the Cinque Ports the mercenary force that they hoped to raise would have difficulty in entering the country. In Kent Simon gained many supporters and the King, who had shut himself up in the Tower among a hostile population, was in no position to resist Simon's demand for the restitution of the Provisions of Oxford.

A truce was arranged for the purpose of mediation, which Henry broke not once but twice. The second time, in December, he all but succeeded in trapping Simon as he lay with a small force outside London at Southwark, but the Londoners succeeded in opening their gates just in time. Although Simon had a large 'country' following the barons were far less united now than they were in 1258; we do not know the exact figures, but many held aloof and a good number supported the King. Having under his command only a minority of the baronage undoubtedly influenced Simon in agreeing that both parties should put their case to arbitration by King Louis and swear to abide by his award. Simon may have believed that under the terms of the arbitration the Provisions of Oxford could be only amended and not abrogated; but we can hardly credit him with not realizing that kings stood for absolute monarchy.

The Mise of Amiens, as Louis's award of January 1264 was called, was completely predictable: the total overthrow of the Provisions and a reversion to the status quo of 1258. It could have but one result: England would be engulfed by civil war. Simon was not present at Amiens, for on setting out for France from his castle at Kenilworth he fractured a leg bone when his horse stumbled, but this did not incapacitate him from taking the field almost as soon as he learned of the award. The campaign which was to culminate in the Battle of Lewes had begun. As is so often the case in war, the side that was ultimately to gain the victory met with early disasters.

Simon divided his army into three, giving his sons Henry and Simon their first taste of command. Henry he despatched into the West Country, where he failed to take Worcester and allowed himself to be tricked by Prince Edward. The Prince, after reluctantly taking the Oxford oath, had for a time showed sympathy towards the cause of reform, but by now his allegiance was firmly to his father. He had managed to get himself shut up in Gloucester Castle, but Simon ordered his son to allow him his freedom on the understanding that he took no part in any fighting. This condition he accepted but soon repudiated, and after securing Gloucester he marched his army to join the King at Oxford, leaving William de Valence to ravage the western marches and prevent Henry de Montfort (who had retired on Kenilworth) from joining forces with his ally Llywelyn. Worse still befell young Simon, who had shut himself up in Northampton. Although at first he repulsed the royal army that marched against him from Oxford, the treacherous Prior of St Andrew's guided the royalists into the city, and after some severe street fighting, in which victors and vanquished performed prodigies of valour, Simon's army was defeated and he himself made prisoner.

Meanwhile, the elder Simon, who had reached St Albans on his way to relieve Northampton, realized that he was too late, retraced his steps to London and marched from there to Rochester, whose position astride the London to Dover road made it of some strategic importance. He soon took the town, but the castle held out. Not wishing to put himself in the position of besieger being besieged, he returned to London on learning that the royalist army – which had made an incredible forced march of 156 miles in five days – was upon him. During these dismal days of April and early May 1264 both sides conducted themselves with that degree of fury and savagery so often associated with civil war. Land was devastated, churches were pillaged, houses were fired, and many innocent men, women and children perished by the sword or in the flames.

No doubt the march to Rochester was a splendid feat, but it is difficult to understand King Henry's overall strategic plan at this time. Why race for Rochester? Would not London have been a more worthy prize? No army could have withstood the rigours of such an ordeal: horses must have died in hundreds and stragglers been left littered along the roads of Kent. But almost at once they were on the move again, and marching still further from London; Tonbridge fell and then Winchelsea. True, Henry was heading for country where the great castles were mainly held by his supporters, but the dark forests of the Weald, ideally suited for ambuscades, were full of hostile bowmen and the army that eventually reached Lewes on 11 May must have been in a sorry plight. There was little enough time to recuperate before further exertions were required, and problems of provender were formidable. Henry, who loved his creature comforts, made his headquarters in the Cluniac Priory of St Pancras, which lies just to the south of the hill on which Lewes is built; Prince Edward, with most of the cavalry, occupied the more advantageously sited castle.

Earl Simon and his army left London on 6 May. Even when battles were of short duration and often conducted almost as set-piece affairs it was important to have a good intelligence system. Gentlemen known as 'espials' were employed by both sides, and those working for Simon seem to have been efficient in their duties, for he was well informed of the royalist army's movements. It was of the utmost importance for him to bring the King to battle, for unless his army was destroyed quickly it would increase in size at the expense of Simon's potential followers, and the disparity in numbers would become even greater than it was already. We do not know the exact route he took, nor does it greatly matter, but by the time the King reached Lewes Simon's army was pitching camp in the densely wooded area around Fletching, a small village some nine miles to the north of Lewes.

There are many conflicting accounts of the numbers engaged in the Battle of Lewes. The chroniclers, as usual, offer fantastic figures ranging upwards to 60,000. The *Chronicle of St Pancras Priory*, however, puts the number of royalists killed at 2,700. But even if this was fairly accurate – and it may well have been, for counting corpses is an easier task than estimating military formations – it does not help us very much, except that we are told that the number of casualties in relation to the total combatants engaged was not noticeably high. Wild statements are often made about the number of knights taking part, and it is interesting that modern research* reveals that at the time of which we are treating there were not many more than 400 knights on the active list – as opposed to those

Collected Papers of N. Denholm-Young, pp.83–94.

47

who were too old to fight. Here again we are not greatly helped, because knights comprised only a very small part of an army, and many fought on horseback (sometimes erroneously called knights) who were either young men aspiring to knighthood, but who had not yet received the accolade, or retainers of one sort or another owing mounted service to their feudal overlord. The King may have had a continental contingent fighting for him, and he was certainly aided by some Scottish barons and their vassals. The most usual estimate made by modern writers puts the royalist army at around 10,000, including some 3,000 cavalry, and the barons' army at half that number with perhaps only 5–600 horsemen. Furthermore, the men from London, who formed a fair part of their army, may have been ardent supporters of the cause, but were inexperienced and ill disciplined soldiers.

There had not been any spectacular changes in arms and equipment since those used by William the Conqueror and described in the previous chapter. The shape of the helmet had altered a little and now completely enclosed the head; the richer knights would wear fine mail with plate reinforcements, and surcoat – in some cases emblazoned with their arms. Plate armour for horses was still in its infancy, but some was being brought in, at great expense, from Poitou and Aquitaine. The cavalryman's principal weapons were the lance, the sword (broad or pointed) and occasionally the mace. The infantry wielded a variety of weapons; they had spears, slings and short bows and by now there were quite a few crossbows in use. The hauberk of mail armour was an expensive item of equipment, and it is fair to assume that many of the infantrymen (especially among Simon's men, for a rebel army always attracted a number of hangers-on) wore quilted leather jackets. The kite-shaped shield was still in use, although it had become shorter.

It is sometimes suggested that to offset his inferior numbers Simon de Montfort hoped to surprise the royalist force. It is difficult to see how this could be so, for on the day before the battle Simon sent the Bishops of London and Worcester to the King with one final appeal for peace. This letter, signed by Simon and Gilbert de Clare, ended with the words 'Given in the Weald, near Lewes, on the first Tuesday after the feast of St Pancras'. If the King did not already know (which is most unlikely) that the rebel army was close at hand, this letter told him so. Simon was no doubt worried by the overwhelming superiority of his enemy, but it was also almost a sacrilegious act to take up arms against your anointed sovereign, and Simon could be expected to make every effort to avoid bloodshed. The letter from the barons was short and most

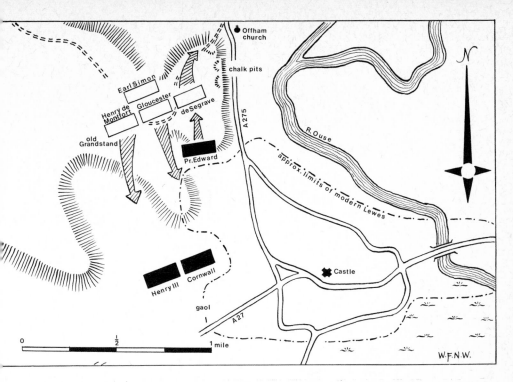

Battle of Lewes. Above: arrows denote Prince Edward's successful charge against the Londoners. Note chalk pits where large quantities of human bones have since been found

conciliatory, begging that the King should be guided by those who had his interests at heart and not by roguish counsellors. We may now detect some spark of grandeur in Henry, shining forth amid the stresses and strains of impending battle – a spark that did not entirely desert him until the day was lost. He returned a blunt refusal: 'Since it manifestly appears by the war and general disturbance already raised by you in our kingdom . . . that you do not observe your allegiance to us, nor have any regard to the security of our person, inasmuch as you have lawlessly oppressed those barons and other our lieges, who adhere with constancy to their truth towards us . . . We, therefore, value not your faith or love, and defy you, as their enemies.' The vials of wrath were overflowing; Lewes was about to be drenched with their lamentable outpourings.

In trying to piece together the story of an ancient battle the historian has to rely principally on the accounts in the various chronicles. Sometimes the chroniclers' tales are tendentious, wisely eulogizing the tactics and behaviour of the victors, but they certainly bring to light in a vivid way the pattern of a long forgotten past, from which we can draw our own conclusions. The reconstruction of the Battle of Lewes is fraught with imponderables, many interpretations are possible, but fortunately certain principles of war have not changed over the centuries and we have two incontrovertible facts upon which to build. We know the approximate position of both armies immediately before battle began, and within the last hundred years or so large quantities of human bones have been unearthed in pits around the site of the present gaol, in the chalk pits of Offham Hill, and in one or two other sites in or near the present town. These mortal remains of some massive disaster are unlikely to have been those of plague victims, for no plague pit would have been left unsealed long enough to contain so many bodies from a small town. Their discovery has helped us to determine those parts of the field where the fighting was fiercest.

The Monk of Lewes records in his chronicle that the battle took place between Prime and noon. Some prominent military historians consider that this account is wrong, for it would have involved the baronial army in the additional strain of a night march through the densely wooded country that lay between Fletching and Lewes. But if, as they suggest, the barons delayed their departure from Fletching to first light (sunrise on 14 May was at 4 a.m.) they could not have reached the top of Offham Hill before 7 a.m. at the earliest. Now almost all the chroniclers agree that the royalists had an outpost at the top of Offham Hill which was withdrawn on the evening of the 13th, except for one man who was surprised asleep at his post by the baronial army. Three hours after sunrise, in a dew-soaked field, the ground reverberating with the thud of a thousand tramping troops? Some soldier, some. sleep. No, if these almost unanimous reports are correct it surely means that Simon's army did arrive on Offham Hill in the early hours of the morning; although that is not to say that battle began as early as Prime (about 5.30 a.m.) – indeed the indications are that the first clash was at least two hours later.

But we go too fast. At the village of Offham Simon had the choice of making straight for Lewes or ascending Offham Hill and deploying his army on the broad plateau at its top. He would have been well informed on the local topography, even if he had not personal knowledge of the grounds. Simon was a most able commander and would have dismissed the direct route immediately, for it necessitated a march in column through a fairly narrow defile flanked by an escarpment to the west and the tidal marshes of the river Ouse that protected the town on its eastern and southern flanks. He would, therefore, have climbed Offham Hill by the sunken track that still exists.

Offham Hill is crowned by a plateau which stretches for about 1,000 yards from the chalk pits at its eastern end to the now dilapidated grandstand of the old Lewes racecourse on the west side; two prominent spurs extend from this plateau almost to the town, divided by fairly shallow re-entrants. Simon drew up his army on the plateau in four divisions, or 'battles' as they were sometimes called, and if we are right about the number of men he had under command he could have covered the whole front of 1,000 yards with his three forward battles five lines deep. This is a further example of Simon's military proficiency, for it was unusual at this time to have a formation in reserve. He took command of the reserve himself, and probably stationed it on the right rear of the army. On his left flank he placed the Londoners under Nicholas de Segrave, a veteran soldier who had escaped from Northampton; he was assisted by Henry de Hastings. The young Earl of Gloucester was in command of the centre battle and the right flank was entrusted to Henry de Montfort, who had with him his brother Guy and Humphrey de Bohun, whose father the Earl of Hereford was fighting on the royalist side. Before leaving Fletching the rebel army had sewn white crosses on the backs and fronts of their tunics, no doubt chiefly for ease in recognition; but as they knelt in prayer, following the usual pre-battle exhortation of their commander, this spiritual symbol may have stirred some into believing that in fighting for their liberties they were also honouring their God.

It is said that the alarm was first given in the royalist camp by a party of grooms who were foraging their horses in the meadows before the town; but surely Prince Edward must have had a watch in the keep of the castle, from where he would have seen the enemy array as soon as they topped the hill, or at first light. There was no element of surprise, nor was any intended, but the hill on which Lewes is built completely obscured the enemy's position from the King. Not only did he have to rely on the castle for information, but it would take a little time for him to lead the bulk of the royalist army round the hill and deploy in front of the town.

On the battle itself we are very short of reliable facts. We only know that Prince Edward, at the head of the cavalry, routed the Londoners on Simon's left flank. He bore a particular grudge against these men for the insults they had heaped upon his mother the Queen when she had attempted to leave the Tower to join him at Windsor the year before; and either on this account, or flushed with the exuberance of inexperienced youth, he pursued them for an unwarrantable distance, not returning to the battlefield until after his father's army had been defeated. Prince Edward was impetuous, but it is unlikely that he advanced upon the enemy without having first informed his father what he proposed doing, and possibly having received permission. That he was in advance of the main royalist army is certain, but probably the King and his brother Earl Richard of Cornwall had deployed for battle at the foot of the two spurs by the time the Londoners and the royalist cavalry left the field after a savage encounter in the area of the Offham Hill chalk pits.

But what would have been Simon's reaction to the departure of the Londoners? No commander with his flank exposed likes to await upon attack from that quarter, and Simon was not to know that Edward was still galloping towards Croydon. He could either fill the gap with the reserve and await the advance of the King in a favourable defensive position, or he could himself advance to the attack on a two-battle front, keeping his reserve intact and partly concealed behind the westernmost spur. The present writer is of the opinion that he adopted the second course. So long as Edward remained off the field the balance in numbers was slightly more favourable to Simon, and his small cavalry force now looked much more dangerous; Simon would certainly have understood the psychological value of attack to any army obviously slightly demoralized by the disappearance of its left flank; and finally we have the evidence of the burial pits round the gaol, which leads one to think that the heaviest, and in this case decisive, fighting took place somewhere in that area.

It seems that contrary to usual practice the King commanded the royalist left, and that his brother (with his son Henry of Almain) led the centre and was opposed by the Earl of Gloucester.* After a short but fierce fight Earl Richard's centre gave way and he was forced to take refuge in a windmill, from which he was later evicted amid ignominious scenes. This left the King facing the full fury of the de Montforts, for Henry and Guy came at him from the front, and it seems probable that victory was clenched when Simon swung the reserve in against the King's left flank. Poor Henry always got himself involved in battles when he would far rather have been building churches, and it is pleasant to record that on this occasion he fought with the utmost gallantry.

Before victory was complete intermittent fighting went on in the town itself and the marshy outskirts to the south, where it is said many lost their lives in trying to escape across the river Ouse. When Prince Edward eventually returned he was too late to rally the royalist forces and the town was already occupied by the rebels. The Prince, like his father and uncle, was made prisoner, but a number of important royalists fled and got to France.

We do not know how many perished on the battlefield or in the swampy marshes of the river. Probably no more than 3,000 men were killed on both sides, and stories of horsemen being sucked to their death in the mud while still in the saddle were certainly exaggerated and probably fabricated. Not many of the barons and knights on either side were killed.

This incident certainly did not delay the Prince's return to the field of battle, as is sometimes suggested, but had he contented himself with the partial rout of his hated Londoners and brought his cavalry back to take part in the main battle would the result have been different? Perhaps we are faced with enough imponderables as it is without having to pose this one, but it is tempting to think that with the weight of numbers and the preponderance of cavalry so greatly in their favour the royalists could have got the rebel army off balance with a flank and frontal attack from which they might not have recovered. If so Simon de Montfort's task would have been left unfinished, for he still had something to offer England.

*Thus Charles Oman, *A History of the Art of War in the Middle Ages*, p.427. Most accounts of the battle give the command of the centre to the King, but Oman's research has led him to a different conclusion. The change from the usual positions was probably due to the hurry and haste of the muster.

CHAPTER 4

The Barons'War

The Evesham Campaign

June–August 1265

*The field of Evesham is not an easy one for visitors to see, because the
battle was fought on what is now private, and for the most part in-
tensively cultivated, ground. The obelisk marked on the Ordnance
Survey one-inch map, sheet 144, a mile to the north of Evesham, is in
the grounds of Abbey Manor House. The owner will often give permission for it to be inspected, but it almost certainly does not mark
the site of the battle. This probably took place around Battle Well,
now an overgrown tangle of grass and rubbish which lies off a rough
track running due west, 100 yards south of Twyford House. Permission can usually be obtained to walk down this track and from it
one gets a very good view of the ground over which the battle was
fought. Today a part of the site is covered with fruit trees, and
although these would not have been there in 1265 the open, cultivated
ground may well have been sparsely clad with larger trees, for Green
Hill was on the edge of Feckenham Forest.*

*A panoramic view of the battlefield, and the line of approach to it
for part of Prince Edward's army, can be obtained by climbing the
Bell Tower in the old abbey grounds, but this can only be done by
appointment with the Vicar of Evesham. The site of the old ford
across the river Avon at Offenham and the clump of willows growing
at Dead Men's Ait, where it is generally thought that many of the
fallen were buried, can be reached by a short walk down Blayney's
Lane, which runs due east just by Twyford House.*

After his decisive victory at Lewes (see chapter 3), Simon de
Montfort probably took up his headquarters at the Grey Friars, a
recent foundation situated just to the south-east of the town wall.
Now he was master of the King and much of the kingdom. He had
reached this pinnacle of power through his superiority in the pro-
fession of arms. His prowess as a ruler was about to be tried.

Simon knew very well that although he had won England by the
sword he could only rule her through the King and with the consent
of the clergy and nobility. Above all his regime would have to be
royal and respectable. It was a task beyond the reach of almost any

54

man not invested with the aura of monarchy; Simon was never able to impose his will on any but a few of his closest confederates, and some of these turned against him. As the months unfolded he more and more assumed the role of a dictator, and many personal defects could be decried; but there were undoubted bursts of beneficent activity, and if in the end his military talent seemed to desert him we must remember that he was around sixty years old, quite an age for those days.

No sooner had the battle been won than emissaries from both sides met to negotiate peace terms. These were hammered out all through the night of 14–15 May, and were known as the Mise of Lewes. We cannot tell what was arranged that night at the Grey Friars, for if a document was drawn up it has not survived, but the release of the Northampton prisoners (which included young Simon de Montfort) without ransom and the imprisonment of Prince Edward and Henry of Almain as hostages for their respective fathers seem certain to have been included in the terms. Once the immediate and important points had been settled in outline Simon left Lewes, taking the King with him. Indeed Henry, now little more than a puppet king with his court circle dismissed, was to accompany Simon on most of his journeys and all the orders were sent out under the royal seal, for it was important to make it appear that they came with the King's full authority, freely exercised.

Simon's power was massive, but so were his problems. The country was a long way from being settled, especially in the north and west, where most of the barons brooded sullenly, awaiting time and opportunity. In France a hostile faction gathered round the English queen, and the threat of invasion – to meet which it was necessary to keep a large force under arms for many months – did not evaporate until the autumn gales made a Channel crossing too hazardous. There was constant correspondence with the French court, for in spite of the lesson learned from Amiens Simon thought it necessary to get French support for his regime – after all Henry was Louis's liegeman – by referring the terms worked out at Lewes to arbitration by Louis. Presumably this time the barons were careful to impose limitations on the points to be settled, but in the event nothing came of the arbitration because of papal hostility towards the baronial cause and the intransigence of the papal legate.

Early in June writs were issued for a parliament to be held in London. Four knights to be elected from each shire were to attend, together with the bishops and magnates. At this parliament 'the community of the realm' were required to give their assent to a provisional form of government that should continue until the peace terms had been finally settled. A triumvirate was established consisting of the Earls of Leicester (Simon) and Gloucester, and Simon's staunch supporter Stephen Berksted, Bishop of Chichester. These three appointed nine councillors by whose advice the King should reign, but the triumvirate, through their ability to dismiss any of the nine, made sure in whose hands the real power resided – and Simon's position was always greater than first among equals, a fact resented by Gilbert de Clare, the young Earl of Gloucester.

Two of the most powerful marcher lords were Roger Mortimer and Roger Leyburn; both had fought against the barons at Lewes and both withdrew to the comparative safety of their border fastnesses on the defeat of the royalist army. From here they were soon in almost open rebellion, refusing to attend the June parliament, or to release their Northampton prisoners, and in the autumn organizing an abortive attempt to rescue Prince Edward from Wallingford Castle. Simon and Gloucester forced them to submit and they were made to surrender the royal castles they held and hand over their prisoners; but in November they again proved contumacious and thinking to make themselves safer destroyed the Severn bridges, including the important one at Worcester. By now Gloucester had become disillusioned with Simon and was inclined to sympathize with his neighbouring marcher lords, but Simon obtained assistance from his Welsh ally Llywelyn and the marchers, fearing to be crushed, sued for peace.

By the end of 1264 Simon seemed almost secure. The north remained unsettled, but the French threat had subsided, at least temporarily, and the more important marcher lords were awaiting deportation to Ireland – to which country in fact they never went. Simon had greatly increased his landed possessions, and he and his family kept Christmas in almost regal style at Kenilworth, while the King celebrated the feast in comparatively humble circumstances at Woodstock. But the winter sun shines with spasmodic brightness, and even as Simon was preparing for his greatest contribution to English history the storm clouds were fast approaching.

The importance of the parliament summoned to meet at London on 20 January 1265 was not in its deliberations – for its principal purpose was to arrange for the liberation of Prince Edward and Henry of Almain, although other matters of national importance became its concern – but in its composition. The calling of a parliament was a long established custom, and knights had often been summoned to attend, but they came mostly to bring information, or receive instruction, and not to take part in important business. On this occasion the writ was broadened to include two burgesses from every city and town as well as two knights from every shire. It was, therefore, a fairly representative assembly, although the higher echelons were carefully chosen. The clergy, who on the whole supported Simon, sent 120 representatives, but only some twenty-three barons known to be favourable to the revolution were summoned. We may suspect that the commons were called because Simon needed their support, but the very fact that they were necessary shows a growing awareness that representatives of shires and boroughs had an integral part to play in the management of the country's affairs. Probably, had Simon survived Evesham, he would not have summoned them to every parliament – for one thing their constant attendance would have proved costly – but the seed had been sown that Edward was to nurture, and from which the modern polity of England would eventually emerge.

It was now that the signs of a widening chasm in the baronial ranks became openly apparent. The Earl of Gloucester was an arrogant young man who resented criticism, such as he received from this parliament for his support for the marcher lords. Moreover, he had been somewhat shaken by the imprisonment of the Earl of Derby – whose numerous offences quite justified Simon's action – and he began to feel insecure. When in February Simon refused permission for the de Clares and the young de Montforts to take part in one of those highly dangerous field exercises that in those days passed for tournaments, Earl Gilbert, accompanied by a number of knights, rode away from Westminster to join up with the dissident marcher lords. It was a quarrel that Simon tried hard to patch up, but although Gloucester made it clear, when later he offered his allegiance to Prince Edward, that he supported much of what Simon stood for politically, mistrust and envy prevented any personal reconciliation.

In May Edward gave Simon the slip. The Prince had been taken to Dover Castle directly after Lewes, and from there to Wallingford; after the rescue attempt at that castle Simon moved him to the greater security of his lake-fortress at Kenilworth. On 11 March, in Westminster Hall, Edward and his cousin Henry of Almain were formally given their liberty in the presence of the King. The ceremony was something of a mockery, for both men remained under close surveillance. However, at Hereford Simon gave Edward permission to take exercise outside the town walls. On 28 May, through a carefully prepared ruse, and some equine prowess, Edward outwitted his guards and galloped to the safety of Roger Mortimer's castle at Wigmore. Under his banner a ring of royalist steel would soon to be forged to contract remorselessly round Simon.

The Battle of Evesham was to last for little more than two hours, but looked at in depth it was merely the culminating episode in a campaign that lasted two months. The actual engagement was aptly summed up by the chronicler Robert of Gloucester: 'Such was the murder of Evesham, for battle it was none.' Prince Edward first outwitted the opposition and then smothered them by sheer weight of numbers. But the interest of the battle lies in Edward's sound strategy, which contrasted so favourably with his rash tactics at Lewes, and the incredible ineptitude of the two Simons, father and son. This extraordinary irresolution and incompetence on the part of the elder Simon started at the end of May when he found himself trapped to the west of the Severn. By this time he knew he would have to fight to retain his position, and he probably realized that the dice were loaded against him. A recent attempt to win back the Earl of Gloucester was clearly seen to have failed when that nobleman welcomed Edward on his escape from captivity; William de Valence and John de Warenne had landed in Pembroke with a small force in early May, and although London was still loyal many of the shires – particularly those on the Welsh border – had declared for Edward.

Simon seems to have been stupefied by the situation in which he found himself. For many days he remained at Hereford doing little except ordering the Bishop of London in the King's name to excommunicate Edward, while all around him the proud, aggressive marcher lords prowled menacingly. The Prince was the first to move, quickly securing Chester, Shrewsbury and Bridgnorth; he then set up his headquarters at Worcester. From here he moved down to attack Gloucester; Simon had reinforced the garrison with some 300 men under Robert de Ros, for it was almost the last place open to him for crossing the Severn. The town soon fell to the royalists, but de Ros held out in the castle for fifteen days. Between 10 and 22 June Simon made a treaty with Llywelyn, whereby in return for many advantageous concessions the Welshman agreed to help him with 5,000 spearmen. This treaty was ratified by the King on 22 June and immediately afterwards Simon decided to march on Monmouth, taking Henry with him.

It is not easy to understand this manoeuvre, unless Simon was interested principally in a personal vendetta against the de Clares, whose lands quickly became a prey to ravage and spoliation. Had he marched direct for Gloucester he might conceivably have relieved the castle before de Ros was forced to capitulate at the end of June. As it was he made for Newport after Monmouth, where he summoned boats from the inhabitants of Bristol, who were still

mail coif with headband   padded coif   tied aventail   padded arming-cap

cervellière   closed helm   closed helm   visored helm

12th and 13th-century head armour

loyal to him, even though their castle had remained in royalist hands since Lewes. When the boats were sunk in Newport harbour by ships despatched from Gloucester, Simon was forced to make a circuitous march back to Hereford through a wild piece of country whose primitive agriculture could scarcely support an invading army. It was a sullen and dispirited body of men, grumbling at the lack of bread and the quality of the Welsh mutton, that reached the comparative safety of Hereford somewhere about 20 July.

Prince Edward, having failed to bring Simon to battle in Glamorgan (although he nearly caught up with him at Newport), withdrew up the Severn and concentrated his now considerable force at Worcester, from where he positioned patrols along the river to give warning of any attempt on Simon's part to force a crossing. Towards the end of June Simon had sent word to his son Simon, who was Warden of the Peace for Surrey and Sussex and currently besieging the royalist castle at Pevensey, to join him immediately. There is a difference of opinion as to the exact date on which the order to raise the siege and march to his father's assistance reached Simon at Pevensey, but authorities agree that if the urgency was conveyed to him correctly he showed unforgivable tardiness.

It is understandable that he would seek reinforcements en route to Kenilworth (which town was presumably the rendezvous), and

59

it is just possible that he made the considerable diversion to London, where he is said to have been on 6 July, for this purpose. Certainly he wasted time in a cruel and wanton attack on Winchester on 16 July, and then he made for Oxford. From here it is alleged that he marched to Northampton. If this is correct – and not all accounts agree – he would have added some thirty miles to his march, and the delay involved could be excused only by a considerable recruitment of men-at-arms from that town. Nearly every account puts his eventual arrival at Kenilworth at 31 July – at least a month after he had received his marching orders. But, as one notable military historian has pointed out,* this date seems very unlikely and, for reasons that will appear shortly, he was almost certainly at Kenilworth by 30 July and probably a day or two earlier.

It is difficult to condemn completely this young commander for his marplot peregrinations round half of southern England, for although they could have further imperilled his father's position they appear to have greatly strengthened his own force, judging by the imposing list of baronial leaders who arrived with him at Kenilworth, not all of whom were at Pevensey. The younger Simon's worst offence was yet to come. He must have known that Prince Edward's army was in the neighbourhood – indeed he might have supposed it to be closer than it actually was – and yet for perhaps two days he took no precautions to safeguard his army. Kenilworth Castle at this time was a very different place from the ruin we know now. John of Gaunt converted it from a fortress to a palace, and in the seventeenth century the lakes were drained and the fortifications dismantled. Then, entirely surrounded by water with access only through well protected drawbridges, and with four massive towers and a keep commanding the inner and outer wards, the castle was virtually inexpugnable. Instead of sheltering the bulk of his army within this great fortress and maintaining outlying picquets, Simon elected to disperse his troops in the town, which with the priory offered more comfortable billets.

By the end of July Prince Edward was in the enviable position of being able to deal with his adversaries one at a time. He chose to march against the smaller army first. Numerically young Simon was almost certainly the weaker, but had his troops been on the alert and within the castle Edward would have put himself at a grave disadvantage in attacking him. However, he received information (some say from a spy called Margot, who posed as a man

*A. H. Burne, *Battlefields of England*, p.47.

in Simon's camp) that his enemy was quartered outside the castle and that no special precautions were being taken. He immediately prepared to march against him, and in the early hours of 1 August completely surprised the sleeping barons, killing or capturing many of their most important leaders. Some, half-naked, managed to escape this merciless slaughter in the streets; Simon was among their number, and finding a boat he gained the safety of the castle. But the royalists took not only important prisoners, but also fresh horses, many banners and a complete supply train which they caught entering the town.

The distance from Worcester to Kenilworth is some thirty-four miles, and with an army that comprised a considerable number of infantry – and there is no reason to suppose that he risked a cavalry raid only – this would have taken Edward at least fourteen hours. It would therefore have been impossible for him to have received the report from his spy and mounted an attack on Kenilworth in the early hours of 1 August if Simon's army had only reached that place on 31 July.

Edward was powerless against those who had taken refuge in the castle, and so, after resting his men for a day, he returned to Worcester on 2 August. It may have been a coincidence – although more likely he had received information – that on the same day as Edward left Worcester for Kenilworth Simon, bear-leading the King as usual, left Hereford. The royalist picquets had been withdrawn for the expedition and so Simon was able to ferry his army across the Severn four miles south of Worcester at Kempsey, where the manor belonged to Simon's old friend Walter de Cantilupe, Bishop of Worcester. This operation took up most of 2 August, and although Edward may have learned about it as he re-entered Worcester his troops would have been far too tired to attack. Simon was therefore allowed to spend the night in peace, and by the morning of the 3rd he had gone.

Now, as always when reliving these early battles, we are again to a great extent in the realms of conjecture. Certain dates and certain facts are assured, but nobody knows what was going through the minds of the two commanders. We can only try to put ourselves in their positions. In saying that Simon may well have been brought to battle at Evesham against his will, and by the superior generalship of Prince Edward, we are on fairly safe ground, and it seems almost certain that, unaware of the disaster at Kenilworth, he was trying to link up with his son, to whom he had sent a message. It is usually assumed that he took the longer route to Kenilworth via Pershore and Evesham in order to put as much distance as possible between himself and his enemy until he could join forces with his son and come nearer to parity in numbers with the royalist army.

On the day before the battle Prince Edward was not to know what was in Simon's mind, but he almost certainly knew that he had taken the Pershore route and that with the delay caused by having to cross the river there he would lie in the Evesham area on the night of 3 August. The river Avon surrounds Evesham on three sides in the form of a U, and the only entrance or exit from the south was by the fairly narrow bridge at Bengeworth. It is hard to understand why Simon led his army across this bridge (itself quite a time-consuming operation) and settled down in the trap. One can only assume that he misjudged the speed with which Edward would move, and perhaps Henry's piety and love of ease led him to the abbey in preference to a night in the open on the safer and strategically sounder left bank of the river.

It seems that Edward was just as surprised as we are that Simon put his army to such a hazard, for if it is true that he marched two columns (his own and Roger Mortimer's) down the left bank of the river he must have thought it more probable that he would have to fight there than in Evesham, which he covered with only one column – Gloucester's. A glance at an old map clearly shows that in those days the road to Stratford and Kenilworth ran to the east of the river past Offenham, Cleeve Prior and Marcliff, then up Buckle Street to Bidford – the present Norton–Harvington road was then at best a small track. Now if Edward had known for certain that Simon had shut himself up in the town, Roger Mortimer's column would have been sufficient to close the gap at Bengeworth and at the same time seal the Kenilworth road. There would have been no point in Edward carrying out the complicated manoeuvre that the chroniclers describe of crossing the river at Cleeve Prior and recrossing it again at Offenham to make a difficult junction with Gloucester's troops, who were marching parallel, but hidden from view, down the Alcester–Evesham road, unless he thought that the enemy might well be met with on the left bank. By the time he reached Offenham he would have learned the true position, and left Mortimer to close the southern exit.

It has been suggested that Edward split his army for the approach march from Worcester and advanced along three different routes; another suggestion is that in order to mislead the enemy he left Worcester by the north and then wheeled right-handed in a wide half circle. We can dismiss this last suggestion at once, for no sensible commander would waste time and energy on such a futile attempt at deception. To advance into battle with columns widely separated presents coordinating problems even with modern methods of communication, but when the only means of communicating was by messenger and the army was moving through fairly close country the difficulty would be immense. Moreover, there was no need for it, because in those days there was no disadvantage in large concentrations of troops. It therefore seems fairly certain that until he reached Dunnington (some seven miles north of Evesham) Edward kept his force concentrated, and then, as mentioned above, divided it into three columns with two crossing the Avon at Cleeve Prior, where the river is only a few feet deep, and the third advancing down the Alcester road.

Once again the royalist army was subjected to a night march. They must have reached Dunnington while it was still dark, for we are told that they were in position on Green Hill by 9 a.m., and the crossing at Cleeve, the march down the east side of the river and the recrossing at Offenham would have taken several hours. Once across the river Edward would have conferred with Gloucester, and as the overriding necessity now was to prevent Simon from breaking out of the trap the royalist line would have been stretched to the utmost to cover the 2,000 yards that separate the two arms of the river. This meant a thin line covering the width of Green Hill and even down to the river on both sides, but a plan would have been

Evesham. The approach of Prince Edward and Simon de Montfort

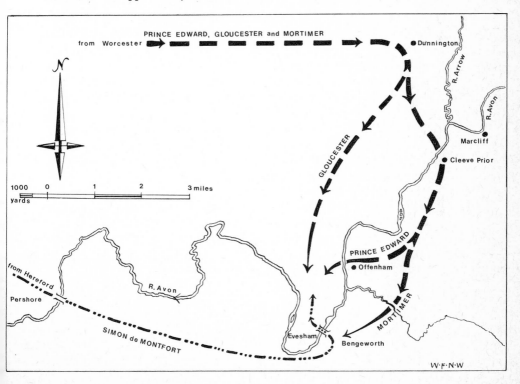

made to swing in the flanks as soon as it was seen at which point Simon would attempt to break through.

On the morning of Tuesday 4 August, while the royalist troops were nearing Evesham, Simon's army was preparing to move out across the bridge and onto the Kenilworth road. Some say that the delay in getting on the move was due to the King insisting on hearing mass first. This may be so, we cannot tell, but whatever caused the delay it was fatal to the slender chance that Simon's soldiers ever had of escaping the slaughter of that day. The tower of the abbey was almost certainly much higher than the present bell tower (built towards the middle of the sixteenth century), and from it a look-out could see far up the river valley and beyond Green Hill. But if the country to the north of Green Hill was wooded an approaching army might have reached the summit of the hill undetected. It was Simon's scouts who first reported the enemy's advance; but Edward marched into battle carrying the standards captured at Kenilworth, and this caused some initial confusion among the scouts. The look-out on the tower would merely have seen a dense column of men advancing along the Kenilworth road, and it seems possible that the delay in standing to arms may have been because for a little while – until the scouts had brought more definite news – these men were thought to belong to young Simon's army. By the time the situation was clarified the royalists were almost in position along Green Hill, and Roger Mortimer's column had closed the bridge.

It was now that Simon realized the full implications of his disastrous decision to enter Evesham, and according to William de Rishanger he was heard to say: 'Let us commend our souls to God, because our bodies are theirs.' But Simon's audacious spirit did not desert him in this hour of crisis. He decided that the best, indeed the only, chance to break through this iron ring was to pack a punch at the centre of the enemy line. Accordingly he drew up his army in a compact, deep column with a frontage that may not have exceeded 100 horsemen, cavalry in the van, followed by the English infantry and Llywelyn's spearmen bringing up the rear. It was about 9 a.m. when the head of the column marched out of Evesham towards Green Hill. The morning sky was loaded with black clouds, and across the darkening countryside the trees stood motionless in the lull that comes before a great storm.

The northernmost ridge of Green Hill, which the royalist army occupied, slopes gently down to a narrow valley and then the ground rises again and there is a slightly undulating plateau for half a mile before the hill descends to Evesham. Prince Edward's position on the furthermost crest would not have been apparent to Simon until his army had gained the plateau, but it would have been no different to what an experienced commander such as Simon would have anticipated. It was in fact an ideal defensive site, for the enemy had to approach in full view for half a mile, which enabled the royalists to see exactly what their intention was and to prepare their encircling movement, and action could be delayed until the rebel army was ascending the final slope. We do not know the numbers engaged on either side, but on the obelisk the battle casualties (which agree roughly with the *Chronicle of Lanercost* figures) are given as 18 barons, 160 knights and 4,000 soldiers. Most of them came from Simon's army, so he probably marched out of Evesham some 6,000 strong, but this number would have been at least halved when the Welsh contingent deserted before the battle was joined. The royalists, even without Roger Mortimer's column, probably numbered nearly 10,000.

At first Simon's punch, delivered at about the junction of Gloucester's and Prince Edward's battles, made some headway; but as soon as the Prince was able to swing in his two wings an avalanche of men, utterly irresistible, swept down upon the barons and the affair became a massacre. No quarter was asked for and none was given. As wounded horses limped from the field, their riders – among them Simon himself – continued to fight on foot until eventually, overwhelmed by the weight of numbers, they sank to the ground in quivering, writhing heaps. Simon had brought the King into battle clad in armour and completely unrecognizable; he only saved himself by constantly shouting until dragged from the fray: 'I am Henry of Winchester, your King. Do not harm me.' In two hours it was all over and some of the bravest and noblest men in England lay dead or dying in the tangled scrub of that tiny valley. Around the body of Earl Simon there lay his son Henry, Hugh le Despenser the Justiciar, Simon's friend Peter de Montfort, Ralph Basset, William Mandeville, John Beauchamp and many others bearing household names. Guy de Montfort was dragged from the field a mass of wounds, and his life was spared. The Welshmen's flight availed them nothing, for they were cut down in hundreds as they made for the river, or drowned in its waters.

As the battle raged the threatening storm broke overhead, and to the clash of arms and screams of wounded men and horses there was added the crash of thunder and the flash of lightning. The countryside trembled in almost total darkness, and later, when

Overleaf: Battle of Evesham with plan inset

Prince Edward's right battle

R·Avon

Offenham Ferry

PRINCE EDWARD and GLOUCESTER

EARL SIMON

WELSH

to Alcester & Kenilworth

from Pershore

Evesham

MORTIMER

N

W·F·N·W

1000 yards

0   ¼   ½   ¾   1 mile

35

Twyford House

left battle

lane to Offenham ferry

Green Hill

Simon

Welsh

Simon's tomb became a holy place, there were those who recalled another such occasion when nature herself seemed to shudder at the time of a great catastrophe.

The fury of the royalists knew no bounds; they butchered the corpses with insensate violence. Simon's body was completely dismembered, the head – according to some accounts – being sent to Roger Mortimer's wife at Wigmore and the limbs distributed in other parts of the country. After the battle the monks of Evesham Abbey were ordered by Edward to bury the dead, and recognizing Simon's mutilated torso they laid it, along with the body of Hugh le Despenser, in the abbey church. What happened to the common soldiery of his army, who although defeated, dead and discredited had in fact shed their blood in a cause that was far from lost, we do not know. Probably they found a mass grave by the river at a place which is called to this day Dead Men's Ait.

The Barons' War smouldered on until the middle of 1267, when the King and Prince Edward made peace with Earl Gilbert, who had once more turned his coat and with a strong force taken possession of London, and the men in the Isle of Ely – always a popular resort for rebels – had been induced to surrender.

The younger Simon had belatedly answered his father's summons for help, but before his troops reached Alcester he learned of the disaster at Evesham and returned sadly to Kenilworth. Before the castle was besieged he left to join other magnates of the baronial party who had escaped from custody, and together they conducted a short and forlorn resistance in the Isle of Axholme. Ordered to abjure the realm, he took up arms once again before leaving the country, when he fought at Winchelsea alongside the men of the Cinque Ports. His subsequent career abroad, and that of his brother Guy, did no credit to the family name. Kenilworth, as might be expected, resisted all attempts at reduction. The garrison scorned the efforts of the most modern siege engines and when in December 1266, near to starvation, they surrendered, secure in their honour, the great fortress remained battered but defiant.

On that fatal morning before Evesham, when he saw the enemy array, Simon is credited with saying (although we do not know who recorded these alleged utterances, for nearly all his close companions were killed), 'They come on well: they learned that from me.' And indeed Prince Edward's conduct of the campaign showed that he was already a fine commander. But he had learned more than the art of war from Simon de Montfort; soon he would become a great king, who understood and espoused the more important causes for which his uncle had fought and died.

CHAPTER 5

The Scottish Struggle for Independence

Stirling Bridge and Falkirk

11 September 1297 and 22 July 1298

The Battle of Stirling Bridge took place on ground that is now entirely built over. The actual bridge was a wooden one thought to have stood about fifty yards upstream from the 'old bridge' that was built about the beginning of the sixteenth century and is still in use for pedestrians. From this bridge the old causeway ran northwards in much the same direction as the present A 9 – only slightly to its west – and the battle took place on either side of this causeway and around the bridge. The best place from which to view the area is Stirling Castle.

The Falkirk site is a matter of conjecture. A possible position (and the one adopted in the following account) for Wallace's troops, which seems to be hinted at by some of the chroniclers and which is a natural defensive position, is to the south of the town and immediately to the south of Callendar Wood. Here the ground slopes down to the Westquarter burn (although the canal would not, of course, have been there in 1298) and was obviously partly a morass in those days. A good viewpoint for this position is from the high ground immediately to the south of Glen Village on the B 8028 road – Ordnance Survey one-inch map, sheet 61. Another possible site for the battle is right in the middle of the present town and cannot be defined.

So utterly vile was the weather on 18 March 1286 that the Chronicler of Lanercost assures us that most men took care to stay indoors. But only five months before King Alexander III of Scotland had married as his second wife the beautiful Yolande, daughter of the Count of Dreux, and after his council meeting in Edinburgh the King was anxious to join her at Kinghorn. His councillors strove, to no avail, to dissuade him from so imprudent a journey, and when he reached Dalmeny, where the sleet swept like a curtain down the Firth and the wind whipped the water to a fury, the boatman added his plea. Alexander little recked his warning and landed safely at Inverkeithing. But by now it was dark and the uniform blackness of the night made riding along that rugged coast perilous in the extreme. The King became separated from his guides; no one knows what happened, for no eye could pierce the darkness. The next morning they found his body lying just above the tide line.

The Scottish throne passed to a three-year-old girl, known to history as the Maid of Norway. Alexander's daughter Margaret was married to Eric King of Norway; she died in 1283 giving birth to the Maid, who was also called Margaret, and less than a year later Alexander's only surviving son followed her to the grave childless. The Great Council had at once accepted the Maid of Norway as the heir to the throne, but in 1285 when the King, who was only forty-two, took a young bride there seemed every chance of another prince. But destiny chose otherwise.

On the death of their king the Scots appointed a regency of six noblemen and prelates – three to rule on each side of the Forth – and for three years, while their young queen was still in Norway, nothing outwardly disturbed the general peace with England that had flourished now for almost exactly 100 years. But Edward I was quick to realize his opportunity. He assiduously courted the friendship of the King of Norway and set about obtaining papal dispensation for a contract of marriage between his son and Margaret of Norway, since the relationship between them was within the prohibited degrees. At a meeting in Salisbury in October 1289 between the representatives of the Scottish, Norwegian and English courts nothing was said about this marriage, although it was agreed that Margaret should come to Scotland and that the Scots would not marry their queen without Edward's prior consent. This was just a short step to a formal contract of marriage between these richly endowed young people.

The Scots, while accepting the marriage, were careful to impose upon Edward certain safeguards affecting their independence. The English king, with the gleaming prospect of the two kingdoms becoming united under one crown – and that the English crown – was prepared to make concessions. He agreed to ensure that the kingdom of Scotland should remain separate from England (although in a saving clause he reserved the right of the King of England 'in the marches or elsewhere'), that Scottish laws, liberties and customs should continue inviolate, and that failing any issue from the union of Margaret and his son Edward the Scottish crown should revert to the nearest heirs, without interference from the English king. These and other rash promises were signed and sealed under the Treaty of Birgham in 1290. Edward was confident; he could afford to wait for a long cherished design.

But the wheel of fortune turns with infuriating caprice. The seven-year-old Maid of Norway left her father's court in September 1290. Great preparations had been made for her arrival in Scotland, and many precious wedding gifts awaited her. But Margaret was never to receive them. On reaching the Orkneys she became very ill, and within a few days she was dead. Scotland was thrown into confusion; the guardians – as the regents were called – found it difficult to avert faction springing up among a dozen or so claimants to the throne, mostly basing their claims on dubious descent from distant monarchs.

Edward was asked to arbitrate and, as the only thing upon which the competitors could agree was their need to remain on the best of terms with the English king, he saw clearly that the path to arbitration led directly to overlordship. There was considerable resistance from the Scottish magnates to his attempt to get them to recognize his suzerainty, for, as they very properly pointed out, only their king could make such a promise; but the competitors had perforce to make concessions, otherwise – as Edward made it very plain – there would be no award. Having thus gained their individual fealty and homage to himself as their overlord, Edward launched himself into the long and tortuous business of arbitration. He was careful to be scrupulously fair and to allow the various cases to be fully postulated before the courts set up for that purpose. It soon became clear that two men had superior claims to any of their rivals – with the possible exception of John Hastings of Abergavenny. They were Robert Bruce, Lord of Annandale, and John Balliol of Barnard Castle. Both were descended in the female line from David Earl of Huntingdon, the younger brother of William the Lion.

Judgement was eventually given – at the end of 1292 – in favour of Balliol, whose case was based on the indisputable fact that through the rule of primogeniture he was the senior descendant of Earl David. Balliol was crowned at Scone on St Andrew's Day 1292. His reign lasted nominally until 1306, although most of it was spent as a prisoner in England or in papal custody. Once he had made judgement Edward quickly showed the Scottish king and people that he regarded King John as no better than his vassal, and he lost no opportunity of humiliating the King before his people. Balliol was summoned to London to hear appeals taken to Westminster from the Scottish courts, and it was even suggested that he should sit as a justice in Yorkshire in his capacity as an English baron. At first Balliol meekly submitted to these power politics, and when at the beginning of 1293 he revoked the Treaty of Birgham and released Edward from his commitments he probably sealed his doom. However, he was not an entirely ineffectual king, nor a complete puppet. He carried through some much needed administrative reforms in western Scotland, and he was at least the nominal head of Scottish affairs – even if, placed between the hammer and the anvil, he allowed himself to be manipulated by his barons – when the nation first commenced its struggle for independence.

In 1294 Philip IV of France and Edward I went to war over Gascony. King John was not only ordered to prohibit all sea communication between Scotland and France, but his personal service, together with a number of his earls and barons, was demanded for the war. Although the country was bedevilled by rival factions with conflicting interests there was sufficient unity to resist this summons to march with Edward, and indeed the 'Auld Alliance' with France, which went back 100 years or more, was reaffirmed in a fresh treaty with Philip – ratified by the Scottish parliament in February 1296.

Rebellion of this sort clearly surprised Edward, who lost no time in putting it down. Leaving French affairs to his brother Edmund of Lancaster, he ordered the levies to assemble at Newcastle in March. Berwick was sacked with a savagery reminiscent of a more barbarous age, and in April old John de Warenne, Earl of Surrey (a veteran of Lewes (see chapter 3)), utterly defeated the Scots at Dunbar. A haul of prisoners, impressive in name and rank, were taken at Dunbar, but King John retired to the north. The English king progressed leisurely through Scotland, demonstrating his puissance by such acts as the removal to England of the Black Rood of St Margaret from Edinburgh and the Stone of Destiny from Scone, and showing his strength in every important town between the border and Elgin. In June Balliol sued for peace. He was summoned to Brechin, where Edward dictated terms that were, not surprisingly, astringent, as a result of which the Scottish king joined the important Dunbar prisoners in England.

Scotland was occupied; her king and many of the most powerful baronial families were in exile or discredited, and of the original guardians only two, James the Steward and Robert Wishart Bishop of Glasgow, were left in the country. The outlook was bleak indeed, but from adversity painful efforts were extorted; a national uprising produced a leader worthy of the embittered and resolute men who rallied to his banner, many of whom were those who had supported the Bruce competitor against Balliol seven years before.

William Wallace was a feudal vassal of James the Steward (or Stewart), a man utterly devoid of fear, of great physical strength and energy, and capable of inspiring men through his enthusiasm for the cause of ridding Scotland of the English. Although he possessed considerable military talent, Wallace was perfectly content to share command of the army with Andrew Murray until the latter's death. He did not attempt to arrogate national leadership to himself, but was as ready to assume responsibility when it was thrust upon him as he was to relinquish it when fortune deserted him.

Wallace raised the standard of revolt in June 1297, and soon most of Scotland north of the Forth was aflame. Many of the higher baronage held land in England as well as Scotland and had much to lose if things went wrong, but their patriotism was never in doubt and in any case there were sufficient of the lesser gentry to hasten the English from this region. Moreover, this was a difficult time for Edward, who was at loggerheads with his clergy over a matter of taxation and in almost open conflict with two powerful nobles, the Earls of Hereford and Norfolk. Much of the onus, therefore, fell on Surrey at Berwick, a man who was no longer capable of speedy and decisive action. He wavered for a long time, but at last realized that he must advance deep into Scotland and force the insurgents to give battle. In the first week of September the English army under Surrey and the greatly hated treasurer, Hugh Cressingham, reached Stirling.

Wallace and Murray had taken up a strong position about a mile north-east of the wooden Stirling bridge on the south-facing lower slope of Abbey Craig. Their left was protected by the loop in the river Forth at that place, and before them a causeway ran to the bridge, flanked by meadows that were passable but wet. There was some delay while the Earl of Lennox and James Stewart volunteered their services to try to persuade Wallace and Murray to disband their force, and again when two Dominican friars were sent – with equal lack of success – on a similar mission. By the morning of 11 September Wallace's defiance made battle unavoidable. But Surrey treated the whole business with unpardonable insouciance. He had already sent away one contingent, because the Treasurer had complained of the expense, and now he held up proceedings through oversleeping.

The bridge was only wide enough for two horses to cross abreast, but two miles upriver, where the Forth meets the Teith, there was a ford where sixty men could cross simultaneously. Making use of

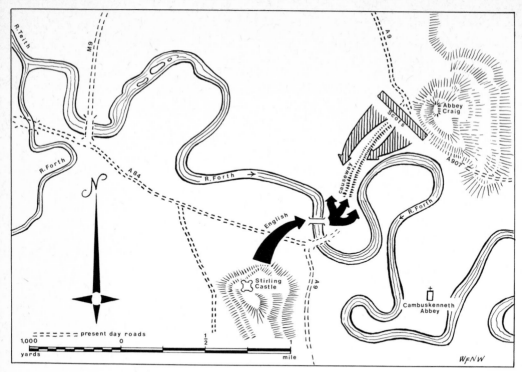

Battle of Stirling Bridge

this crossing to deliver a flank attack was virtually the English-men's only hope of success, but when Sir Richard Lundy suggested it the egregious Cressingham persuaded Surrey that it would be a completely unnecessary waste of time. Accordingly the men-at-arms were sent over the bridge. With what feelings of exultation must the Scots have witnessed this incredible piece of folly; and no sooner had a fair proportion (faultlessly adjudged by the Scottish leaders) of Surrey's knights crossed the bridge than Wallace and Murray unleashed their men along the causeway and over the meadows. The confusion was indescribable, for the attack suc-ceeded brilliantly in cutting the English army in two. The men on the far bank were insufficient to cope with the weight of attack, and Surrey was powerless to reinforce them at a rate greater than two by two. Some of the more lightly clad Welshmen escaped by swimming the river, and a few knights fought their way back before the bridge was destroyed – either by the Scots or on Surrey's orders – but most of the men who had crossed perished in the fray, in-cluding Cressingham, who chose the path of repentance like a true knight. The Scots did not get off unscathed, and Andrew Murray can probably be numbered among their casualties, for his death

74

shortly afterwards seems to have been due to a wound received in this battle.

Surrey then entrusted Stirling Castle to Sir Marmaduke Tweng, who was one of those who had fought his way back over the bridge, and made all haste himself to Berwick. The Earl of Lennox and James Stewart, who with commendable foresight had sat quietly on the fence, now seeing which way matters had gone called out their men in time to intercept the heavily laden baggage train, which they plundered close to the place that was soon to be the scene of a more disastrous English defeat.

Stirling Bridge decided very little. The English had been smitten, but not too grievously, and the battle showed them two things. First, that heavy cavalry were vulnerable to determined and resolute infantrymen, making proper use of their pikes* and bills, and, second, that the Scots were not only in deadly earnest, but were a force to be taken seriously. The lessons of this rebellion were not lost on Edward: he determined to tame these trouble-some clansmen to their yoke.

Not long after Stirling Bridge William Wallace was knighted and raised to the position of sole guardian. An honourable, but un-enviable, post in the circumstances. In the summer of 1298 Edward set up his headquarters at York and ordered the host to assemble on the borders ready for the advance into Scotland. Although there was no Marshal's Register for that year we have a better idea than is often the case, from horse-lists that have survived and the Scottish Roll for the year, of the numbers involved in the English army. Edward would seem to have mustered some 2,500 heavy cavalry (almost all the cavalry of Edward I's reign was armoured, only a few light horse being used in his battles) and the April infantry levies were for 12,500 men – 1,000 each from Cheshire and Lancashire and the rest from Wales. However, it seems probable that there were also some levies, or volunteers, from the border garrisons, making the infantry total a little in excess of 15,000. These figures are for the campaign, and by the time detachments had been hived off for special duties, such as garrisoning captured castles, the numbers for the actual Battle of Falkirk would be slightly less.

*At this time the pike, which was not quite such a long-handled weapon as that to be used by the Scots at Flodden (see pp. 203-4), was usually called a spear; but as this may conjure up the picture of a short-handled weapon of the type hurled by some Zulu warrior, premature use has been made of the words pike and pikemen. The bill was a kind of halberd, wielded like a two-handed axe, and was used more by the English than the Scots.

At the beginning of July the army crossed the border and marched through Lauderdale to Fala, the Braid Hills and Temple Liston,* a few miles to the west of Edinburgh. Feeding an army of this size in a land that the Scots (and English) had largely laid waste presented a formidable problem, for regular supply trains were not yet a feature of the commissariat, and supply by sea was most uncertain. The English and Welsh soldiers suffered great hardship, and there was at least one ugly incident, involving casualties and much bitterness, when Edward rashly permitted the Welsh contingent to enjoy a shipment of wine that had unfortunately arrived unsupported by more solid substance. Although Wallace could hardly be expected to take to the hills and leave Scotland south of Stirling at the mercy of the invader, no one seemed to know where his army was. Dirleton and two other castles were taken by that militant prelate Anthony Bek, Bishop of Durham, in the interlude; but so grave was the supply position that Edward was on the point of turning back when news was brought to him by the Earls of Angus and March† that the Scottish army was in Callendar Wood beside Falkirk, only fifteen miles away. Edward immediately advanced and the English bivouacked that night (21 July) just east of Linlithgow.

Wallace has sometimes been criticized for offering battle with considerably inferior numbers, but he really had little alternative, and having decided to fight he took up a strong position on the southern slope of Callendar Wood with the Westquarter burn running below him.‡ Another burn ran down from Glen Village; where the two met they overspilled, and in the naturally boggy ground a fair-sized sheet of water was formed which was not immediately visible to the English troops. In spite of Stirling Bridge the Scots were still very fearful of the English armoured horse, and Wallace (who was possibly the first man to adopt the formation) organized his troops into what later became the famous schiltron. This was a tight circle or square of perhaps as many as 1,500 pikemen, with the front ranks kneeling, their pikes at an angle of forty-five degrees. The whole formation bristled like a porcupine

*Now called Hallyards.
†This was before the days when the Douglases held the title of Angus, and this earl was Gilbert de Umfraville; March was Earl Patrick, also of Dunbar, who had been an adherent of the English cause for some while.
‡See description of battlefield at beginning of chapter. The chroniclers give very scanty information as to the site of the battle; the present writer agrees with the location favoured by Professor G. W. S. Barrow.

Scottish clansman c. 1300. He wore a mantle (or plaid), saffron shirt, and sometimes a ring or chain mail byrnie, or quilted gambeson

and presented a living *cheval de frise*. In between the schiltrons were positioned the archers under Sir John Stewart and in the rear the cavalry. The schiltrons were further protected by wooden stakes, but it is hardly likely that in the time available anything could have been constructed that would seriously have hindered heavy cavalry. Edward, who may have been somewhat shaken from being trodden on by his charger during the night, and was anyway unimpressed by the strength of the opposition, wished to send men and horses into battle fed and rested, but his barons

*English longbowman.
Wearing chapelle-de-fer
and quilted gambeson*

W.F.N.WATSON

were fearful of being taken unprepared,* so he gave orders for the vanguard, under his adversaries of the previous year Norfolk and Hereford, to advance to the attack. The Bishop of Durham commanded the second battle and the third, under Edward himself, was held in reserve.

On meeting the boggy ground the Earls felt round to their left and the Bishop did likewise to the right. Bek, probably with better military intuition than his impetuous second-in-command Ralph Bassett, wanted to hold back in order to synchronize his attack with that of the left, and allow the reserve to come forward. Such foresight was met with some uncanonical advice from Bassett and the attacks duly went in. Considerable success was achieved early on, for the Scottish cavalry left the field having hardly struck a blow, and the archers were ridden down and most of them, including their commander Sir John Stewart, killed. But when the English horse turned upon the schiltrons, now hopelessly isolated, they failed to pierce the steel wall. However, Edward's army was strong in archers using the comparatively new and formidable weapon, the longbow. This weapon took a dreadful toll of the closely packed Scottish infantry, and as the gaps in the ranks increased from the inexorable hail of arrows and sling missiles the cavalry were able to crash their way through the crumbling ranks and complete the discomfiture of the Scottish foot. The schiltrons had proved their worth against armoured horse, for we know that there were more than 100 horses killed, but they were no match for the combined attack of horse and bow, and as yet they had not learned to be effective on the move. Wallace and most of the Scots magnates escaped into the great forest behind, but they left a vast number of the rank and file dead or dying on the field of battle. Casualties among the English were comparatively few, and they lost only two knights of rank.

Edward first used the longbow in his Welsh campaign, in which country longbows made from elm were known to have been in use as early as 1150, but Falkirk was the first battle of importance in which the power of this weapon was felt. As it dominated the European battlefield for the next 200 years and gave the English (who curiously enough were the only nation to make full use of it) a superiority in firepower over all her adversaries, we should pause to examine its characteristics.

The bow was made from yew – Spanish or Italian yew being

*In fact it was the Scots who were unprepared. Wallace himself was away on patrol when the English were first sighted.

Overleaf: Battle of Falkirk with plan inset

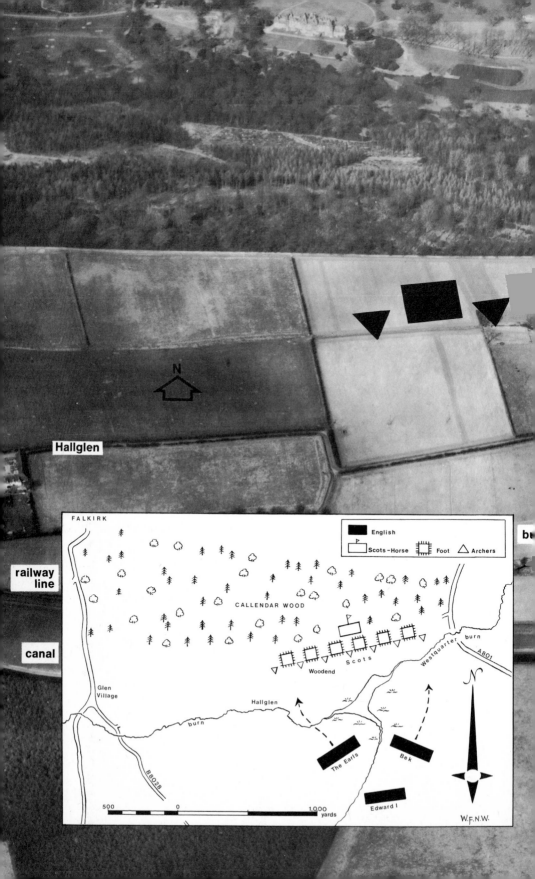

Hallglen

railway line

canal

FALKIRK

English

Scots-Horse   Foot   Archers

CALLENDAR WOOD

Scots

Woodend

Westquarter   burn

A801

Glen
Village

Hallglen

burn

B8028

The Earls

Bek

Edward I

500   0   1,000
                              yards

N

W.F.N.W.

CALLENDAR WOOD

Woodend

SCOTS

Westquarter burn

The Earls

Bek

Edward I

preferred to the native species – and was five foot six inches to over six foot in length. The draw weight of a military bow (when drawn thirty-six inches to the ear) would not have been under sixty pounds and could have reached ninety according to the user. The normal practice range was 220 yards, but arrows could be fired much further when the bow was elevated. Arrows were about three feet long with a triangular broad head; the fletching was of goose feather, or preferably peacock feather, which was stiffer than goose; the feathers of crane, swan and other birds were also used. The strings of bows were of hemp, or silk, and at a later date than Falkirk would have been dressed with some water-proofing glue.

Archers wore quilted jackets – very seldom mail – and they carried from a dozen to twenty-four arrows bound together in a sheaf suspended from the belt. They were also usually armed with a dagger or short sword for in-fighting. A good archer would discharge twelve arrows in a minute with considerable accuracy up to 220 yards. At a range of more than 200 yards arrows would not easily penetrate a mail hauberk, and certainly not plate, but at shorter ranges their penetration power was very considerable. Much of the destruction was wrought among the horses, for even the large and valuable Spanish destriers ridden by the great men of the time could not be entirely protected, and a grounded knight was as helpless as a tortoise on its back.

With defeat in battle the strident voices of discontented vili-penders are quickly raised, and yesterday's hero becomes tomorrow's galoot. So it was to a great extent with William Wallace. From being the sole guardian of the realm, elected to rule the country on behalf of the exiled king, he became little better than a guerilla captain. Nevertheless, for the next seven years, whether leading Scotsmen in their homeland or champion-ing their cause on the continent, he steadfastly refused to submit, and the name of Wallace became synonymous with nationalism. Finally, a hunted fugitive with a price upon his head, he was basely betrayed. He was led captive through the streets of London to be butchered under Smithfield's trees.

But the torch that Wallace had lit was soon to be carried by another, whose courage and tenacity of purpose qualified him in every respect to become the ruler of a race of men as tough and determined as any on earth. Robert Bruce was a young man of divided loyalties; but when at last, albeit through a deed of shame, he seized the reins that fate had thrown him, Scotland was to rediscover the true spirit of her people.

CHAPTER 6

The Scottish Struggle for Independence

Bannockburn

23–4 June 1314

The greater part of the battle area is now built over and it is very difficult to get a clear idea of what happened from walking the ground. However, from the higher ground around Foot o' Green (one mile south-west of Bannockburn) the visitor can visualize the Scots' position on 23 June and the English attack across the Bannock burn – although at the time of writing (January 1973) it is not possible to say whether the new motorway now under construction will interfere with this view. Again one can get a fair idea of the Carse (now cultivated farmland lying to the east of the railway) and Broomridge by going down the side road in Bannockburn that leads north from the A 9 towards the A 905 (Ordnance Survey one-inch map, sheet 54). There is a track running parallel to the railway line which leads almost to the burn somewhere near the place at which the English army must have crossed on the night of 23–4 June.

Fortunately, it is not necessary (although very pleasant on a fine day) to drive, or walk, all round the battlefield, because the National Trust for Scotland have an excellent exhibition at the monument, which is just off the Glasgow road (A 80) at Bannockburn. Here they have a very good model of the field of battle and they also have an audio-visual account of the lead-up to Bannockburn and of the battle itself. This exhibition is open during the months of April to September inclusive.

The Bruces, who were of Norman origin, gained favour and considerable property under Henry I of England and David I of Scotland. The Robert Bruce, known as the Competitor, who was the future king's grandfather, was not only a large English land-owner, but had been for a time Governor of Carlisle. This accounts for the fact that the family, like many others in the same position, were often found fighting for the English king although they may have held Scottish land and titles. King David had given the Robert Bruce of his day the lordship of Annandale, and through marriage the family later acquired the earldom of Carrick.

The Competitor's grandson, also called Robert Bruce, was born – probably at Turnberry Castle – on 11 July 1274. This Bruce, the son of an undistinguished father, was born and reared a Scot, and after early years of double allegiance, doubts and disappointments was to gain through conquest the throne denied to his grandfather through arbitration. We have evidence from the opening of his tomb at the beginning of the last century that he was six feet tall – which was very tall for those days – and powerfully built; concerning his features we know nothing, but of his character we are well informed. In the early days there was clear evidence of a hasty temper and lack of control, but on assuming a position of responsibility he kept in leash this dark and explosive side. Instead there developed qualities that fitted him to bring his country safely through some of the most desperate years of her history: a belated but sincere patriotism, a steel-like composure in the face of all dangers, an ability to bear defeat with fortitude and a resilience to rebound to victory, and above all and in great measure the human touch, combined with a willingness to share and endure all that he asked of his men.

Shortly after Falkirk (see pp. 75-82) Edward had to leave Scotland, and the nationalist party had a chance to gather up the pieces and make a fresh appraisal of their position. Robert Bruce and John Comyn, the younger of Badenoch, were elected guardians. We do not know if Bruce fought at Falkirk; two years previously his family were known to be loyal to Edward, but in 1297 he had thrown in his lot with the nationalists, so he could well have been under arms against the English at Falkirk. Certainly he learned some lessons from the way that battle was fought. However, we are still in the period of Bruce's double allegiance. When at the beginning of 1300 it was decided to take action against dissidents in his own part of the country – where his father had always remained pro-English – he resigned the guardianship, but did not immediately offer his sword to Edward.

The fate of the border Scot had been for some time now – and indeed was to continue to be with little respite for a further 300 years – one of involvement in acts of terrorism, guerilla warfare and large-scale raids. But for the first three years of the new century it might be said that the Scots succeeded in holding their own, and with a reversion to a single guardian (Sir John de Soules) diplomatic activity supplemented, if it did not actually replace,

Engraving from impression in British Museum of Robert the Bruce's second great seal

strife in an attempt to bring King John back to his own. In 1301 a strong incursion into the south-west of the country under the Prince of Wales, to coincide with an advance into Selkirk by his father, met with only limited success – largely due to the efforts of Robert Bruce, whose castle of Turnberry held out until the late autumn.

But the year 1302 was one of gloom for Scotland, heralding the disasters of 1303 and 1304. Early in that year Bruce turned his coat yet again, and from being a passive supporter of the patriots became an active opponent, offering the English king the assistance of his armed retainers. At almost the same time the French defeat at Courtrai lost the Scots the assistance of King Philip, and Pope Boniface VIII also withdrew his support for the nationalist cause.

Edward's invasion of 1303–4, which took him once more as far north as Elgin, was at first by no means a triumphal progress. John Comyn and Simon Fraser seriously mauled the English army south of Edinburgh and both Stirling and Brechin Castles put up a stern and resolute defence against the most powerful siege engines. Not long after the fall of Stirling peace terms were arranged from which the Scots emerged quite favourably. They were to be allowed their own laws and customs (Edward reserving the right to be consulted on any alterations), prisoners were to be released free of ransom, and no reprisals were to be taken. One man only was beyond any act of mercy: William Wallace was proscribed and his life when captured was forfeit. But in spite of these fairly generous terms and a willingness on the part of Edward to meet the Scots in full consultation on their form of government the country was to all intents and purposes occupied and under the tutelage of English administrators: a position not very different to that pertaining directly after Falkirk.

Edward's nephew, John of Brittany, was appointed Governor of Scotland, and he was advised by a Scottish council which included both Bruce and Comyn of Badenoch. In 1304 Bruce's father died in England and Edward at once conferred upon the son the family titles and lands, for he felt assured of the young man's loyalty. But in that very summer, quite unknown to Edward, Bruce was in communication with William Lamberton, Bishop of St Andrews, who although a member of the ruling council was a completely dedicated nationalist. These secret negotiations, in which the two men formed a compact to help each other in case of need, almost certainly ranged over a possible successor to King John in the interest of the nationalist cause. Now Comyn was John Balliol's nephew and in default of any children his heir apparent; here was an obvious stumbling block to any aspirations that Bruce may have had to the crown. However, we may be fairly sure that what happened in the church of the Friars Minors at Dumfries two years later was not premeditated murder.

It is a measure of Robert Bruce's courage and daring that just at a time when everything seemed to be going his way – a second marriage to an influential Irish lady, great possessions in England and Scotland, the trust and favour of the English king – he should suddenly decide to hazard all for a prize which, although the most dazzling gift that fortune could bestow, might be grasped, if at all, only on the other side of a river of blood both wide and deep that most would fear to cross. To achieve his object the full cooperation of John Comyn was essential. The two met in the church at Dumfries while Edward's justices were in session at the castle. What exactly happened before the high altar in that church we shall never know; but it is reasonable to suppose that Comyn, as many other Scottish noblemen would have been, was appalled at any idea of overthrowing his legitimate sovereign, no matter how ineffectual that sovereign might be. There had never been more than a thin veneer of friendship between the two, and high words may have been spoken when suddenly Bruce lunged his dagger into the unsuspecting Comyn, and before his uncle Sir Robert Comyn could come to his rescue Bruce's companions had completed the woeful deed. They then slew Sir Robert as well. The Bruce faction, who seem to have ensured themselves of adequate support, now took possession of the town and seized the castle, in which the terrified justices were still assembled.

Having imperilled his immortal soul in the eyes of friend and foe, Bruce must have realized that there could be no turning back. The speed and success with which he consolidated his position in the south-west of the country between 10 February 1306 when he slew the Red Comyn and 27 March when he had himself crowned at Scone show that although he may have intended to delay action until after Edward I (who was clearly on the way out) had died, his plans for a coup d'état were well advanced. He, or his supporters, succeeded in capturing five important castles, and only the refusal of Sir John Menteith to surrender Dumbarton prevented him from having complete control of the Firth of Clyde, the door through which succour could come from Ireland.

Only hazy details survive of the coronation of King Robert I; it seems that there were two ceremonies, one on 25 and another on 27 March. Three bishops, Wishart – in whose diocese the murder had been committed and who had absolved Bruce from spiritual damnation – Lamberton and Murray, the Bishop of Moray, were present, together with at least three earls, – Lennox, Atholl and Menteith.*

The Earl of Fife, whose presence was most needed (because by tradition the Earls of Fife had the privilege of placing the Scottish kings on the Coronation Stone), was completely under Edward's control, but his sister the Countess of Buchan – whose husband was a cousin of the Red Comyn's – inspired by loyalty to an ancestral duty put pride of race above petty faction and hastened to Scone in time to crown the new sovereign on 27 March.

Edward reacted strongly, appointing Aymer de Valence (Comyn's brother-in-law) as his representative in Scotland with wide and ferocious powers. De Valence soon captured, and sent to England, the troublesome bishops Lamberton and Wishart, and in June he

*Alan Earl of Menteith, not to be confused with Sir John Menteith the keeper of Dumbarton Castle.

Horse armour (bards). Trappers (left) of mail, or cloth, sometimes quilted or studded, were worn from the 12th century. By early 14th century all-round defences of solid plate had been developed (right). Costly and weighty, they appear not to have been much used in war apart from the testière or chamfron protecting the horse's head

caught Bruce's army unprepared at Methven, near Perth, and completely destroyed it, forcing Bruce to fly with but a hundred or two supporters. Travelling west and south into Argyll and then Ayr, his small band suffered a further defeat at Dalry, after which his queen, and certain other ladies, were sent off in the care of Bruce's brother Nigel, the Earl of Athol and James Douglas to the supposed safety of Kildrummy Castle on Donside. But this place fell to de Valance in September and the party made off north-wards to seek sanctuary at St Duthac at Tain in Ross-shire. This availed them little, for they were seized by the Earl of Ross, a staunch supporter of Balliol, and sent to England. Edward's infamous behaviour towards these ladies was one of the most discreditable acts of his reign. It is true that the Queen was placed in honourable captivity, but her sister-in-law and the Countess of Buchan were confined to iron cages and hung from the walls of Roxburgh and Berwick Castles respectively, while Bruce's daughter, a very young girl, was for a while similarly treated in the Tower of London. Nigel Bruce was hanged at Berwick, and to complete the family discomfiture two other brothers, Thomas and Alexander, were captured a few months later and suffered a similar fate.

The defeat at Methven had one redeeming feature for Bruce,

which was that it forced him to adopt the guerilla tactics that from now on served him so well right up to the time when through his brother's over-chivalrous conduct he was obliged to give battle at Bannockburn. We cannot trace in detail the long years of endeavour and endurance during which Bruce's resilient spirit and sturdy body kept the flame of revolt alive. Slowly but surely, through a series of small-scale engagements based on surprise and mobility, large areas of Scotland were won to his cause. There are months early on when we lose all trace of Bruce's movements; hunted from one hiding place to another he seems to have left the country, or at least the mainland, for a while. Then in the summer of 1307 came the first taste of victory at Loudoun Hill, where his men defeated de Valence in a small engagement, and a few days later Sir Ralph de Monthermer was roughly handled and forced to take refuge with his men in Ayr Castle.

The death of Edward I in 1307 brought a welcome respite, for his son, although a brave fighter with campaign experience, was not cast in the warrior mould of his father. He preferred less arduous pursuits to warfare and it was not long before he had troubles and difficulties that kept him at home. However, he had no intention of relinquishing the pressure upon Scotland, which was maintained, as before, first through the governorship of John of Brittany, and then by Aymer de Valence. But from 1308 the tide gradually began to turn in Bruce's favour. By the end of that year he was in control of Scotland north of the Tay, and had won recognition from Philip IV of France, and in March of the following year Bruce was able to hold his first parliament at St Andrews. Edward II stirred himself into action in 1310 and 1311, but the considerable armies that he brought into Scotland were unable to achieve anything except to infuriate Bruce and his now considerable following, who replied with devastating raids into most of the northern counties, where Bruce was able to raise huge sums of protection money.

By 1313 the reduction of Lothian was almost completed and it could be said that with the exception of a few strategically important castles Bruce was in control of almost all Scotland, and a truce with the northern counties had been proclaimed. The year preceding Bannockburn might be called the year of the castles, when with reckless heroism, and a commando style worthy of the best Achnacarry* tradition, Bruce himself and a few of his more daring captains waded moats and scaled walls at the head of small bands

*Lochiel's seat was used as the commando training centre in the 1939–45 war.

of picked men. Falling upon the enemy from their scaling ladders and forcing them to surrender after fierce hand-to-hand combat, they took by stealth and storm Perth, Roxburgh, Linlithgow and Edinburgh Castles. Here was leadership of the highest quality from men hardened by constant fighting, in command of troops trained by example and not by precept. At this time the English had none to match them.

By the spring of 1314 the only castle of any real importance still in English hands was Stirling. Edward Bruce had laid siege to this castle for almost three months in 1313, and had then agreed to a proposition by its hard pressed castellan Sir Philip Mowbray that if an English army had not relieved him by midsummer's day 1314 – which was then a year ahead – he would surrender the castle.* This chivalrous, but unwise, gesture had no doubt been prompted in part by the difficulties that Edward was known to be having with his barons – some of whom had recently killed the hated favourite Piers Gaveston – which might be expected to keep him at home. But it was a challenge that no English king could afford to neglect, and was to give Edward the necessary spur to attempt the reconquest of Scotland. It was a piece of folly that earned for its instigator a severe rebuke from his elder brother, because it committed the Scottish king to an open conflict with the might of England, which was something that for the past six years he had been studiously avoiding.

As the deadline approached Edward made preparation to cross the border with a formidable host, drawn mostly from the northern and Midland counties and many parts of Wales. Orders also went out for a large number of ships and sailors to mobilize for the purpose of transporting supplies and troops north, and to ferry men over from Ireland – Bruce's father-in-law, the Earl of Ulster, commanded the Irish contingent. We have considerable information concerning the extent of this call-up, but we do not know exactly how many men responded – although the death of Gaveston had rallied many barons to the King's side who were now prepared to send their full feudal muster – nor how many deserted before the battle was joined. It seems probable that the English king eventually arrived at Bannockburn† with a force not far short of 20,000

*By the custom of those times a castle was considered to have been relieved when the relieving army had come within three leagues (nine miles) of it.

†In those days the scene of the battle was within the parish of St Ninians and Bannok was a sub-division of this parish. The battle was eventually to be called after this small place, and *not* after the famous burn.

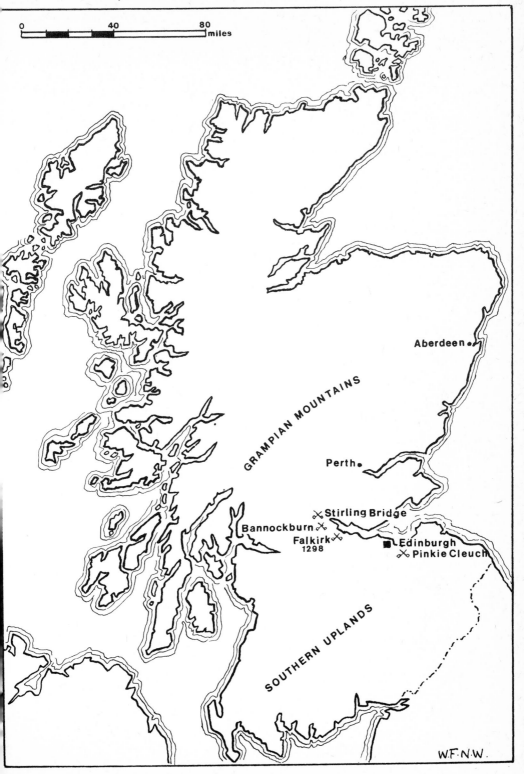

0   40   80 miles

Aberdeen •

GRAMPIAN MOUNTAINS

Perth •

⚔ Stirling Bridge

Bannockburn ⚔
Falkirk ⚔
1298   ■ Edinburgh
            ⚔ Pinkie Cleuch

SOUTHERN UPLANDS

W.F.N.W.

men, of which 2,500 were heavy cavalry. Of the 16–17,000 infantry we have no means of telling how many were archers, although in the first writs (subsequently cancelled) 5,000 had been summoned from a total of five counties, and more from Wales. Undoubtedly Edward was well supplied in this important arm, which makes it all the more astonishing that he made such little use of it. The baggage train was immense in size and value; for Edward, confident of victory, had brought into Scotland every kind of aid to a life of luxury.

We are in the realms of conjecture when trying to put a figure on the number of men with which King Robert could meet this great English array. It has to be remembered that even now not all of Scotland was behind their king; there were those prudent enough to hold off and a few bold enough to oppose. Moreover, the guerilla tactics adopted hitherto would not have required a large force. We may therefore place some confidence in Barbour's* figure and say that the Scottish infantry numbered no more than 7,000 and was probably nearer 6,000, and that there were 500 Horse (smaller and carrying lighter armour than their English counterpart) under the Earl Marischal, Sir Robert Keith. In addition there were perhaps as many as 3,000 men known as the 'small folk', who possessed the enthusiasm but not the training of the more regular soldiers and whose discipline might be suspect.

Edward followed the route taken by his father before Falkirk, but he seems to have allowed too little time in which to move so vast a host, for we find the army being hustled along in the great heat of that June in order to keep the tryst with Sir Philip Mowbray within the allotted time. Some twenty miles was covered on Saturday 22 June, and by that night the army had reached Falkirk. Bruce had ordered his troops to assemble in Torwood, which forest stretched from a point north and west of Falkirk almost to the Bannock burn, and was separated from the New Park only by the cultivated ground in the valley of the burn. Here he drew them up in four battles, with his own forming the rearguard as he fell back to a strong defensive position.

This was in New Park, an extension of the older King's Park, which had been fenced by Alexander III in 1264. It was a fairly well wooded area rising not too steeply to a broad plateau. The actual park was about a mile long and almost two wide, and we must presume that there was an entrance on the south side not far up from the Bannock burn. The road from Edinburgh to Stirling ran

*John Barbour of Aberdeen, *The Bruce*, 198.

92

through Torwood and passed just to the east of New Park. The Scottish king adopted a somewhat irregular formation, for he had to be prepared for more than one contingency. Edward could not outflank him to the west on account of the denseness of the woodland, but he could attempt a frontal attack, or he might pass below the escarpment and either try to turn the position from that flank or make straight for Stirling Castle. Bruce therefore placed his own battle on the right, occupying the ground from near the burn to about where the present monument stands; on his left was Edward Bruce whose own left was turned back overlooking the low ground below; the Earl of Moray's men were positioned still further back near St Ninians Church to guard the road, and in reserve were the cavalry and the battle nominally commanded by Walter the Steward, but as he was only a youth it was actually commanded by James Douglas. The 'small folk' were left in a valley between Coxethill and Gillies Hill. Against the possibility of a frontal attack the position had been further strengthened by a series of pits, or pots as they were called, which were camouflaged and in which sharpened stakes awaited horse and man.

From this position the Scottish king despatched Sir Robert Keith to spy out the English host. The Earl Marischal was greatly perturbed at the overwhelming strength of the enemy; the whole chivalry of England seemed to be moving through the forest. The knights, sitting their great war horses with the sun glinting off their basinets and burnished armour, their colourful banners caught in the light summer's breeze, made a deep impression which Sir Robert anxiously conveyed to his king. Bruce wisely suppressed such a disturbing report and told his soldiers that the English were advancing in disarray.

At some place near to present-day Bannockburn Sir Philip Mowbray joined Edward and pointed out to the King that technically the army had relieved Stirling Castle, and that not only was there no need for the garrison to surrender, but in all probability Bruce, whose force was very small, would not risk a fight. However, Edward was in no mood to stand on technicalities; he was there with a huge army to subdue the turbulent Scot once and for all. Edward's van was commanded jointly by the Earls of Hereford and Gloucester* (a tactless arrangement, for the two were usually

*Gilbert de Clare, Earl of Gloucester, was Edward's nephew and only in his early twenties. It is easy to confuse him with his stepfather Ralph de Monthermer, who from 1298 until the death of his wife Joan (Edward's sister) in 1307 was given the style and title of Earl of Gloucester.

at loggerheads) and they appear to have wasted no time in going into the attack. If they did not act under orders it was certainly Edward's intention that they should attack, for although the afternoon was by now far advanced he would not have wanted the foe to escape overnight, and to guard against this – and perhaps with the alternative task of relieving the castle garrison – he sent Sir Robert Clifford and Sir Henry Beaumont, with about 600 horse, along the foot of the escarpment to cut off the expected retreat of the Scots.

As every schoolboy knows, the Battle of Bannockburn opened with the English knight Sir Henry de Bohun (who was in the van with his uncle the Earl of Hereford) tilting his lance at the Scottish king. Bruce mounted on 'ane gray palfray litill and joly', and easily distinguished by the gold circlet or small crown worn above his helmet, was examining the forward positions of his battle, when the English van came up the wooded slope. Eager for personal glory, Sir Henry spurred his charger forward, but Bruce on the more nimble, smaller animal had no difficulty in side-stepping the thrust, and, in Barbour's immortal sentence, 'Scher Henry myssit the nobill Kyng'. But the noble king did not miss Sir Henry; turning in his saddle he 'cleft de Bohun to the brisket'. Thus the battle started on a sorry note for the English. Soon the whole of their force that had crossed the burn was hotly engaged by King Robert's battle, possibly helped by that of his brother Edward. The fight was no minor skirmish, but a savage encounter in which the English were worsted. Gloucester was unhorsed, and narrowly escaped capture, and perhaps in the withdrawal the pots took some toll. But the force regained the main English army without much loss and Bruce recalled the pursuing Scots – which speaks highly for his control and their discipline.

Meanwhile, Clifford's cavalry had got almost opposite St Ninians Church without Moray taking any action. The King, with whom he was standing at the time, chided his nephew 'that ane rose of his chaplet was faldyn'; stung by the rebuke Moray at once advanced his small infantry force down the hill towards the cavalry. According to the chronicler Sir Thomas Gray,* Clifford was delighted by their coming and was heard to say, 'Let them come on, give them some ground.' But Moray's schiltron remained steady in the face of repeated charges and took heavy toll of horse and men – including the chronicler's father, also called Sir Thomas Gray, who was captured, and Sir William Deyncourt who was killed.

*Sir Thomas Gray of Heton, *Scalacronica*, p.141.

94

*Bannockburn: detail
from mural by William
Hole in Scottish National
Portrait Gallery*

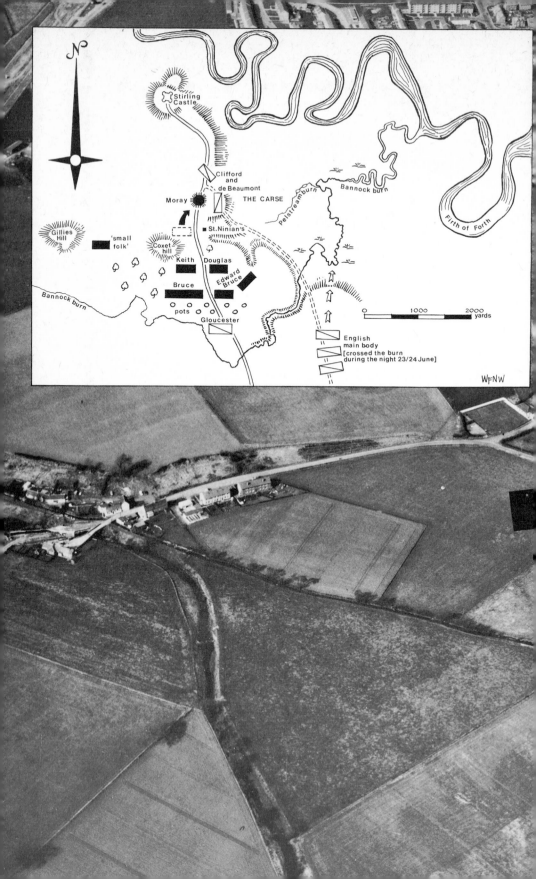

N

Stirling
Castle

Clifford
and
de Beaumont

Moray

THE CARSE

Pelstreamburn

Bannock burn

Gillies
Hill

'small
folk'

Coxet
hill

St.Ninian's

Firth of Forth

Keith

Douglas

Bruce

Edward
Bruce

Bannock burn

pots

Gloucester

0   1000   2000
                    yards

English
main body
[crossed the burn
during the night 23/24 June]

WFNW

Moray

Keith

Douglas

monument

Edw.Bruce

Edw.Bruce

Bruce

pots

Gloucester

Eventually, unable to break this solid phalanx, Clifford's men drew off badly mauled; some rode back to the English lines, while others made for the castle.

The first day of the Battle of Bannockburn was over. It had been one of triumph for the Scots, for they could congratulate themselves on two important achievements. The teaching they had received from their king, that the schiltron if properly handled and resolutely manned could resist cavalry, had been gloriously vindicated; and the repulse of the English on two fronts had raised their morale to a high pitch, while at the same time reducing that of their opponents to a dangerously low level. Later that night, as the weary, dispirited English were floundering across the Bannock burn, the Scottish leaders were to learn that the chance to stem the tide of invasion was now within their grasp.

What could Edward do? He now realized that a frontal attack against that strong position must fail, nor could he ride round the flank with impunity. But below the escarpment was a large plain called the Carse. It is now known that the Carse was not a huge, swampy morass in those days, although where it bordered the Forth it may have been impassable for cavalry; but for the most part there was a good depth of clay above the soggy peat, and in spite of scattered pools and wet patches there was no reason why a battle could not be fought there. Edward argued that if the Scots were so foolish as to offer battle on this plain they would be devoured by his huge army, and anyway he was assured that the sight of it deployed for battle would be enough to disperse them leaving the road to Stirling clear. Moreover, the great heat of the day had made it imperative to water the horses, and so in the evening of 23 June he made for the burn and prepared to cross.

The Bannock burn and its tributary the Pelstream were tidal higher up their course than they are now, and the banks of the burn were in some parts much steeper. Here was a formidable obstacle, and the crossing place had to be chosen with care and at low tide if possible. We hear accounts of doors and beams being brought to assist the horses over the pools; but clearly it would have been impossible in that scarcely populated area to find sufficient timber in time to enable a huge cavalry host to ride dry shod. If any timber was brought it must have been with a view to helping the baggage train across wet areas, but in the event it is much more likely that the baggage never crossed the burn. For most of that short night the crossing would have continued, and we can readily imagine

98

what a long, tedious process it must have been, with horses slithering and falling in the mud, their riders exhausted almost beyond endurance.

Maybe Bruce was wondering whether he was strong enough to meet the English in open battle in the plain, although it seems improbable that his courage and constancy should have deserted him at this hour. However, Sir Alexander Seton, for reasons we do not know, deserted the English camp that night to tell the Scottish king of the plight of Edward's army, and that he only had to attack to gain the victory. Advice that must have seemed bold indeed as with the coming of the dawn the Scots looked down upon the assembled array of English might drawn up in all its clanking panoply of war. But Bruce knew that a grave risk must be run, for now was his only chance of victory. We must admire the spirit of the man as he contemplated the peril that impended, convinced of the justice of his cause. It was Monday 24 June, St John's Day, and after he had addressed his army – a speech that comes down to us from the Abbot of Arbroath, and well calculated to stir the hearts of all those who could have heard it – he gave the order to advance.

Exactly where the Battle of Bannockburn was fought will never be known. Ever since Doctor W. M. Mackenzie produced convincing reasons as to why it was not fought on the traditional site (the original Scottish position in New Park), but somewhere on the Carse, historians have been striving to pinpoint the location. It is possible to argue a case for two or three sites. An examination of the ground seems to indicate that the fight must have taken place to the east of Broombridge, and from what we know of the battle from the various chroniclers it seems to have been fought in a very restricted area. This brings us to the site suggested by General Sir Philip Christison,* and if we say that Edward's army was drawn up in the land lying between the Bannock burn and the Pelstream, near the railway line and just north-west of the Skeoch steading, we may not be far wrong.

King Robert advanced his battles in echelon with Edward Bruce leading on the right. As they came forward the Scotsmen knelt briefly in prayer. Edward appears to have been astonished even at this late hour that they meant to offer battle, and is reported to have said, 'Those men kneel to ask for mercy', to which Sir Ingram de Umfraville replied, 'You are right, they ask for mercy, but not from you. They ask it from God for their sins.' Not only the King but the whole English army appear to have been taken unawares,

*Bannockburn: A Soldier's Appreciation of the Battle, p.19.

and there was a hasty scramble to get to horse. The young Earl of Gloucester, impetuous as ever, rode into battle without his surcoat, which may have cost him his life. As on the day before, the mailed knights of the English van could make no impression on the bristling hedgehog of pikes. But the fighting on this right flank must have been very fierce and Bruce found it necessary to bring Moray's battle into line alongside Edward Bruce's. A little later Douglas was brought into line and so the Scots were fighting on a three-battle front with the King's force in reserve.

The slaughter in the English van was heavy. Gloucester was among the first to be killed, but before the leading troops retired in confusion many another knight lay dead on the field, including Sir Robert Clifford and Sir John Comyn, the son of him whom Bruce had slain at Dumfries. Much the same was happening all along the line: at no place could the English break through the schiltrons, and at every attempt the Scottish pikes took a heavy toll, especially among the horses. Whenever an English division – and there were ten of them – broke, the confusion among the infantry as loose and wounded horses surged around was considerable. Edward II did not lack courage; he was a brave fighter, but unlike his father he was no general, and he had not learnt the lesson of Falkirk, that cavalry needed supporting fire if they were to break the Scottish schiltrons. Not until his horse had been sorely bent and almost broken did he bring up archers on the Scottish left – they were probably firing from the north bank of the Pelstream. Then a dangerous situation developed for Douglas's men. But this was the great chance for Bruce to use his small band of cavalry. He ordered Keith into the attack, and the archers were soon swept back into the now sadly struggling English army. The cry went up among the Scots to press on; the English were unable to manoeuvre in the circumscribed area in which they had been caught and the Scottish schiltrons were rolling them up remorselessly.

When he saw the plight of the enemy, some of whom had already begun to attempt the difficult escape across pools and burn, Bruce ordered the Highlanders and Islesmen, comprising his own battle and hitherto held in reserve, to go forward. The result was almost decisive; the demoralized English had already begun to waver when they saw the royal standard leave the field. Edward had no wish to desert his army, but the Earl of Pembroke (Aymer de Valence) and Sir Giles d'Argentine, who were responsible for his safety, insisted that he made haste for Stirling Castle. The Earl went with him, but once his king was safely off the field the gallant Sir Giles, recognized as one of the leading knights of his day, rode back into the fray to be killed. With their king and their fighting spirit gone the English army was ready to break; at that moment the 'small folk', utterly unable to restrain themselves any longer, emerged from their position over Coxethill. For the English this was the end; they would not stay to fight what appeared to them to be fresh reinforcements. It was now every man for himself and the army broke up in all directions. Many perished in the burn desperately striving to avoid the Scottish pikes; a strongish party managed to reach the high ground round Stirling Castle and others fled towards Falkirk and home, but terrible casualties were inflicted and all the baggage fell intact into Scottish hands. A vast army, reckoned by many to hold the professional primacy of Europe, had been brought to its knees by the skill and daring of a small, determined force, led by one of the great captains of history.

Sir Philip Mowbray refused King Edward sanctuary in Stirling Castle, for the excellent reason that it could now no longer hold out, and so the King with a fairly strong escort made his escape through the King's Park and behind the Scottish army. Bruce was more interested in dealing with the large body of fugitives who had made towards the castle, and so the pursuit of Edward was left to Douglas and a small force. They failed to catch him, and from Dunbar Edward took boat to Berwick. The English losses in the battle were grievous, not so much in numbers as in the men of high rank who rode with the cavalry. There were probably 300 or more men-at-arms slain, and besides these knights, squires and mounted retainers many infantrymen were killed in the battle, drowned in the Forth, or perished on the way home. Some important prisoners, including the Earl of Hereford, were taken, in Bothwell Castle on the Clyde. Escaping from the battlefield they sought sanctuary with the constable, who having admitted them promptly made them prisoner. Hereford was exchanged for the Scottish queen, her daughter, her sister-in-law and the Bishop of Glasgow. Sir Marmaduke Tweng and Ralph de Monthermer were returned without ransom, but there were around 500 for whom ransom was demanded. After Sir Philip Mowbray had surrendered Stirling Castle he changed sides and followed Bruce. Of the Scottish casualties in the battle little is known, but the ratio of men killed to the numbers engaged would certainly have been considerably smaller than with the English army.

'Robert de Bruce was commonly called King of Scotland by all men, because he had acquired Scotland by force of arms.' Thus the

Overleaf: Bannockburn, second day's battle, plan inset

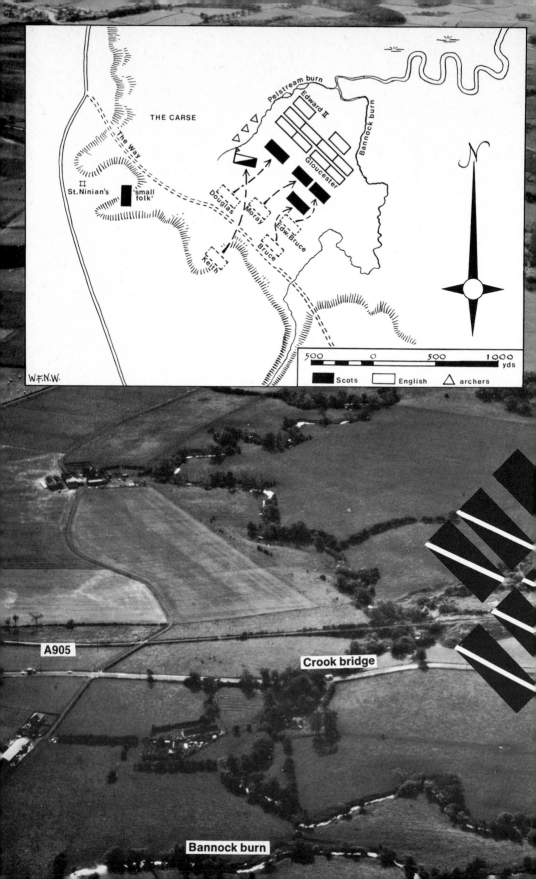

THE CARSE

Pelstream burn

Edward II

Bannock burn

The Way

St. Ninian's

'small folk'

Douglas

Moray

Gloucester

Edw. Bruce

Bruce

Keith

N

W.F.N.W.

500   0   500   1000
                          yds

■ Scots   □ English   △ archers

A905

Crook bridge

Bannock burn

N

BANNOCKBURN

...och

Bruce

Keith

Edw. Bruce

Moray

Douglas

Gloucester

...ward II

Pelstream burn

archers

Chronicle of Lanercost. Certainly Bruce had won Scotland by the sword, but until his sovereignty was recognized by all his task was not complete. The English king and the Pope steadfastly refused him recognition; his great victory at Bannockburn had yet to be consummated.

The story of the next fourteen years is mainly one of plunder and pillage, fire and sword, throughout the border areas and northern counties of England, for Bruce came to realize that these were the methods by which he would most speedily gain his ends. The principal exponents of these acts of terrorism were Sir James Douglas and the Earl of Moray; so devastating were their attacks that as in earlier years a large sum of money was raised through blackmail, and many northern Englishmen who could not buy the raiders off changed their allegiance and became 'Scottish'. To begin with Edward Bruce was also among the raiders; but the Irish, inspired by Bannockburn, sought help from King Robert to free them from the English, and it suited the Scottish king well to send them his brother. Edward met with some small success, but soon after being crowned king he was killed fighting at Dundalk in 1318.

Edward II's only large-scale attempt to avenge Bannockburn in 1322 was a dismal failure. An ill-found, unmounted force with few archers was quite unable to bring the mobile Scots to battle, and a near starving army was forced to sue for peace. A thirteen-year truce was arranged at York in 1323, and soon afterwards the Pope was persuaded to recognize the Scottish king.

Edward III, on his accession in 1327, offered a more lasting peace but, like his father, would not hear of Scottish sovereignty. It was not until after a further hopelessly abortive campaign that the English realized the need for more subtle tactics. In the spring of 1328 a marriage was agreed upon between King Robert's son David and Joan, King Edward's six-year-old sister, and in May of that year the English king recognized Scotland's absolute independence. The treaty, which had been framed in Edinburgh, was ratified by the English parliament on 4 May at Northampton. In July of that year the young couple were formally married at Berwick, and in June 1329 Pope John XXII granted to Robert Bruce and his successors the right, long in abeyance, to receive anointing and coronation.

Thus at last all that this great man had fought for had been achieved; but the papal bull came six days too late, for on 7 June 1329 the strife and struggle of a lifetime ended. King Robert I died at his palace at Cardross. His going left a void that would soon prove serious.

CHAPTER 7

The Wars of the Roses

A General Survey

1455–71

The story of the Wars of the Roses is one of the most complicated in all our history. The great families of England, with their large bands of armed retainers, often clouded the main issue with personal feuds. The fact that they constantly intermarried and that titles and estates frequently passed through the female line is a further cause of confusion to the student of those times. The dynastic quarrel between the houses of York and Lancaster spanned more than thirty-five years, during twelve of which there were fought as many battles as there were years, and the English nobility scowled upon each other with lineaments of fury, while the great slaughter on battlefield and block left their hatreds and vendettas behind. This chapter endeavours to trace in outline the events that led us to this period of turmoil and distress, and to present the principal facts. In subsequent chapters five of the more important battles will be discussed in detail. See table giving brief descriptions in chronological order of the principal battles of the Wars of the Roses on p. 186 and map of England and Wales showing the sites of the battles on p.187.

Edward III had seven sons. The Wars of the Roses chiefly concerned the descendants of the second (surviving) son, Lionel Duke of Clarence; those of the third, John Duke of Lancaster; and the fourth, Edmund Duke of York. Edward was succeeded by his grandson Richard II, but in 1399 Henry Earl of Derby, the eldest son of the Duke of Lancaster, seized the throne, had Richard murdered, and established the ruling dynasty of Lancaster. Like most usurpers he did not have matters entirely his own way and had to fight to retain his throne, notably against Owen Glendower in Wales and the lords of the northern marches. His most serious clash was with the old Earl of Northumberland's warrior son, Henry Hotspur; the Percys, having helped Henry to the throne, had become disaffected to him after the Battle of Homildon Hill (1402), and decided to ally themselves to Glendower and the Duke of Clarence's grandson Edmund Mortimer. However, on 21 July 1403 the King successfully defeated and killed Hotspur just north of Shrewsbury in a battle memorable for being the first in which both sides used the longbow. A little later Glendower was forced back into his Welsh mountains and eliminated as a serious threat. In due course Henry was succeeded by his son Henry V, who dying in 1422 left an infant as his heir, and England was faced with a long minority.

Henry VI was born in 1421 and during the years immediately following his father's death affairs in England and France were managed by his uncles the Dukes of Bedford and Gloucester. In 1437, two years after Bedford's death, Henry began to assume personal control. He proved over the years to be a kindly, pious man, who was easily led; but he was not unintelligent, and at brief intervals showed that he had a will of his own. His misfortune was that in this age of rule by kings he was mistakenly loyal to a faction who constantly mismanaged affairs of state. He stands condemned as the man chiefly responsible for the Wars of the Roses, because he headed an administration that was incompetent and untrustworthy, while he himself was too weak to cope with the passions and artifices of these fierce and dangerous times.

We are not concerned with the early years of Henry's reign. One by one the men who led the nation – Gloucester, Cardinal Beaufort, the first Duke of Somerset, the Duke of Suffolk – disappeared by fair means or foul, until in 1450 the King's principal counsellor was Edmund Beaufort, second Duke of Somerset, who for the past few years had been busy losing every important town and province in France which Henry's father had so gloriously conquered. By August 1450 the whole of Normandy had gone and only Gascony remained. In twelve months' time that too would be lost and by 1453 the English were left with just a precarious foothold in Calais.

The country was full of bewildered, discontented ex-soldiers, who had been driven out of France and disbanded; robbers roamed the roads and woods, and the evils of unlawful 'livery and maintenance' were weakening traditional loyalty to the crown and binding the lesser nobles and their tenants to their more powerful neighbours, who thus formed independent armies. The King ruled not so much through Parliament as through his chosen council – dominated largely by the Beauforts. In 1455 a bride had been found for him from France, and Margaret of Anjou was already exhibiting signs of that courage, determination and masterful spirit which were the hallmarks of her character. She greatly favoured Somerset, and was said to have been responsible for Richard Duke of York's removal from France and banishment to the lieutenancy of Ireland.

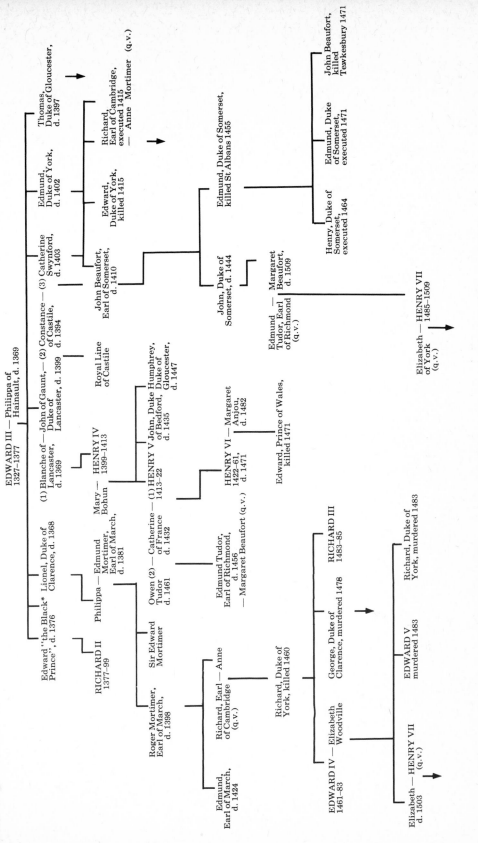

EDWARD III — Philippa of
1327–1377   Hainault, d. 1369

Edward "the Black* Lionel, Duke of (1) Blanche of — John of Gaunt, — (2) Constance — (3) Catherine   Edmund,   Thomas,
Prince", d. 1376   Clarence, d. 1368   Lancaster, Duke of   of Castile,   Swynford,   Duke of York,   Duke of Gloucester,
d. 1369   Lancaster, d. 1399   d. 1394   d. 1403   d. 1402   d. 1397

RICHARD II   Philippa — Edmund   Royal Line   Mary — HENRY IV   John Beaufort,   Edward,   Richard, Earl of Cambridge,
1377–99   Mortimer, Earl of March,   of Castile   Bohun   1399–1413   Earl of Somerset,   Duke of York,   executed 1415
d. 1381   d. 1410   killed 1415   — Anne Mortimer (q.v.)

Roger Mortimer,   Sir Edward   Owen (2) — Catherine — (1) HENRY V John, Duke Humphrey,   Edmund, Duke of Somerset,
Earl of March,   Mortimer   Tudor   of France 1413–22 of Bedford, Duke of   killed St Albans 1455
d. 1398   d. 1461   d. 1432   d. 1435 Gloucester,
d. 1447

Edmund,   Richard, Earl — Anne   Edmund Tudor,   HENRY VI — Margaret   John, Duke of   Henry, Duke of   Edmund, Duke   John Beaufort,
Earl of March,   of Cambridge   Earl of Richmond,   1422–61,   Anjou,   Somerset, d. 1444   Somerset,   of Somerset,   killed
d. 1424   (q.v.)   d. 1456   d. 1471   d. 1482   executed 1464   executed 1471   Tewkesbury 1471
— Margaret Beaufort (q.v.)

Richard, Duke of   Edward, Prince of Wales,   Edmund — Margaret
York, killed 1460   killed 1471   Tudor, Earl Beaufort,
of Richmond   d. 1509
(q.v.)

EDWARD IV — Elizabeth   George, Duke of   RICHARD III   Elizabeth — HENRY VII
1461–83   Woodville   Clarence, murdered 1478   1483–85   of York   1485–1509
(q.v.)

Elizabeth — HENRY VII   EDWARD V   Richard, Duke of
d. 1503   (q.v.)   murdered 1483   York, murdered 1483

THE HOUSES OF YORK AND LANCASTER

* Edward III's second son
William died in infancy

Political agitators and military adventurers found ready material to hand in these dark days. One such man, calling himself Jack Cade, marched on London at the head of a large band of Kentish men in the summer of 1450. His army was eventually dispersed and he himself killed, but it was a typical example of the lawlessness of the times. Possibly Cade had Yorkist backing; certainly his Articles of Complaint included a demand for the expulsion of the ruling clique and the recall of the Duke of York. Anyway, with the present government discredited both at home and abroad, the Duke felt strongly the need for action.

He left Ireland in August 1450 and landed in Wales. Henry recalled the Duke of Somerset from Calia and made half-hearted attempts to intercept York, but on these failings he weakly submitted to receiving him and listening to his complaints and demands – without, however, acceding to them. Although York's open enmity for Somerset could have sparked off civil war at any moment, it seems almost certain that neither now, nor when fifteen months later he led a more threatening march on London, did he seek the kingdom. He was, however, head of the house that finally prevailed in the Wars, and we should look briefly at his strong claim to the throne (see chart on p. 107).

Richard II left no issue. As early as 1385, however, he may have recognized his cousin's son Roger Mortimer, fourth Earl of March, as his heir apparent; such at any rate was the substance of a later Yorkist legend. March's claims were inherited from his mother Philippa, daughter and heiress of the Duke of Clarence, who in the year of her father's death (1368) had married the third Earl of March (died 1381). Roger was killed in Ireland in 1398, leaving a son of only six and two daughters, the elder of whom (Anne) married the Earl of Cambridge, son and heir of Edward III's fifth son, the Duke of York. Early next year the death of the King's uncle the Duke of Lancaster precipitated the events that were to lead to Richard II's deposition and the destruction of any hopes the young Earl of March may have had of succeeding to the throne. On Lancaster's death Richard sentenced his son and heir Henry of Bolingbroke (then in temporary banishment from England) to perpetual exile, at the same time confiscating the enormous Lancastrian inheritance. Faced with a choice of poverty-stricken exile or rebellion, Henry chose the latter, and in a rapid campaign seized the kingdom and the crown. By 1450 the Lancastrian dynasty was represented only by the childless Henry VI. The Mortimer claim to the

Henry VI, artist unknown, National Portrait Gallery

throne had descended, after the death of the fifth Earl of March (1424), to the son of his elder sister Anne – Richard Duke of York.

His claim *de jure* was probably superior to the King's, but the Lancastrians had won the throne, and York at this time only wished to dispute the way in which the exercise of royal power had fallen into the hands of a clique or faction. His mistrust and dislike for Somerset, however, went deeper. In 1407 Henry IV had carefully regulated the descent of the crown in an Act of Parliament which had never been repealed, and while recognizing the legitimacy of his Beaufort half-brothers he had specifically debarred their line from any claim to the throne. Save for the childless king, Henry IV's line was extinct, and Richard of York was unquestionably his heir. But Somerset was in direct male descent, through the Duke of Lancaster, from Edward III, and all that was needed was for the favourite to slip an Act through Parliament repealing Henry IV's prohibitory clause. Thus the two men glowered upon each other suspiciously with a cold, enduring antagonism.

York had good reason to feel aggrieved at being excluded from the King's council, for his talents as an administrator and soldier were probably superior to Somerset's. He saw clearly what was wrong with the country, and he believed himself capable of putting those wrongs to right. For a little while he took no overt action, but having failed to move the King by constant supplication he determined to rid the country of Somerset and purge the government, if need be by force. Early in 1452 he marched south from his castle at Ludlow at the head of a large army. London closed its gates against him so he camped at Dartford. The King, with a much bigger army, moved to Blackheath. Civil war seemed imminent, but neither side wanted it and York realized that he was in no position to fight. He had committed high treason, but he was far too strong to be punished. On taking a solemn pledge not to disturb the peace again he was given his freedom, and the country gained a short respite from the horrors of internecine strife.

The following year, 1453, was crowded with momentous events. While further and final disasters in France – which culminated in October with the surrender of Bordeaux – were being inflicted upon his armies, the King was dramatically released from his troubles. A sudden start plunged his feeble mind into oblivion, and for fifteen months he remained in this state of suspended animation, declaring on his recovery that he remembered nothing. Parliament was faced with having to appoint a regent. The court favourite, Somerset, had been successfully impeached by the Duke of Norfolk for the French catastrophes and was in the Tower, but Queen Margaret felt that her claim was paramount. She was, however, somewhat preoccupied, for on 13 October 1453 – after eight barren years – she produced a son. Parliament hesitated and procrastinated, but eventually the Yorkists won the day and in March 1454 the Duke was appointed Protector and Defender of the Realm. He was also given the captaincy of Calais, recently held by Somerset.

The country remained comparatively quiet until at Christmas 1454 the King recovered his senses. He wasted little time in reversing most of what York had done and in restoring Somerset to freedom and responsibility – including the captaincy of Calais. York retired to his castle of Sandal, near Wakefield, where he and the Yorkist lords brooded sullenly upon the scene. All the evils that Somerset had inflicted upon the country seemed about to be repeated; moreover, not only all that York stood for, but his very life, was now only prey to time and occasion. He determined upon a resort to arms. In the middle of May 1455, at the head of 3,000 men, he marched south. The first blood in the Wars of the Roses was about to be shed. But we should pause to examine the composition of the forces which were soon to sear England with the flame of war.

The pernicious effect of unlawful livery and maintenance – which has already been touched upon – meant that the Wars of the Roses were fought between private armies under the command of the more important barons supporting one side or the other – and occasionally changing their allegiance. The heads of these great families were virtually petty kings within their own domains, and by giving their badge and livery to almost any rascal who applied they could command large armies – the Duke of Norfolk put 3,000 men and cannon into the field during a private quarrel in 1469, and at about the same time the Earl of Warwick had very many more armed retainers proudly flaunting his badge of the Bear and Ragged Staff. There was frequently a bitter rivalry, and sometimes private warring, between these great families; this was largely responsible for the ruthless extermination of important prisoners that was such an unpleasant aftermath of most of the battles, but on the other hand it tended to make the Wars mainly an affair of the aristocracy. Both sides were, for obvious reasons, usually anxious to spare the common man as far as possible; hence reprisals were few and far between and although there were inevitably cases of sack and plunder these were comparatively rare.

These great lords of the land did not march to war at the head of ill armed rabbles; for the most part their retainers were equipped with up-to-date arms and armour. There had been many changes since Bannockburn, which was fought more than a hundred years earlier. Although the longbow had a further span of sixty years to run, already the improvement in armour – especially the completeness of plate – had considerably lessened its destructive power. Until tackled at close quarters the man-at-arms was almost invulnerable, for gunpowder was still in its infancy. Both sides – particularly Warwick, who employed Burgundian mercenaries at the Second Battle of St Albans – used a limited number of hand-guns. These were very primitive and unreliable weapons, fired by means of a touch-hole on the top of the barrel near the breech. Cannon, which was soon to end the rule of feudal despotism, was at this time still very unwieldy, and although employed in many of the battles by both armies it was really only the heavy ordnance, such as the great bombards used at the siege of the northern castles, that made any mark. Probably the most useful weapon was the halberd, introduced into England at the end of the fourteenth century, although it and the bill were now giving way to the pike.

Horse armour had undergone little recent change, but the man-at-arms (who in the Wars of the Roses mostly fought on foot) now wore a new style of helmet; the basinet with its close-fitting visor had been replaced by a continental introduction called the salade. This was a curious-shaped helmet with a long projection at the back and a movable visor; it was worn with a mentonnière, which was a plate fastened to the breastplate and moulded to cover the lower part of the face. Towards the end of the Wars the more orthodox-shaped armet was used as a helmet. The breastplate was still globular, but was stronger, being reinforced by what was called a demi-placcate and with gussets of plate adapted to the movement of the arms. The shield was no longer carried, which necessitated greater protection by plate armour on the left, or vulnerable, side of the man. The ordinary infantryman was somewhat less well protected; a longbowman usually wore a hat and gorget of banded mail, and a hauberk of overlapping scales of leather, but the arbalester might expect to be given a helmet and complete plates for his legs.

Mention has been made of the great families, and something must be said concerning the man who more than any other was responsible for putting Edward Duke of York on the throne – Richard Neville, Earl of Warwick, known to history as the Kingmaker. His father was the second son of the Earl of Westmorland by his second marriage with Alice de Montacute, through whom he inherited the lands and title of his father-in-law the Earl of Salisbury. These lands were mostly in Wiltshire and Hampshire, and it is interesting to note that in general the Yorkist support came mainly

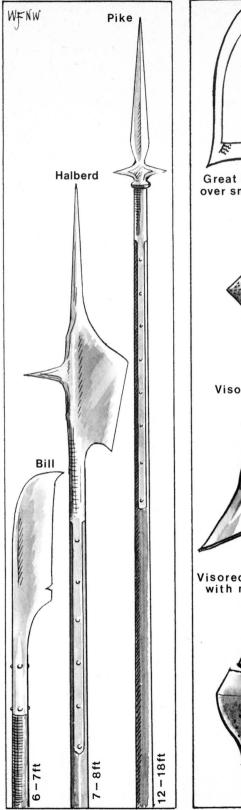

WFNW

Pike

Halberd

Bill

15th-century
pole arms and
head armour

6–7ft

7–8ft

12–18ft

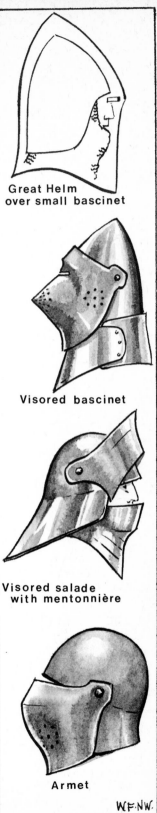

Great Helm
over small bascinet

Visored bascinet

Visored salade
with mentonnière

Armet

WF.NW.

from the south and from Wales and the marches, while the Lancastrians drew their strength from the north. Richard Neville was Salisbury's eldest son, and following the wise example of his father he too married an heiress, Anne Beauchamp, daughter of Henry, fourteenth Earl of Warwick. Richard, therefore, in due course succeeded not only to the vast possessions of his father and father-in-law, but also to both titles, Warwick being the premier earldom of England. Furthermore, his aunt Cicely Neville had married the Duke of York, and so Warwick was fighting first for his uncle and then – until he turned against him – for his first cousin.

We know little enough about Warwick's private life, but his public record stamps him clearly as a man built upon a larger scale than almost all his contemporaries. He was a fearless fighter and tireless organizer, although not a conspicuously talented general. His excursions into diplomacy were often successful, for he was a courteous man of much charm, but they were not always wisely undertaken. Immensely popular with the rank and file, he was at first loyal to the cause he championed; but in the end injured pride proved stronger than loyalty.

This was the man, now aged twenty-seven, chiefly responsible for his uncle's victory at St Albans on 22 May 1455. We left Richard Duke of York, with Salisbury and Warwick, marching south at the head of 3,000 men. On 20 May they sent a letter from Royston to the Chancellor explaining their reasons and demanding the removal of Somerset, and a similar letter, but couched in deferential terms, was sent to the King from Ware. However, Henry never received it, for on learning of the Yorkist approach he had moved out of London (which was pro-Yorkist) and headed for Leicester. With the King were the Dukes of Somerset and Buckingham and the Earls of Pembroke, Northumberland and Devon – the last named having recently deserted York, with whom he had marched in 1452.

The King halted at St Albans on learning that York was at hand. He set up the royal standard in St Peter's Street, and after some unsatisfactory parleying awaited the Yorkist attack. He had under command little more than 2,000 men, so the Duke of York held the advantage in numbers. St Albans was an open town, being at that time still under the jurisdiction of the abbot. Only a partially filled-in ditch presented any obstacle, and this was not properly manned by the Lancastrians, who preferred to rely principally on barricading the two roads leading from the south into St Peter's Street. These barricades were under the command of Lord Clifford, and the Duke of York obliged him by a frontal attack, which made no headway. But Warwick, acting either on information or intuition,

114

Petardier. A petard contained inflammable material and explosives. It was thrown into the faces of the advancing enemy

crossed the ditch at an undefended spot and forcing his way through the back of the houses in Hollywell Street gained access to the main street, where he fanned out and took both the barriers in their flank. The Lancastrians were thus divided and the troops manning the barriers being attacked from two sides soon fell back, allowing the Yorkists to pour into the town.

The whole affair was little more than a street scuffle lasting only half an hour. The total casualties were probably less than 150, but the Duke of Somerset, the Earl of Northumberland, Lord Clifford and many other Lancastrian noblemen lay dead; the Yorkists lost Lord Clinton and Sir Robert Ogle. The Duke of Buckingham had been wounded by an arrow in the face, and the King, standing forlornly by his standard, received a flesh wound in the neck before taking refuge in a tradesman's house, where the Duke of York found him and immediately assured him of his fealty and devotion. The time of bitter hatreds and savage reprisals among the families of the nobility was still five years away; now the victors behaved with moderation. York caused a parliament to be summoned within four days of his victory, and many of the important offices of state were given to men of his faction. Warwick became Captain of Calais in place of Somerset, and was the only man to retain his position when Margaret of Anjou and the court party once more gained the ascendancy at the end of 1456. He was thus available to succour the Yorkists with his garrison troops when hostilities broke out in earnest in 1460.

The four years following the First Battle of St Albans saw an uneasy truce in the land. The Yorkist government, which was terminated in October 1456, struggled with the problems of the time. The Lancastrian power was always formidable, and apart from a short period when Henry was again incapacitated by illness they had the magic of the crown on their side. In 1457 York was once more given the lieutenancy of Ireland for a period of ten years. Presumably this was to get him out of the way, but if so the attempt failed, for when at last in 1459 Margaret felt herself strong enough to act and sent out writs in the King's name for an armed assembly to gather at Leicester on 10 May York was at Ludlow – although apparently in no hurry to arm.

All that summer Margaret was busy raising troops in the counties of Lancashire and Cheshire, but there was no action before September. By then York had realized his peril and sent urgent messages to his brother-in-law Salisbury, who was at his Yorkshire estate of Middleham, and to Warwick in Calais, to join him at once. Soon armies were marching throughout England: Warwick north-west from Kent, Somerset north-east from Wessex (the two nearly clashed), Salisbury from Yorkshire to Ludlow, and when the Queen learned that Salisbury was on the move she dispatched Lord Audley to intercept him. This he did on 23 September at a place called Blore Heath, just east of Market Drayton (see also p.186). Salisbury had but 3,000 men and was outnumbered by perhaps as much as three to one, but he was forced to fight. He took up a strong defensive position with one flank resting on a wood and the other protected by baggage carts; Audley's first attack was mounted and repulsed with heavy loss, and so were two subsequent ones made with dismounted troops. The battle lasted for most of the afternoon, but when Audley had been slain and his lieutenant Lord Dudley captured the Lancastrians had had enough; 500 deserted to the enemy, the remainder fled the field.

Salisbury, although victorious, was in a dangerous position between two superior Lancastrian armies. Thanks to the antics of a crazy friar, who kept firing a cannon all night, he managed to leave Blore Heath undetected and join York at Ludlow. A few days later Warwick arrived with a contingent of trained soldiers from Calais. But Henry displayed unwonted determination and vigour. He was now in the area of Worcester with an army that may have num-

116

bered 30,000 men, with which he planned to deal swift and exemplary chastisement to all who would not accept his pardon. York faced this vast host behind the river Teme at Ludford, but the peril of his situation was plain for all to see; soon Andrew Trollope, with many of the Calais men, deserted, and the disheartened Yorkist army dispersed in the night. The Duke and his youngest son made for Ireland, while Warwick and his father, together with York's eldest son, struck south and took ship from Devon to Calais. No longer officially its captain, Warwick nevertheless gained entry to the town and was soon holding it against his nominated successor Henry Duke of Somerset, who had inherited much of his father's puissance at the Lancastrian court.

On 26 June 1460 Warwick, who had visited Ireland at Easter to concert plans with York, left Calais with Salisbury and the Earl of March (York's son). They landed near Sandwich with 1,500 men and were unopposed, for the Lancastrian army was centred mostly in the Midlands. On 10 July Warwick's force encountered Henry's army encamped in a strong position just outside Northampton (see also p.186). The Earl attacked on a three-battle front, and his task was made considerably easier by the treachery of Lord Grey of Ruthen, whose soldiers were ordered to help Lord March's right battle over the fortified ditch and mound. With these men across the ditch the Lancastrian position was untenable. Once again the total casualties (about 300) were small compared with the loss in the higher echelons: the Duke of Buckingham, the Earl of Shrewsbury, and Lords Beaumont and Egremont (Northumberland's brother) were among the Lancastrian fallen. The King, who appears to have taken no part in the battle, was conducted back to London with every mark of respect; his wife, on learning of the defeat, retreated north with her son.

York was still in Ireland, but when Warwick had won the greater part of the kingdom for his cause he came to London. Here at last he declared his true colours and claimed the crown. But he had acted prematurely: neither the lords temporal nor spiritual wished to change the dynasty at this time. A compromise was reached whereby Henry should rule for his lifetime, and should be succeeded by York. It seemed an admirable expedient, but it failed to take into account one important factor. Henry might agree to disinherit his son, but Margaret certainly would not.

The indefatigable queen, helped by the Duke of Somerset (now back from his abortive attempt on Calais), the Earl of Northumberland and other northern noblemen, immediately set to work organizing another army based on York. They soon had a force of 15,000

15th-century plate armour

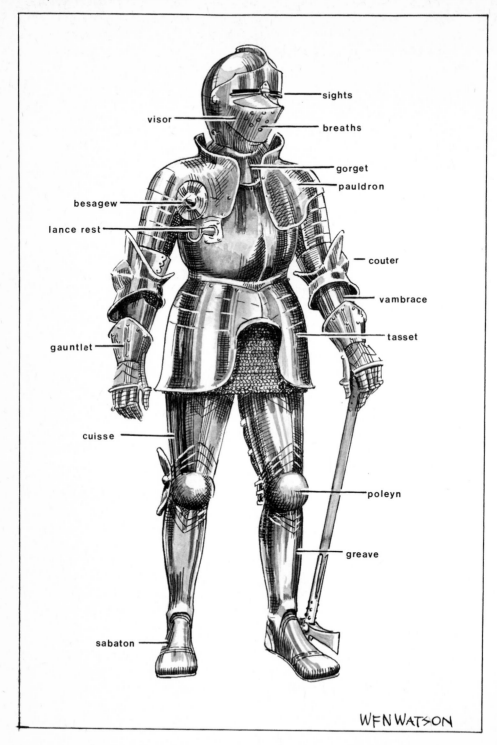

sights

visor

breaths

gorget

pauldron

besagew

lance rest

couter

vambrace

gauntlet

tasset

cuisse

poleyn

greave

sabaton

WFN WATSON

armed men. York hurried north and spent Christmas at Sandal. Five days later the Lancastrians with superior numbers fell upon his army (see also p.186). Details of the Battle of Wakefield no longer exist. Possibly the Yorkists were taken by surprise; certainly they suffered a crushing defeat and both in the mêlée and after the battle was over their enemies took a fearful revenge. Richard Duke of York fell in battle; his young son the Earl of Rutland was caught fleeing the field by Lord Clifford, who personally stabbed him to death; Salisbury was captured that night and executed the next day. Their three heads were sent to adorn the walls of York, that of the Duke being exposed to mockery and malice by the adornment of a paper crown. It is said that the Yorkists lost 2,000 men to the Lancastrian 200. There were to be other disasters, but none so great as this. However, the cause was not lost, for Edward Earl of March (now Duke of York) was to prove himself a fine soldier and a popular prince. But the struggle now became far more bitter, for a new generation took over the ugly business of avenging their fathers: Lord Clifford had already opened his account.

Warwick was not present at Wakefield, but lay at his castle on the Avon; on learning of the disaster he at once made for London with his troops. The Queen's army was marching south towards the capital and on the way committed what were by far the worst ravages of the war, sacking Stamford, Grantham, Peterborough, Royston and later St Albans. In so doing the Lancastrians alienated their cause still further with the common people of the south, and there was much sympathy for the Yorkists gathering to defend the capital. However, Warwick marched from London to meet the Queen's army and allowed himself to be surprised near St Albans: 'the prickers came not home to bring tidings, how near the Queen was, save one, who said that she was yet nine miles off.' This time he himself was taken in the flank and his army soundly beaten (see p.188 or chapter 8 for a detailed account). The way to London lay open – there was no occasion throughout the Wars on which any town closed its gates to a victorious army. But Henry, whom Warwick had taken from London to witness the battle and who had as a result been united with his queen, forbade the Lancastrians to advance on the city, having been sickened by the sack of St Albans. It was an honourable decision but fatal to his chances, for when at last he did dispatch a force to seize Westminster it was too late.

The Second Battle of St Albans was fought on 17 February 1461. On 2 February the young Duke of York, now just three months short of his nineteenth birthday, had taken the first steps in a tale of broadening glory that led him to the throne. In a battle of whose details we know nothing he defeated the army of the Earls of Pembroke and Wiltshire at Mortimer's Cross (see p.188). The beaten army was pursued to Hereford and the Lancastrian losses were said to have been heavy. The two earls escaped, but in the ceaseless bloodletting that was now to become such an unpleasant feature of these rancorous times Owen Tudor (who had married Henry V's widow), Sir John Throckmorton and eight other important prisoners were beheaded. Young Edward of York then marched to meet Warwick, and although he was too late for St Albans he joined the Earl in time for them to re-enter London ahead of the Lancastrian force.

The Yorkists had now crossed the Rubicon; there could no longer be any pretence that their loyalty still lay with the King, for the King was firmly in the hands of the Queen and in no circumstances could they treat with Margaret. There had to be a new dynasty. On 4 March Edward Duke of York rode from the family home of Baynards Castle to Westminster, where he was officially acclaimed King Edward IV. England now had a man on the throne cast in the true mould of a king. Tall (he stood six feet four inches), handsome and of a pleasing disposition, he was to prove himself a brave fighter and a very capable general. Possessed of considerable intelligence he was capable when he exerted himself of governing wisely, but he had a broad streak of indolence and hedonism. He much preferred to leave matters of state to his cousin Warwick, and to enjoy the fruits of his kingdom. It was a mistake that nearly cost him his throne.

The new king had no time for dalliance in London; he had to march north to subdue the unconquered Lancastrians who were assembling in large numbers around York. On 29 March 1461 there was fought at Towton (see p.188 or chapter 9 for a detailed account) the bloodiest, and perhaps the most decisive, of all the battles of the Wars of the Roses. The Yorkists gained a complete victory in that part of the country where the Lancastrian strength was greatest. Edward, whom we must now call the King, spent the next three weeks in York. After the battle there were plenty of noble Lancastrian heads to replace those of his father and others that had grinned down upon the city since Wakefield.

The next three years belong in a special way to Queen Margaret. We can only condone her behaviour if we remember that she was a princess of France, and although a queen of England she was without a throne; her interests centred round her husband and her son, for England she cared not a straw. Nevertheless, we can have nothing but praise for her indomitable courage in the face of

15th-century hand-gun and hand-culverin

defeat, anxiety and extreme hardships, for her determination, her perseverance and her skill. The royal fugitives hovered between Scotland and northern England; in Scotland and in France she had two allies, for it was the policy of these countries to keep England divided by backing the weaker cause. Margaret's peregrinations cannot be gone into here; sufficient to say that for Scottish aid she gave away Berwick, and for French she mortgaged Calais. She became a supplicant at the French and Burgundian courts, and with the aid of the devoted and competent Pierre de Brézé, and a slice of English treachery, she gained the important northern castles of Alnwick, Bamburgh and Dunstanburgh. To regain them Edward was forced to ship his heavy ordnance – the pride of his military arm – north, and the Earl of Warwick took charge of the siege operations (see p.189).

Edward, although ruthless when occasion demanded, could also be magnanimous. In 1462 he not only pardoned the Duke of Somerset, but took him into his confidence and showed him great favour. Such generosity was ill received by his supporters and ill repaid by the recipient, who at the end of 1463 renegued with his followers to

121

Henry. Warwick's brother Lord Montagu, who was Warden of the East March, was escorting the Scottish envoys to York to treat with Edward when Somerset and Sir Ralph Percy confronted him on 25 April 1464 at Hedgeley Moor, between Morpeth and Wooler; it was a small affair in which the Lancastrians were worsted, and Percy, who disdained flight, was killed (see p.189). But on 15 May a more serious engagement was fought near Hexham in a meadow on the south side of the Tyne (see p.189). Here the Lancastrians had taken up a position that offered no hope of escape, and in a short, sharp encounter Montagu virtually surrounded them, and those who were not killed had no alternative but surrender. Somerset was among those who were taken and executed on that same day; Lords Hungerford and Roos suffered the same fate two days later.

The war in the north was now virtually at an end; it was left to John Tiptoft, Earl of Worcester and Constable of England – a man as cruel as he was cultured – to bring Lancastrian nobles and knights to trial by the score with a view to execution. Henry, who was in nearby Bywell Castle during the fight at Hexham, made good his escape and wandered about the Lake District for the next year before being betrayed. He arrived as a prisoner at the Tower on 24 July 1465.

Edward was a valiant man of war, but he loved peace; he loved it for what he could get from it by way of ease and enjoyment. So far, for the most part, he had been content to let the powerful Neville family run the kingdom for him, and had he let matters go on in this way the Wars of the Roses might now have been over. But the King had a will of his own; he would not be thwarted and when he was he could quickly slough off his indolence and let it be known that he was the master, a soldier with a sword in his hand and a man to be reckoned with. His quarrel with the Nevilles lasted six years, but in the end he triumphed.

It concerned first his marriage to Elizabeth Woodville, or Wydvile, which had occurred in 1464 and been kept a carefully guarded secret. To Warwick and other magnates, who thought that this was just another harmless flirtation, the announcement that he had actually married this comparatively lowborn Lancastrian widow came as a deep shock – especially to Warwick who had plans for a French bride. But more damaging was their difference over foreign affairs, for here the matter was raised above a purely family quarrel. Warwick was convinced that a French alliance was essential to forestall any possibility of a Lancastrian revival borne upon French arms; while he was working hard to this end, Edward was all the time negotiating behind his back with the Duke of Burgundy.

Just as Warwick was bringing his negotiations to a successful conclusion Edward, in 1468, announced his pact with the Burgundian court, which included the marriage of his sister Margaret to Charles the Bold.

Such public humiliation could not be tolerated. Warwick laid his plans with care. He won over the King's brother the Duke of Clarence, to whom he married his daughter and co-heiress Isabella. Next he stirred up trouble in the north, where a man calling himself Robin of Redesdale headed a tiresome insurrection that necessitated the King marching against him. As soon as he learned that the King had left London, Warwick and his new son-in-law crossed from Calais with a number of trained soldiers and entered London in something like a triumph. Edward, learning of Warwick's landing, now became seriously alarmed; he fell back on Nottingham to await reinforcements from Wales under the Earl of Pembroke.* But these were cleverly intercepted by the northern rebels, who getting between them and the King met Pembroke at Edgcote – some five miles north-east of Banbury – on 26 July 1469 (see also p.189). The previous day Pembroke had had a disagreement with the Earl of Devon,† who had gone off with all his archers, and so Pembroke fought at a grave disadvantage. Even so although at first repulsed he rallied his Welshmen and might have won the day had not an advance party of Warwick's troops joined the fight at the critical moment. The slaughter was considerable, both sides losing men of consequence. Pembroke, and later Devon, were among those of the defeated army to be executed.

The King found himself unable to rally his scattered forces, and at Olney was made to realize that he was Warwick's prisoner. He was conveyed to Middleham, where he was treated with the respect due to his high rank, although left in no doubt as to where the power now lay. Edward decided to dissemble; he professed himself penitent and ready to mend his ways. In due course he was liberated. However, any outward healing of the breach between these two powerful men was only on the surface. Warwick continued to plot and another insurrection – this time in Lincolnshire – required the King once again to march north. In a battle near Empingham on 12 March 1470 – known as Losecoat Field from the way in which the rebels hastened their flight – the King defeated Sir Robert Welles before Warwick could join him (see p.189). The

*Sir William Herbert, recently created Earl of Pembroke in place of Jasper Tudor.
†Sir Humphrey Stafford, recently created Earl of Devon, in place of Thomas Courtenay who had been beheaded after Towton.

defeated leader then confessed that Warwick was the instigator of the revolt and that he had intended to place Clarence on the throne. Warwick fled the country, and being refused entry into Calais he eventually landed at Honfleur.

Louis XI saw his chance. Here was Warwick crippled, beaten and discredited; in Anjou were Margaret and her son mortified, moneyless but indomitable. If he could but persuade these two deadly enemies that together their cause could triumph he would at the same time relieve the pressure on France. A wide and bloodstained gulf separated Warwick and Margaret, but eventually Margaret accepted Warwick's plea for forgiveness, and as a pledge of his new found allegiance to the house of Lancaster his daughter and co-heiress Anne was to marry the Prince of Wales. Louis supplied money and ships for the invasion of England.

In only six months after Empingham the wheel of fortune had turned full circle. Edward, from being supreme and seemingly secure in his kingdom, with his dangerous rival a fugitive abroad, was himself scurrying to safety in Friesland. Warwick's landing in Devonshire had taken the King by surprise; he was without support in the north and the force that was with him in Yorkshire was small and not entirely reliable. He was wise to seek safety in flight. Henry VI, resigned to whatever fate might impose, was restored to the throne at Michaelmas 1470 by the man who five years before had led him to the Tower crying 'Treason, treason and behold the traitor'.

Edward's return to England in March 1471 and his defeat of the Lancastrian armies first at Barnet and then at Tewkesbury were prodigies of daring and determination that clearly portray the dynamic force of the man. No sooner had Charles of Burgundy realized that Warwick's policy was to aid France against him than he readily supplied Edward with money, ships and more than a thousand German mercenaries. Landing at Ravenspur,* he overcame the sullen resistance of the citizens of York by declaring that he came only to claim his paternal inheritance, upon which assurance they opened their gates to him. His march south, gathering reinforcements as he went, was swift and skilful. Montagu had 4,000 men assembled at Tadcaster ready to oppose him, but Edward evaded this force and when he reached Nottingham he was strong enough to declare his real intention and reassume the royal title.

Warwick learned when he was at Coventry what Edward had known for some time, that the treacherous Clarence had reaffirmed his loyalty to the King (Edward). With Clarence against him and

*This port at the mouth of the Humber, where Henry IV also landed, has long since been swallowed by the sea.

124

Montagu still in Yorkshire, Warwick felt himself unable to offer battle at Coventry. This suited Edward admirably. He marched on to London, where he was admitted virtually unopposed. He left it again the next day, Easter Saturday 13 April, to fight the Battle of Barnet (see p.189 or chapter 10 for a full account). With him went the wretched Henry, once more bereft of everything but his simple dignity and moral virtue, to witness the death in battle of his recent champion the Earl of Warwick, together with Montagu and many other lords and knights of both factions. It was an expensive victory for Edward, but with the death of Warwick the hopes of Lancaster were all but gone.

Queen Margaret had shown considerable reluctance in answering Henry's and Warwick's constant calls to join them. We do not know her reasons, but contrary winds could not be the full explanation, although they certainly delayed her in the end. She eventually landed at Weymouth on the day that Barnet was fought. The news of that disaster – brought by Somerset – temporarily overwhelmed this dauntless woman; she wished to return to France immediately. But her son, who had perhaps inherited his grandfather's military qualities, soon rallied her flagging spirit. The Lancastrians were not without hope of reinforcements in the west and Jasper Tudor – once more Earl of Pembroke – commanded a large force. And so she agreed that the army should march for the Welsh border. It was a race against time; both armies covered long distances in a day, and the Lancastrians, brought to battle at Tewkesbury, were in a badly exhausted state (see p.190 or chapter 11 for a full account of the battle). Here they were shattered and scattered; the Prince of Wales was cut down together with many other noblemen. The Duke of Somerset* sought sanctuary in Tewkesbury Abbey, from where he was removed for execution. Jasper Tudor, who was not at the battle, skulked in Wales before escaping to Brittany with his nephew Henry, who would one day return.

Edward IV was now triumphant. An attempt by the Earl of Kent's bastard to take London had been forestalled, and a rising in the north had been quickly subdued by the Earl of Northumberland. On 21 May the King entered London in state with Queen Margaret his prisoner. That very day Henry VI was reported to have died 'of pure displeasure and melancholy'; Richard Duke of Gloucester is often thought to have been the particular cause of this 'displeasure'. The Wars of the Roses were not quite over; but for fourteen years the sword slept in the scabbard.

*He was a brother of the duke executed after Hexham, and the third holder of the title to die in the Wars.

CHAPTER 8

The Second Battle of St Albans

17 February 1461

The battle was fought in three distinct phases. The first phase took place in the centre of the town around the fifteenth-century watch tower, which still stands, and over much the same ground as the First Battle of St Albans. It is impossible to be certain about the exact site for phases two and three, but the second and principal battle was fought either on Bernard's Heath (a northern suburb of the town), or more probably on ground to the west of Sandridge. Warwick's rearguard action took place south of Nomansland Common.

Bernard's Heath is now very much built over, although a part of the great ditch constructed by the Belgae is unspoilt. But the Sandridge–Nomansland area is still mostly open country. A good idea of the ground over which the fighting took place can be obtained by driving along the B 651 road to Nomansland Common, and along the minor roads leading off the B 651 west from Sandridge. The watch tower can usually be ascended on application to the museum (situated near the Roman town), and from the top a very good view of the city is obtained. The Lancastrian approach march and the first phase of the battle can be studied from this vantage point, but the rising ground to the north obstructs any view of Bernard's Heath and the land beyond.

The Second Battle of St Albans (see also pp. 119-20) is perhaps the most interesting of all the battles of the Wars of the Roses; not from a tactical standpoint, for we know all too little as to how it was fought, but from the point of view of strategic appraisal of both commanders. It also presents a fascinating exercise in trying to make a credible picture of a whole fight from a few clearly established facts.

The overwhelming Lancastrian victory at Wakefield in December 1460 (see pp. 117-19) and the subsequent elimination of Richard Duke of York, came too late to have a decisive influence on the war. By now the quarrel had bitten too deep; anger and hatred, far from being subdued at the death of the Yorkist leader, strengthened the arm of strife. And anyway there could be no Lancastrian victory while King Henry, captured at Northampton, remained a puppet king in Yorkist hands. In fact Wakefield merely gave fresh impetus to the struggle. Queen Margaret hastened from Scotland to York, where her council were unanimous in calling for a march on London to free the King; and the Earls of March and Warwick – both with fathers to avenge – who were on the Welsh border and in Warwickshire respectively, at the same time realized the urgency of securing the capital. Thus we see the two sides girding themselves for yet another trial of strength.

Warwick received the news of Wakefield on or about 3 January and lost no time in getting to London. But once there a strange inertia seems to have come upon him; for a whole month he did virtually nothing. He does not seem to have been in touch with his protégé, the nineteen-year-old new Duke of York, Edward, until after Edward had defeated Jasper Tudor, Earl of Pembroke, at Mortimer's Cross on 2 February (see p. 120); he made no personal attempt to settle certain disaffected areas in the home counties; and he issued no commissions of array, nor took any steps to recruit men in the important Midland counties, but relied chiefly on his large Kentish following. On the other hand he does seem to have taken infinite pains in procuring many strange devices for a defensive battle. When Warwick eventually marched out of London he certainly had a formidable and well armed force, but the total – and surprising – lack of intelligence concerning his enemy's progress obviously inhibited him from making a constructive plan.

Warwick was not normally a sluggish and incompetent commander, and his performance immediately before and at the Second Battle of St Albans seems to have been out of character; but it could well have extinguished Edward of York's prospects of ever becoming king, and it was largely responsible for the poor opinion that Edward always held of his cousin the Kingmaker as a military commander. Edward himself set about raising men for his march on London as soon as he learned of Wakefield; he had in fact started at the head of some 10,000 troops when news reached him of the Lancastrian rising in Wales. He turned back to defeat Pembroke, but then he would have been better employed hastening to join Warwick (his victory was gained more than a fortnight before St Albans) than chasing his opponents and chopping off their heads.

Queen Margaret left York somewhere around 20 January at

the head of an army that may at first have numbered 40,000 men. The northern Lancastrians had rallied to her in good numbers, but the bulk of her army comprised moss-troopers from the borders – rascally ruffians in the game solely for what they could get from it. Andrew Trollope, who it will be remembered deserted to the Lancastrians after Blore Heath (see p. 116), is usually credited with having the overall command. This may seem strange, for he was certainly not in command a month later at Towton, and there were such distinguished persons as the Duke of Somerset (a favourite and not an insignificant commander), the Duke of Exeter, the Earls of Northumberland, Devon and Shrewsbury and Lord Clifford also in the field. But, together with the Queen, this distinguished soldier may well have formulated the Lancastrian plan, which was bold, imaginative and, for those times, unorthodox. We know the army's route as far as Royston from the trail of pillage and destruction and the burning towns it left behind. From Royston the Lancastrians probably marched down Icknield Way to Luton, and on learning of a 200-strong Yorkist contingent in Dunstable they made a short detour in order to wipe out the whole force. This was completed by the afternoon of 16 February.

The Earl of Warwick left London on 12 February, accompanied by, among others, the Dukes of Norfolk and Suffolk, the Earl of Arundel, Lords Bourchier, Bonville and Montagu and Sir Thomas Kyriell. He did not consider it safe to leave Henry in London, so the King was brought along, eventually to be placed under a tree from where he could brood agreeably upon the discomfiture of his enemies. The size of Warwick's army is given variously as between 9,000 and 30,000 men. The figure of 30,000 is probably much too high, but as is so often the case we have only the haziest idea of the numbers engaged. Almost certainly the Lancastrians had the edge, although by the time the Queen's army reached Dunstable the majority of the wild northerners had amassed their quota of loot and gone off home. Gregory* says that she went into battle only 5,000 strong; it is unusual for a chronicler to err on the low side, but this is surely too few. Perhaps some 20,000 men fought at St Albans, of which Warwick had rather less than half.

On reaching St Albans on the evening of the 12th Warwick halted. His intelligence was sadly lacking, for although there is reason to believe that he knew the Lancastrians were crossing his front from east to west, the first real intimation he got of the enemy's whereabouts was when they attacked his flank. He

*The Historical Collections of a Citizen of London in the fifteenth century, ed. James Gairdner, p.212.

apparently spent four days in preparing a defensive position (which in the event had to be hastily altered), confident that his enemy would oblige him with the usual frontal attack. But this was to be a most unusual battle, and Warwick himself – no doubt partly on account of his lack of information – was the first to abandon orthodoxy.

He took up a position that stretched from St Albans to Nomansland Common, which lies four miles to the north; he did not, of course, hold an unbroken line, but covered this long front with four unconnected defensive positions. The right flank probably rested on the high ground immediately south of Nomansland Common; the centre on the ridge west of Sandridge; the left either in Beech Bottom or on the high ground of Bernard's Heath; and on the extreme left in the town by the watch tower he stationed a strong body of archers. There remains the question of the troops at Dunstable. Quite likely these were a small band of local volunteers hastily brought together, for the chroniclers tell us that they were commanded by a butcher, who appears to have escaped the slaughter and later hanged himself out of shame.

We have a very full description of the devices used to protect at least some of these positions. On the ground were placed huge caltrops, which were spiked lattices that would effectively break up a cavalry charge, while the infantry were taken care of by stout nets measuring twenty-four feet long by four feet wide, fixed upright by iron rods with a nail standing upright at every second knot – the meshes being wide enough to allow the defenders to fire arrows through them. In addition there were many hundreds of pavises (door-shaped shields of thick wood) supported by stakes, from behind which archers and arbalesters discharged arrows and quarrels through holes pierced for that purpose. Warwick had some cannon and his Burgundian mercenaries were using the hand-gun, a weapon little known in England then, that 'wolde schute bothe pellettys of ledde and arowys of elle lengthe with VI fetherys, III in myddys and III at the other ende, with grete myghty hedde of yryn'.* These hand-guns were in fact more lethal to the operator than to the enemy. A section of the Burgundians called petardiers were employed throwing 'wylde fyre', which belched from an ignited earthenware pot that they flung in the faces of their enemy – another hideously unreliable weapon.

In those days when communications were of a most primitive kind, why did Warwick abandon one of the most important prin-

*ibid., p.213.

ciples – concentration of effort – and disperse his force in so dangerous a way as to invite defeat in detail? One eminent military historian* asserts that from Harpenden two roads led to London, one via St Albans and the other via Hatfield, and that Warwick wanted to cover them both. But a look through some old maps reveals no sign of a road running from Harpenden through Nomansland to Hatfield, nor does one seem to be mentioned by the chroniclers. Possibly, not knowing the exact line of the enemy's advance, he wanted to ensure that he was not bypassed, and by throwing out strongly defended positions on a wide front he hoped that the one eventually attacked could hold out long enough for him to bring up support. In fact when one of his positions was attacked he was unable to succour it in time to save it. There is little point in trying to guess Warwick's reasons when we have only fragmentary – and often contradictory – accounts of the actual sites he occupied and the part that his defensive works played in the battle; but the latter were on a big enough scale to indicate that, apart from the uncertainty born of bad intelligence, the Yorkist commander was sadly lacking in the offensive spirit.

The Lancastrian plan of attack – and, as I have suggested, we may perhaps see the Queen's questing mind at work here – was almost as unorthodox as Warwick's defensive position. Throughout the Wars of the Roses well laid plans were frequently vitiated by the presence of a traitor in one or other camp; so it was at St Albans. A Kentish squire by name of Lovelace (whom the French chronicler Jehan de Waurin states had been captured at Wakefield and only released in order to play the traitor†) sent Queen Margaret the Yorkist plan of defence, and indicated his intention of bringing his men over at the decisive moment of the battle. Armed with this information the Lancastrians rejected the customary thrust at the heart, and determined upon a flank attack – as unprecedented as it was unsporting. The initial point of attack would be the archers in St Albans, and once they had been disposed of the army was to swing left against the Bernard's Heath position. Dunstable to St Albans is twelve miles, and in order to gain surprise the approach march was to be made at night.

The hard core of the Lancastrian army still remaining under arms had had a lot of marching, and on 16 February a tough skirmish in Dunstable. All this was now followed by a night march down Watling Street, which was no longer a nice paved way, and by

*A. H. Burne, *Battlefields of England*, p.84.
†*Anciennes Chronicques d'Engleterre*, II, p.264.

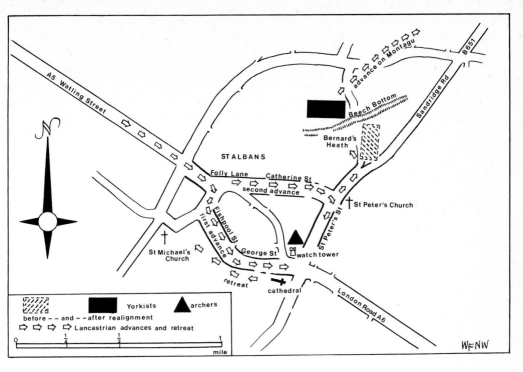

Above: The second battle of St Albans (first phase). Below: The second battle of St Albans (second phase, note east-west orientation)

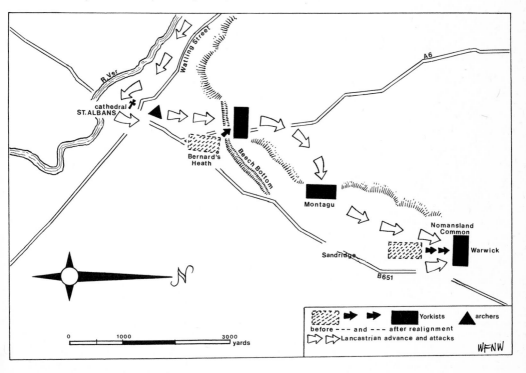

dawn on 17 February, as the troops crossed the river Ver and ascended what are now Fishpool Street and George Street, they must have been feeling far from fresh. The town barriers were not manned, but round the watch tower and Eleanor Cross the archers, although a comparatively small force, resisted with such spirit that they pushed back the Lancastrian advanced guard, who retreated precipitately on the main body by St Michael's Church. Clearly this narrow way could not be forced; a scouting party was sent out who soon reported that the archers could be outflanked by an advance up Folly Lane and into St Peter's Street via Catherine Street. This was successfully accomplished, and presented the archers with an unpleasant situation, for the rear of the Lancastrians was only moving away from St Michael's Church when the van was in St Peter's Street; the Yorkists had therefore to watch two fronts. But the second phase of the Lancastrian plan, to roll up the Yorkist left flank, could not be put into operation until the archers had been liquidated as a fighting force. For the second time in less than six years the streets of St Albans became a battleground; and in a restricted area where deployment was difficult these highly skilled bowmen were able to give so good an account of themselves that the morning was well advanced before they were done with.

Thus far, with the exception of the exact sitings of Warwick's positions, we are on firm ground. All of it has been recounted by one or more contemporary, or near contemporary, chroniclers. But now we are forced into the realms of conjecture. No detailed account of the rest of the fight exists, and one can only be constructed from the few threads of surviving evidence. The student of military history has the chance to open his own window upon the past, for the official one has long since been closed.

We have seen that Warwick's left-hand defensive position was in the Bernard's Heath area, immediately north of the town. At the bottom of this small patch of heath there is still a length of the great ditch that the Belgae dug before the Roman occupation; at one time it stretched from the town through Sandridge almost to Wheat-hampstead, and the portion still extant is even now some thirty feet deep. It was of course a natural defensive position, and it is possible – as some historians assert – that Warwick's men held it in the first instance, and on learning of the Lancastrian attack in St Albans pulled out onto the high ground facing south instead of west, and that the main fight took place there.

We know that the Bernard's Heath troops did not go to the aid of the archers, who were left to their fate, and most contemporary accounts refer to only one further main engagement and a rearguard action. The main engagement must have been fought either on Bernard's Heath or on the high ground above Sandridge a mile or so to the north. In spite of Gregory's inference that the complicated defensive equipment was rendered useless through the flank attack, we have Andrew Trollope's word that he was incapacitated by a wound received from a caltrop, so at any rate some of the protective devices must have been re-aligned in time to receive the attack. If the Bernard's Heath contingent held the line of the ditch they may not have had any further artificial protection – and anyway they would have had little time to dismantle it and drag it to the high ground. It therefore seems more likely that they withdrew behind the limited protection of the Sandridge post which, under Warwick's brother Lord Montagu, bore the brunt of the main attack.

The precise spot on which the battle was fought cannot be known for certain, but we have sufficient information about the fighting to enable us to make a reasonable reconstruction of events. The February air was chill and keen; and as the Lancastrian host, each man wearing besides his lord's livery the white ostrich feather on crimson and black (the badge of the young Prince of Wales), advanced upon the Yorkist ranks, snowflakes began to fall from a leaden sky. We are told that the buffeting wind sweeping flurries of snow into the eyes of the Yorkists played havoc with their shooting, and made the task of their hand-gunners more perilous than ever. These troops were, of course, outnumbered, but relied upon what they hoped would be their superior firepower to hold the enemy at bay until Warwick could strengthen their ranks with the men from Nomansland. But amid the falling snow and yellow fog of powder smoke, loud explosions followed by jagged pieces of metal that tore through the Yorkists ranks told a tale of exploded guns. Soon the fire from these unreliable weapons ceased altogether, and as the opposing ranks closed the fighting was sword to sword, axe to axe, with Montagu trying to shore up his wavering line and Trollope trying to crush him before reinforcements could arrive.

The Abbot Whethamstede asserts that the Yorkists would have won had their endurance equalled their valour at the outset; but there is a limit as to how much battering the smaller army can withstand in close quarter fighting, and Montagu's men fought for many hours before, judging themselves abandoned as the archers had been, the last bonds of discipline snapped. What, meanwhile, was Warwick doing? He certainly never lacked physical courage and the one account that credits him with leading a cavalry charge with fresh troops may well be true, but much of his time seems to have been spent in striving to hold his timorous lieutenants in leash. There were those who argued that to reinforce failure was foolish, and that it would be wiser to withdraw the right wing from the field while it was still intact, and march to join the Duke of York. But Warwick eventually managed to overcome such caitiff counsel and set off with these fresh troops to relieve his hard-pressed brother.

It was at this stage of the battle, just as Warwick had managed to get the right wing on the move to reinforce his centre, that the Kentish squire Lovelace went over to the enemy with his troops. Naturally this had a most demoralizing effect, and in any event it was by now too late to save Montagu. His men, who had resisted with the utmost constancy against superior numbers, had already broken, leaving their commander to be captured. As they poured back in disorder, closely pursued by the victorious Lancastrians slashing and thrusting with intent to kill and destroy, the atmosphere was heavy with defeat. However, Warwick, whose nerves were of steel and who seemed unaffected by the strain of the day and the imminent peril, now managed to save the Yorkists from utter rout and ruin. Somehow he stabilized a line above Nomansland Common, and here until dusk he stood at bay against the howling Lancastrian wolves. No doubt the enemy, who had marched all night, had had a stern fight and were without their wounded commander, preferred to hunt Yorkist fugitives along the patchwork of hedges to tackling a fairly formidable force of fresh troops; but in any case Warwick's final stand, and his orderly withdrawal from the field with 4,000 fighting men, went some way to atone for his lamentable lack of generalship in the early stages of the battle.

Throughout the Wars of the Roses both sides so often owed their victory to the odium of military treachery that one hesitates to predict what the result might have been had the losing commander not been betrayed. At St Albans the defection of Lovelace may have hastened the end, but Warwick never seemed to have a grip on the battle, and in hoping for victory from an already inferior force rendered more so by his curious dispositions he was asking his men to perform a prodigy of war.

The chroniclers are fairly consistent in estimating the numbers killed in this battle, and a figure of about 2,300 is usually accepted. On this occasion very few men of importance fell in the battle; however, the unpleasant practice of slaughtering prominent prisoners of war was now becoming commonplace. King Henry had been placed in the care of Lord Bonville and Sir Thomas Kyriell, who after the battle conducted him to Lord Clifford's tent,* where amid scenes of much joy he was reunited with his queen. It is said that his guardians had been offered a safe conduct, but they were brave men to place themselves in the empoisoned hands of Queen Margaret on such a tenuous understanding. Their fate was probably inevitable, but the manner of it – if correctly recounted by the chroniclers – was particularly loathsome. The Queen had them brought before the Prince of Wales, and said: 'Fair son, what manner of death should these knights, whom ye see here, die?' to which the boy, not yet eight years old but clearly aware of what was expected of him, replied, 'Let them have their heads taken off.' Lord Montagu's life was spared, possibly because he had been Henry's chamberlain, but more likely because Somerset's brother was a prisoner of the Neville faction in Calais. The only Lancastrian of distinction killed was Sir John Grey of Groby, whose widow Elizabeth was soon to become Queen of England.

At St Albans Warwick may have lost his reputation for victory, but he retained his courage and resolution. He accepted responsibility, made no accusations, levelled no reproaches; intent only on continuing the struggle, he led the remnants of his army across the miry roads and tracks that led, not to London, for that would have been hopeless, but westward to Chipping Norton, where he joined the Duke of York.

From the ashes of defeat would come a new flood of strength welling from depths as yet unplumbed. Warwick determined that he would palter no longer with a puppet king in whose name a plundering horde had recently ravaged many of the principal towns of England. There was no sense in striving to prop up a broken reed. Only a year before he had been vehement in opposing any change of dynasty, now he saw the need for a new effulgence to dazzle and to dominate. A fortnight after the Yorkist defeat at St Albans the young man whose badge the losing army had worn was proclaimed Edward IV at Westminster.

Before March was out the stigma of St Albans was to be expunged; Warwick wasted no time in assembling a new army reforged on the anvil of monarchy and ready to strike hard and swiftly at the enemy. Queen Margaret had withdrawn her army to Yorkshire; the new king was eager for pursuit, and the heavy hand of vengeance was to be laid upon the Lancastrians in the slaughter of Towton (see p.120 or chapter 9 for a full account).

*In some accounts Lord Clifford is said to have commanded the Lancastrian army, but this is most unlikely. There is, however, no reason why he should not have received the King.

DEVELOPMENT OF WEAPONS

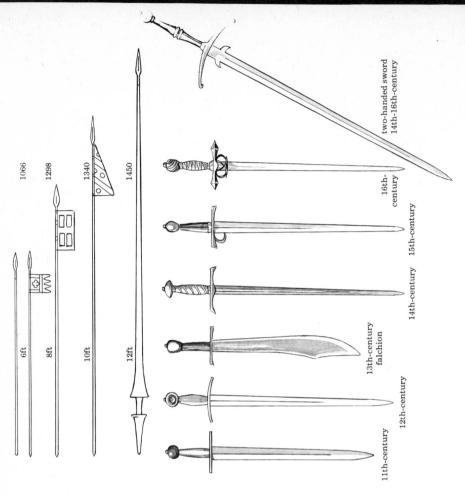

1066 · 1298 · 1340 · 1450

6ft · 8ft · 10ft · 12ft

11th-century · 12th-century · 13th-century falchion · 14th-century · 15th-century · 16th-century · two-handed sword 14th-16th-century

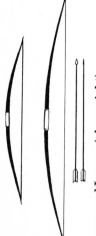

Spears and Lances (above right)

The spear or javelin used by both Saxon infantry and Norman cavalry appears from the Bayeux Tapestry to have been 5 to 6 feet long, and to have been used both for thrusting and casting. 13th and 14th-century illuminated manuscripts show spears lengthening and developing by the 15th century into the heavy, tournament-type spear or lance

Longbow and Shortbow (above)

The shortbow used until Edward I's time (c. 1270) was about 3 or 4 feet long. The 6-foot longbow with a pull of 60 to 90 pounds, developed first in Wales, became by the 14th century the national weapon of the English. Arrows were 3 feet long and had heads of various shapes: broad, leaf-shaped for use against horses, long and narrow for piercing armour. The longbow was used from the 14th to 16th century. Short, hunting bows were still used by some Scottish clansmen during the Civil War

Swords (right)

Beginning as a fairly short weapon mainly for cutting and slashing, the sword tended to grow steadily stiffer, longer and more pointed through the centuries, and so better suited for thrusting as well as cutting. There were many minor variations within the main development, but the 13th-century falchion was a particularly unusual weapon designed to increase the weight and penetrating power of the cut, as armour improved. The 6-foot long two-handed broadsword was a 14th-century invention. It achieved little popularity in England but found great favour in Scotland in the 14th to 16th century, being called the claymore ('claidheamh mor'—great sword)

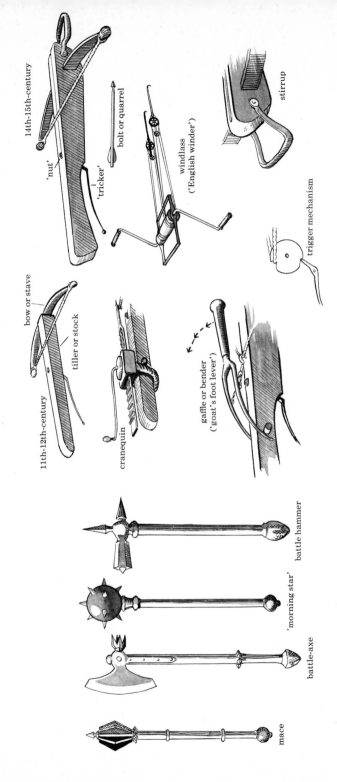

14th–15th-century

'nut'

'tricker'

bolt or quarrel

windlass ('English winder')

stirrup

trigger mechanism

bow or stave

tiller or stock

11th–12th-century

cranequin

gaffle or bender ('goat's foot lever')

battle hammer

'morning star'

battle-axe

mace

Arbalest or Crossbow

The crossbow was spanned by pulling the cord back with both hands while the archer's foot steadied the front end on the ground, in later models with the aid of a stirrup. These later more powerful bows required first a hook attached to the belt and eventually spanning devices such as the windlass, the cranequin and the simpler 'goat's foot lever'. The bolt or quarrel was a stout, heavy missile about a foot long, fletched with vanes of parchment, wood or leather, often angled to impart spin. Little used in England as a military weapon after the development of the longbow, the crossbow reappeared during the Wars of the Roses when foreign mercenary troops were brought in

Maces, Battle-Axes and Battle Hammers

Heavy maces with flanged or spiked heads, battle-axes and battle hammers were used by horsemen from the 11th to 15th centuries. For crushing or piercing heavily helmeted heads, they must have been useful weapons in a mêlée

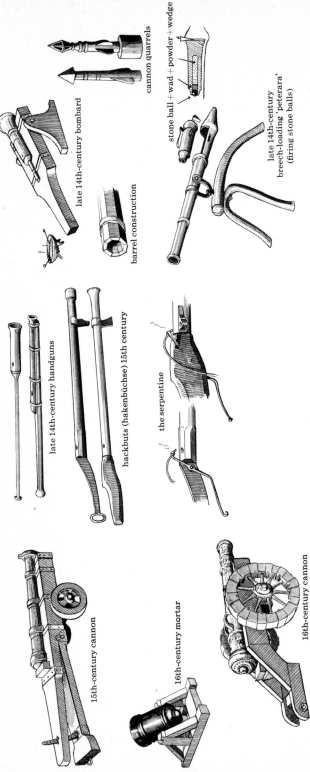

cannon quarrels

late 14th-century bombard

stone ball + wad + powder + wedge

barrel construction

late 14th-century
breech-loading 'peterara'
(firing stone balls)

late 14th-century handguns

hackbuts (hakenbüchse) 15th century

the serpentine

15th-century cannon

16th-century mortar

16th-century cannon

Handguns
Late 14th century handguns
The earliest handgun was essentially a miniature cannon, a barrel as short even as 8 inches, fixed to a wooden or iron stock or tiller which was held against the chest or tucked under the arm. Some required 2 men to handle them. Like the cannon, the handgun was fired by means of a red hot wire or coal. It was in use from the late 14th century until the end of the 15th

Guns
Cannon were used from the mid-14th century

onwards. Early ones were constructed of a series of wrought-iron bars welded together longitudinally. They fired stone balls or cannon-arrows (quarrels) which were a natural development from the crossbow bolt and the ballista missile. Many early cannon were breech-loaders: the chamber containing powder, wad and ball was plugged into the breech, being held firm with wedges. The guns were fired by means of a red hot iron rod or wire. Breech-loaders were soon abandoned in favour of the doubtless safer and more efficient muzzle-loader

Hackbuts (hakenbüchse) 15th century
The hackbut was a larger and more advanced handgun, which could presumably be hooked over a wall or other cover to absorb recoil. The stock was of iron or wood. Developed in the early 15th century, it appears to have still been in use at Pinkie Cleuch, though it is possible that the name persisted after the invention of the slow match, which soon led to the addition of a simple device, the serpentine, to carry the lighted match to the touch-hole, and so to the development of the arquebus or matchlock musket

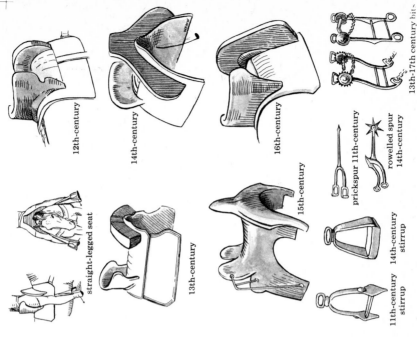

12th-century

14th-century

16th-century

13th–17th century bit~

straight-legged seat

13th-century

15th-century

prickspur 11th-century

rowelled spur
14th-century

14th-century
stirrup

11th-century
stirrup

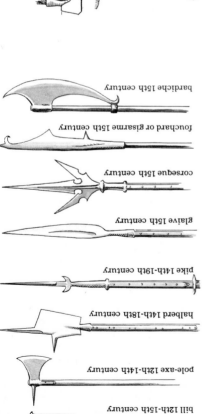

bardiche 15th century

fouchard or glsarme 15th century

corseque 15th century

glaive 15th century

pike 14th-19th century

halberd 14th-18th century

pole-axe 12th-14th century

bill 12th-15th century

Pole-Arms

Originating from agricultural and hedging implements (axes, scythes, bills) mounted on poles, pole-arms were in use by infantry throughout the 11th to 18th centuries, becoming steadily longer, more elaborate and more varied. Most of the 13th to 16th century ones included a point for thrusting, a heavy blade for cutting and a rear spike or hook for dragging horsemen from their saddles. A feature of most is the long steel straps or 'langets' from the head down the shaft, to prevent the lopping off of the head by enemy horsemen

Saddles (right)

The medieval knight rode with a straight leg. His saddle had a high pommel and cantle, of which there were many varieties, both for protection of the lower trunk and thighs, and for assistance in resisting the shock and pressure of an opponent's weapons and body. A straight legged seat necessitates long spurs. These were originally prickspurs, but rowels were introduced in the early 14th century. Bits were very long cheeked and extremely severe

CHAPTER 9

The Battle of Towton

29 March 1461

Towton is two and a half miles south of Tadcaster on the A 162 road. Immediately south of Towton the road forks, and about a mile along the right fork (B 1217) there stands, on the right of the road, the battle monument. It is usually held that the Lancastrian line was just to the south of the monument, stretching from the edge of the high ground on the west to a little way across the A 162 road on the east. The Yorkist battle line was on the cross ridge beyond the slight depression that runs directly in front of the Lancastrian position in an east-west direction.

The land, which is much as it was at the time of the battle, except that then it was open heath land and now it is neatly cultivated but still mainly unenclosed, is all privately owned. A public footpath runs across the southern part of the battlefield, but probably the best view is obtained from the highest point of the B 1217 road in the area of the monument. A bridle path leads from Towton to Stutton (it follows the line of the old London road), and about half a mile along it the river Cock is bridged at the same spot as where the great slaughter took place in 1461. Very little is changed here. On the north side of Saxton Church can be seen Lord Dacre's tomb; he was buried there after the battle, together with his horse.

At the beginning of his reign Edward was undoubtedly much under Warwick's influence. It was Warwick who first put kingship into Edward's head, and it was he who organized the great military and civilian gathering in St John's Fields, Clerkenwell, two days after their entry into London, at which the people loudly acclaimed their new sovereign. But Edward, although only nineteen years old, was by no means Warwick's puppet; he had a mind of his own, and when he stirred himself to use it – particularly in military matters – he showed what a keen instrument it was. Moreover, as we have seen, his confidence in Warwick as a commander had been somewhat shaken by St Albans, and there is evidence that he placed more reliance in his (and Warwick's) uncle, William Lord Fauconberg, during the forthcoming Towton campaign.

There were two strangely contrasting pleasures in Edward's life:

the pursuit of leisure and the pursuit of war. When there was no fighting to be done he was foremost among the lotus-eaters; but the slightest smell of battle stimulated him to tireless industry. The speed with which he made the journey from Chipping Norton to London, and the exertions he made to mobilize an army after he had reached the city, were manifestations not only of his readiness to assume his new responsibilities, but also of his determination to stake all on building a reputation worthy of his kingly office. Warwick, who had received another contingent of Burgundians under the Seigneur de la Barde, was dispatched on 7 March to recruit men from the western Midlands; the Duke of Norfolk went to East Anglia to levy his formidable number of retainers; on 11 March Lord Fauconberg left London at the head of a strong infantry force, and on the 12th or 13th Edward himself set out for the north.

The Lancastrian army which, against all advice, King Henry had prevented from marching on London until it was too late, began its withdrawal to the north on 26 February. The holocaust from which Henry had saved London was reserved for numerous smaller towns; for the large, unruly section of mosstroopers among the Lancastrian soldiery, who had been deprived of what they regarded as the legitimate spoils of victory, considered all land south of the Trent as foreign and therefore fair game. Queen Margaret was well aware that without a triumphal entry into London to take possession of the city her army's effort at St Albans was but a hollow victory. Warwick had been deeply smitten, but she was herself too well endowed with the attributes of the warrior mind not to know that he would soon be burning for revenge. The Lancastrian leaders had the choice of three great rivers behind which they could select a strong position that would afford the army reasonable prospects of success, the Don, the Aire and the Wharfe. They chose the Aire. But in the first instance Margaret, whose guiding hand was probably still at the helm, directed them to the Tadcaster–York area, there to await the arrival of reinforcements from those northern counties which most favoured the Lancastrian cause.

Somewhere north of the Trent (we do not know exactly where) Edward, who had been following the trail of ravaged towns and burnt out homesteads blazed by the Lancastrians, was reunited with the advance elements of his army. The Don was crossed unopposed, but soon afterwards news was received that the enemy were massing behind the Aire. On Friday 27 March, from his camp at Pontefract, Edward sent a detachment under Lord Fitzwalter to reconnoitre the river crossing at Ferrybridge and if possible to seize and hold it.

Towton (see also p.120) is often considered to have been the most decisive battle of the Wars of the Roses, for this overwhelming Yorkist victory was gained in the heart of Lancastrian country, and the melancholy toll of Lancastrians who perished on the field or by the axe made serious inroads into their leadership. This assertion is open to argument; but what bears no contradiction is that it was the bloodiest battle, with the greatest number of combatants engaged, ever to be fought on British soil. And yet it is a battle upon which the contemporary chroniclers bestowed only a few lines. Perhaps the best account comes from the pen of Edward Hall, written some seventy years later. The principal facts stand out clearly from the meagre accounts, but there are many contradictions in detail, not least in respect of the numbers of men who fought and of those who were killed. Hall, in computing a figure of 48,660 Yorkist soldiers, states that he took this from the pay roll – an impeccable source, but there were many on the pay roll who were non-combatants. His estimate of 60,000 for the Lancastrian army is probably too high. Edward may have started the battle with just under 40,000 fighting soldiers, against an enemy numbering a few thousand more.

King Henry and his queen, together with their son, remained in York. Unlike at St Albans, where we do not know for certain who commanded the army, it seems that now the Duke of Somerset, although only twenty-four years old, was put in overall command. It could not have been a very enviable post with such as the veteran Earl of Northumberland, Andrew Trollope, the Duke of Exeter and Lord Dacre breathing down his neck. It was never a part of the grand design to hold the Yorkists on the line of the river; in those days it was usually better tactics to harass the enemy while he attempted a river crossing and then allow him to come up against a strongly held position with the river at his back in the event of defeat. Accordingly the main army was drawn up on the ridge that rises from the York plain between the villages of Towton and Saxton, while Lord Clifford was sent forward to dispute the crossing of the river.

The Yorkist detachment commanded by Lord Fitzwalter found the Ferrybridge crossing unguarded. The wooden bridge had been broken down, and much of that day was spent in repairing it. The night of Friday 27–8 March was passed by Fitzwalter's troops on the north bank of the river, but clearly proper precautions against surprise had not been taken. On the Saturday morning, as a cold, translucent green sky was gradually extinguishing the stars, Lord Clifford and his men swooped down upon the unsuspecting Yorkists and swept them back across the bridge they had so laboriously re-built. Lord Fitzwalter was asleep when the enemy pounced, and coming out of his lodging to investigate the noise was promptly killed.

The contemporary chronicler William Gregory states that War-wick was present at this skirmish and slightly wounded in the leg. Hall casts him in the highly dramatic and somewhat uncharacter-istic role of the hysterical messenger of defeat: hastening back to the King with the tidings, he dismounted, drew his sword and hav-ing cut his horse's throat with it proceeded to kiss the hilt and ex-claim, 'Let him fly that will, I will tarry with him that will tarry with me.'* The story must remain apocryphal; it is most unlikely that Warwick was present at this fight, although his bastard brother was killed with Fitzwalter.

Edward, at any rate, remained absolutely calm. As soon as he learned that Clifford commanded only a strong raiding force he ordered Lord Fauconberg to cross the river four miles upstream at Castleford and cut off the Lancastrians' retreat. Fauconberg's column comprised troops led by Sir Walter Blount and the re-nowned Kentish captain Robert Horne. Their mission was entirely successful. Clifford, realizing his predicament, made a hasty re-treat, with Fauconberg always at his heels. The Yorkists finally closed on their prey in the picturesquely named Dintingdale valley.†
Here a sharp fight ensued and before the Lancastrians could regain their main body they had suffered many casualties including Clifford (who for some reason had removed his gorget and received an arrow in the neck) and John Neville.‡ The death of these two men would have cast considerable gloom over the Lancastrian host, for they were both experienced and valued leaders.

Lord Clifford and his men had almost gained the safety of their own lines, for Somerset had decided to make his stand on the low plateau south of Towton, which rises to 100 feet above sea level out of the vast York plain. The rise is scarcely perceptible on all sides except the west, where from the valley of the Cock Beck the ground ascends steeply and parts of the slopes are wooded. At its top this plateau is crossed by the east–west depression of Towton Dale,

---

Hall's Chronicle, p.258.
†This valley, which is marked on the 1850 Ordnance Survey six-inch
  map, lies between Saxton village and the A 162 Tadcaster–Ferrybridge
  road.
‡Brother of Ralph, second Earl of Westmorland; this branch of the
  family were mainly Lancastrians.

which on the east side is little more than a dip, but where it drops into the river it forms a considerable gulley. At the time of the battle, when populations were small and only the best land in the immediate vicinity of the villages was cultivated, all this ground was open heath land. The little river was then a more formidable obstacle, for besides being in spate at the time of the battle and therefore in parts up to five feet deep and fast-flowing, the banks were lined with marshy ground, which near the bridge north-west of Towton assumed the proportions of a treacherous quagmire.

The Duke of Somerset awaited the enemy somewhere along the top of this plateau. In order to follow the course of the battle and the appalling slaughter that ensued it is not essential to know the exact position of the two armies, and there is no contemporary account that pinpoints these. Most historians are agreed that the Lancastrian line was situated immediately south of the battle monument, stretching from the bluff that falls sharply down to the river on the west side to a point a little way across the main Tadcaster–Ferrybridge road on the east; and that the Yorkists drew up for battle at the top of the ridge immediately south of the dip. Therefore the opposing forces faced each other across this shallow (except at the extreme west end) depression.

This opinion among historians may well be right, but it was for the Lancastrians almost what we would now call a reverse slope position, and the time was some way on before this became an accepted battle position. The forward slope of the depression was insignificant, except in one small area. It must also be remembered that Somerset had more than 40,000 men to draw up in battle order, and even allowing for the fact that both armies almost certainly fought in column of divisions he would have needed a good deal of space. The accepted position denied him some 400 yards of ground that would have been available 300 yards further south with his right resting on Castle Hill Wood, and here he would definitely have had a forward slope position.

The evidence for the generally accepted site of the battle rests almost entirely on legend: a field known as Bloody Meadow, on the west of Towton Dale, grave pits, and a 'bur tree' behind which the arrow that killed Lord Dacre was fired. The grave pits are authentic, but they do not necessarily indicate the initial position of either army; neither for that matter does the name given later to a field – although it helps – and the 'bur' or elder tree has long since disappeared and then, as now, there must have been a great many in the area. In accepting the majority opinion, therefore, it must be realized that there is at least one alternative site for

144

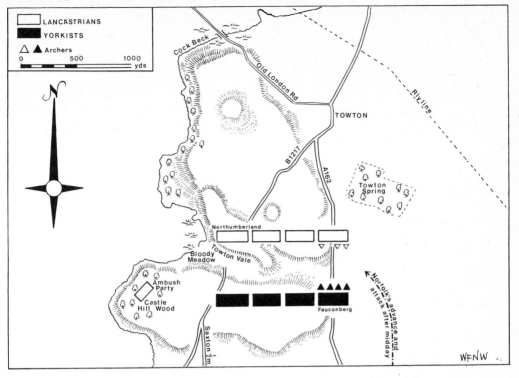

Battle of Towton. Note Bloody Meadow: Slaughter here was extremely heavy and survivors escaped across the Cock over the bodies of the fallen

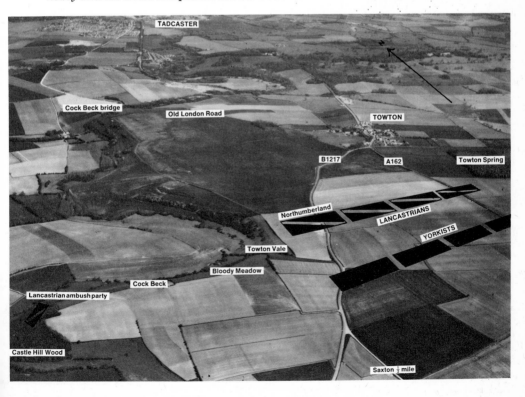

this murderous battle. However, having accepted it, it is logical also to agree that Somerset may well have placed a strong ambush in Castle Hill Wood: there would have been no very great risk in doing this and a resolutely led force on the enemy's flank could do much damage.

The Lancastrians made no attempt to support Lord Clifford, or in any way cover his withdrawal; instead they remained inactive for the whole of Saturday 28 March, awaiting the arrival of the Yorkist army. Edward had left Pontefract and crossed the river as soon as he had learned that Clifford's force had withdrawn with Fauconberg in pursuit. The main body probably crossed the river at Castleford, for the bridge at Ferrybridge was being either rebuilt or greatly strengthened to take the cannon and supply wagons. In this approach march of nine miles no doubt Edward and Warwick led the way, but later in the day Fauconberg and his victorious troops would have rejoined the army and Fauconberg then assumed command of the vanguard.

The head of the Yorkist army reached Saxton village well before dark, but a large army always has stragglers and the wagon train was still far back. Edward wisely decided to postpone the issue until the following day. The Yorkists advanced to within half a mile of their foe, but it was a wild and bitter night with a whiff of snow in the air and the wind – then from the north – deadened the sound of their approach. The men of both armies lay down on the cold ground with no protection from the elements. Sentries were posted, and as darkness gradually enveloped the landscape straining eyes would seem to detect parties of enemy stealthily approaching. But soon the few trees, which stood in elemental solitude on that windswept plateau, surrendered their weird shapes to the night, and all was quiet, save for the whine of the wind.

The morning of 29 March, which was Palm Sunday, dawned cold and cloudy. The wind had now gone round to the south and as the Yorkists prepared to advance to the crest of the plateau it began to snow. Edward was in no hurry to engage, for he was still short of the Duke of Norfolk's contingent,* but he would not have waited too long with so powerful an army to his front. The chroniclers mostly agree that the fight, including the immediate

---

*The Duke of Norfolk was a sick man; he died the following November. He may or may not have fought in person, but certainly his troops arrived on the scene late in the day and had a decisive influence on the battle. Some accounts say that Norfolk was left at Pontefract to follow on with the reserve; but it seems more probable that his contingent was always a day's march behind.

146

pursuit, lasted for ten hours – a long time for those days – so it must have started before 10 a.m., for by 8 p.m. it would have been almost pitch dark. We do not know the order of battle, nor the formations adopted, but from the meagre accounts of the fighting, and the knowledge that vast numbers were employed in a limited space, it is reasonable to assume that both armies fought in column of divisions (or battles) and not in extended order as was usual. And we do know that Lord Fauconberg commanded the Yorkist van and was responsible for the first successful phase of the battle.

The strong south wind that blew snow into the Lancastrians' faces put them at a grave disadvantage, the full significance of which seems to have escaped even so experienced a soldier as Andrew Trollope who, together with Northumberland, commanded the Lancastrian van. Fauconberg advanced his archers a few paces and ordered them to fire a single volley into the enemy and then withdraw to the main body. The volley took some effect and the Lancastrians immediately returned the fire, but the combination of a headwind and the withdrawal of the Yorkist archers caused their arrows to fall short by '40 tailor's yards'. However, so bad was their fire discipline that they continued to loose off arrows until their quivers were empty. Fauconberg then advanced his archers again, this time to keep up a steady fire not only with their own arrows, but also with the many that had fallen harmlessly from enemy bows. Those they did not return were stuck in the ground to impede the oncoming troops, for the Lancastrians were the first to advance.

Cannon appears to have played no part in this battle – indeed the Yorkist guns may not even have arrived on the field in time – but the archery was a sufficient irritation to the Lancastrians to cause them to close with their enemy. As they entered the depression, and marched steadily up the slope towards the inexorable firing line, their casualties were heavy – especially on the west above Bloody Meadow where the slope was at its steepest – but once the two armies were joined in the savagery of hand-to-hand combat their very weight of numbers gave them some advantage, and the wind and snow were of less worry to them. This desperate contest was fought upon an unprecedented scale between at least 80,000 men in a very circumscribed area. It was a soldiers' battle, for there was little that the commanders could do, except to keep feeding fresh men into the fray to take the place of wounded or fallen comrades. A dreadful ardour inspired all ranks; men thirsted to be at their enemy's throats to kill and be killed. It was said that in places the dead lay so thick on the ground that the troops from the rear divisions were marching over a carpet of bodies to get at their foe.

For three hours the struggle continued thus. Some pauses were inevitable, but for the rival commanders there was no respite. Casualties among the leaders were heavy, and those still fighting had the constant task of shoring up the front lines with ever-dwindling reserves. The Yorkist left may have felt the effects of the Castle Hill Wood ambush, while the centre and right were holding on grimly, but by around midday fortune, indifferent to sacrifice though smiling upon numbers, clearly favoured the Lancastrians. Edward remained cool and resolute; he was everywhere to encourage by word and example; although only nineteen he displayed a nerve of steel. The Yorkists were indeed lucky in their leaders, for the young king had invaluable support from such as Warwick and Fauconberg. But by now only one man's name could have been on all lips. Where was the Duke of Norfolk?

Slowly, but surely, the Yorkists were giving ground; back now nearly to the southern edge of the plateau, hacking and thrusting with sword and bill amid gaps that were gradually widening, for it was becoming increasingly difficult to fill them. But just as the battle had reached its crisis, the spirit of hope was rekindled throughout Edward's rapidly weakening army: out of the gloom there appeared the Duke of Norfolk's banners. Marching through the ancient hamlet of Sherburn in Elmet with what speed they could muster in the slush and snow, his men had arrived on the right of the Yorkist army and they wasted no time in taking up position. It was now a little after midday and Norfolk's arrival marked the turning point in the battle. But it did not cause any immediate panic or disintegration among the Lancastrian soldiers; stubbornly they fought on, still almost shoulder to shoulder, and the issue remained in doubt until the now extended Yorkist line could turn the Lancastrian left. At first, almost imperceptibly, the Yorkists regained their lost ground, and then more noticeably the Lancastrians began to give way. A trickle to the rear gradually spread into mass flight. By the late afternoon this tremendous trial of strength was over. The Lancastrian army was in full retreat.

As always in those days, when men attempted to flee encumbered by armour or heavy equipment, it was in the retreat that the heaviest losses occurred, and the nature of the terrain played a decisive part in this. We can therefore believe that the slaughter in the field known as Bloody Meadow would have been very heavy, for it was a veritable trap with the river on one side and

148

on the other a steep slope that left only a narrow, marshy passage of flat ground. The obvious line of retreat was towards Towton and along the old London road, which had been the Lancastrian line of advance; but this involved the crossing of the swollen stream by a small wooden bridge surrounded by a marshy quagmire. So long as they were on the plateau we hear of pockets of Lancastrians turning at bay and fighting with great courage and desperation to stave off defeat, but as soon as the steep decline to the London road and the river was reached all semblance of discipline seems to have disappeared, and men rushed headlong to the crossing. The ghastly scene of destruction by steel and water has often been described; men were slaughtered, or trampled into a watery grave, in such thousands that the chroniclers probably did not exaggerate when they said that the survivors crossed the Cock over the bodies of the fallen, and that the water still ran red when it joined the river Wharfe three miles downstream.

Not all the Lancastrians would have converged on the bridge at Towton; no doubt some of those fighting on the left would have tried to reach Tadcaster across country, but accounts of further fighting on the 30th between Towton and Tadcaster would seem to be inaccurate. Mopping up went on almost to the gates of York; Sir John Denham and Sir John Wenlock were sent in pursuit with a strong cavalry force and killed many with little resistance.

The numbers of those who perished on the field of battle, in the waters of the Cock, or in the pursuit beyond its banks will never be accurately known. Polydore Vergil, writing some fifty years after the battle, gives a figure for both armies of 20,000, of which he says 10,000 were wounded and made prisoner (some of whom died). This is the lowest estimate and is of interest in mentioning prisoners, for most authorities say that there was no quarter given. The Monk of Croyland heads the list with a figure of 38,000 and Hall is not far behind with 36,776; in the Paston letters we get a total of 28,000 of which 20,000 were Lancastrians, and this latter figure is supported by another contemporary writer, the Abbot Whethamstede. The truth may lie somewhere between Polydore Vergil's and Paston's figures, and is sufficiently horrifying without accepting the probably exaggerated higher numbers.

Particular attention was paid, as in most of these battles, to cutting down men of rank. The list of Lancastrian peers and knights who fell is formidable indeed. The Earl of Northumberland was carried off the field badly wounded, only to die the next day; Lords Dacre, Clifford, Neville, de Maulay, and Welles were killed, and among the knights to perish were Sir Andrew Trollope, Sir

Henry Stafford, Sir John Heyton and Sir Richard Percy. Thomas Courtenay, Earl of Devon, was made prisoner, and on the Monday when Edward rode into York the Earl's head was needed to replace that of Edward's father, which had adorned the walls since the Battle of Wakefield (see p. 119). Later in the month the Earl of Wiltshire was captured and he too was executed. Henry and Margaret were hustled out of York with a small escort and headed for the safety of the Scottish border; the Dukes of Somerset and Exeter also made good their escape. The Yorkists lost few men of rank. Lord Fitzwalter, Sir Richard Jenney, Warwick's bastard brother, and Robert Horne were the only prominent men to be killed, while Lord Scrope of Bolton was severely wounded.

Edward had won this, his first major engagement, on merit. There seems little doubt that although well supported by more experienced men he was not content to act as their parade ground fugleman, but was in active command of the army from the day of assembly until the march into York. The Lancastrians may have suffered from divided leadership; certainly the affair at Ferry-bridge and the subsequent fate of Lord Clifford and his men showed a lamentable lack of generalship, and the first phase of the battle was lost through inexperience or indifference on the part of the vanguard commanders.

In the space of ten hours a sizable slice of the English aristocracy and gentry had been dealt a crippling blow. But if the limbs are lopped the trunk remains. Despite the devastation to their ranks during the Wars of the Roses scarcely an English peerage became extinct,* and fifty years later when a similar disaster overtook the Scots at Flodden (see chapter 13) their ancient nobility showed the same powers of recovery. The fact remains that the total casualties in this one battle were almost a third of those suffered throughout the Wars of the Roses. Lurking foes across the Scotish border and the Channel must have wished that they had been in a position to take advantage of this cataclysm. No one could be certain that they were not. For this reason Edward left Warwick and his brother to guard the north, while he and most of the other magnates went south to London for the happier duty of preparing for his coronation.

*Succession through the female line was partly responsible for this survival.

CHAPTER 10

The Battle of Barnet

14 April 1471

Although the actual site of this battle is surprisingly free from buildings, there are, unfortunately, sufficient to make it difficult to view the complete positions of the rival armies from the ground. However, it is fairly easy to trace these, and the course of the battle, piecemeal, by driving and walking the ground. The A 1000 road north from Barnet leads to Hadley Green, and just north of this Barnet suburb the road forks to Kitts End, where the monument known as the High Stone stands. Warwick's advance from St Albans took him along the Kitts End road to the High Stone.

Hadley Green is on a plateau which stretches to Barnet, and just south of the High Stone it widens to almost 2,000 yards; on this ridge both armies took up their positions. The plateau, at 400 feet, is the highest ground between London and York. Warwick's line probably ran across Hadley Green and a little way to the north of Hadley church (the present church was built after the battle); it would have stretched from a point west of the A 1000 across to where the ground starts to fall away north of the road called Camlet Way – just above Monken Hadley Common. Edward's line was about 300 yards to the south of Warwick's; it overlapped Warwick's on the right and was itself overlapped on the left. It therefore stretched, on the right, to Monken Hadley Common.

The return of Edward IV to England, his landing at Ravenspur on 14 March 1471, and his march to London have already been recorded in outline (p. 124). The Earl of Warwick's position in the kingdom, and the manoeuvring of the rival forces during the month that followed Edward's landing, need to be looked at in rather more detail in order to set the stage for the Battle of Barnet (see also p. 125). The brief period of Lancastrian restoration, which lasted from October 1470 to April 1471, marked the apogee of Warwick's power. He had married his eldest daughter Isabella to the Duke of Clarence and, so he thought, won that somewhat slippery royal gentleman to his side; his younger daughter Anne was married to Edward Prince of Wales – a match that he hoped might gain him the confidence, if not the friendship, of Queen

Margaret and the Lancastrian lords, by most of whom he was still regarded with deep mistrust; and above all it was Warwick, not the worn and wearied Henry, that ruled the kingdom.

But Warwick sat uneasily in Westminster. He ruled without the aura of monarchy, and, added to this grave disadvantage, his undoubted popularity with the lower classes did not extend to the merchants who, with their capitalist guilds, controlled the trade of London. These men viewed with considerable disapproval Warwick's attempts to align himself with the King of France in opposition to the Duke of Burgundy, whose territories now provided them with their best markets. Moreover, Henry's queen proved most reluctant to respond to her husband's urgings to join him in London; she was not prepared to bring her son from the safety of France until she was satisfied that no skulduggery was afoot. Her constant procrastination may have suited Warwick personally, but he was aware that her presence in the capital, and more importantly that of her son, might bring about a change of heart and strengthen the Lancastrian cause in a way which Henry alone could never achieve.

Warwick was sure that Edward of York, whom he had served so long and of whose abilities as a soldier he was perfectly aware, would attempt to regain his kingdom. The army that Warwick had promised King Louis of France would never cross the Channel, for by February 1471 every man was needed to secure the country against invasion. Warwick had reason for confidence: he had made his dispositions wisely, and the ring of steel with which he girdled the country had few gaps. The north had always favoured the Lancastrians, and now the powerful Neville family buttressed their support; his brother John, Marquis of Montagu, had an army at Pontefract, and although the loyalty of the Earl of Northumberland (whose title had recently been restored to him by Edward) was suspect, it was not thought likely that he would join Edward. The Earl of Oxford and Lord Scrope of Bolton were in charge of the east coast; the Earl of Pembroke was in Wales; the Dukes of Clarence and Somerset* and Lord Devon were raising the south-west; the men of Kent always rallied to Warwick, and the Bastard of Fauconberg was off the south coast with a fleet.

*There is a sharp difference of opinion among historians (near contemporary to modern) as to whether Somerset fought at Barnet, or whether – like Devon – he was in the south-west until the arrival of Queen Margaret. The writer is of the opinion that although he may have gone to the coast, he had returned in time to command Warwick's centre at the battle.

Warwick himself remained in London until on the news of Edward's successful landing he left the capital in charge of Henry, aided by Warwick's brother George Neville, Chancellor and Archbishop of York, and hurried into the Midlands to raise more troops.

Edward, having found the East Anglian coast too strongly guarded, landed at Ravenspur with less than 2,000 men. At Nottingham, where he felt strong enough to declare himself king, he was joined by Sir Thomas Parre, Sir James Harrington, Sir William Stanley and Sir William Norris, all of whom brought men, and by the time he reached Leicester Edward had a force of some 4,000 troops, which probably equalled that commanded by Warwick. The latter was still expecting Clarence to join him, and Montagu – who had made no attempt to intercept Edward on his march south* – had been ordered to bring his army of perhaps 3,000 troops to join Warwick, who had meanwhile shut himself into Coventry. Here he refused battle, and he also had some scathing remarks to make about the Duke of Clarence who, after he had deserted his father-in-law and made his peace with his brother at a meeting of their two armies near Banbury, persuaded Edward to offer honourable terms to Warwick and his followers should they surrender.

The road to London was open, and Edward took it, leaving Warwick, who had disdained surrender, behind the walls of Coventry. He celebrated Palm Sunday at Daventry and was at St Albans for the night of 10 April. Warwick had sent urgent messages to his brother George Neville to hold London for up to three days, by which time he would arrive and hope to take Edward in the rear. Oxford, whose troops had had to run before Edward at Newark, and Montagu had now joined Warwick, whose combined force was probably slightly in excess of what Edward commanded, even after Clarence's accession. But Edward was not to be caught between two fires. George Neville, in an attempt to rally the Londoners' patriotism, paraded the wretched Henry through their streets; but the citizens, whose interests he had squandered and whose sacrifices he had ignored, were not impressed. There were many Yorkists in London; Edward's queen, in sanctuary at Westminster, had recently given birth to a son; and the City merchants had everything to gain from Edward. The

*It is difficult to understand Montagu's lapse. As a result Warwick suspected his brother's loyalty, but this suspicion was proved quite unfounded. Possibly he thought himself too weak to attack and was waiting for Northumberland to act. The latter's neutrality undoubtedly saved the Yorkist cause.

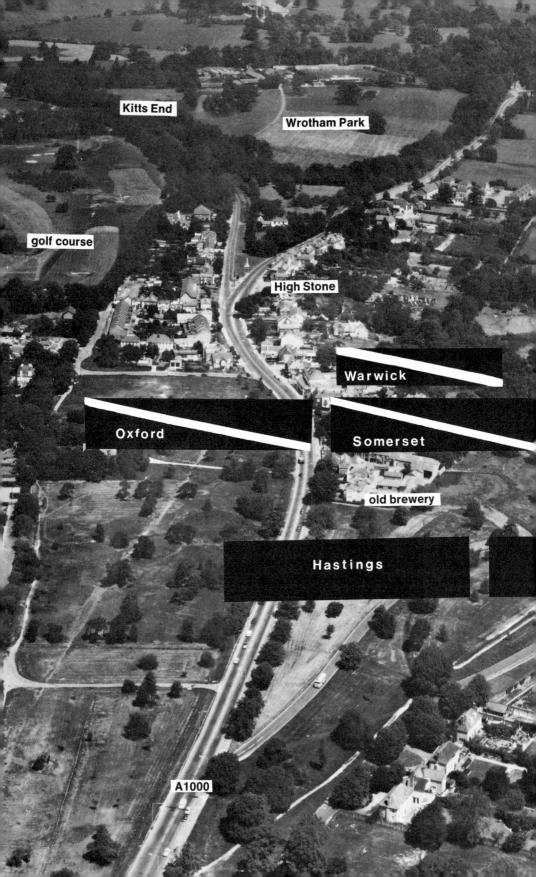

Kitts End

Wrotham Park

golf course

High Stone

Warwick

Oxford

Somerset

old brewery

Hastings

A1000

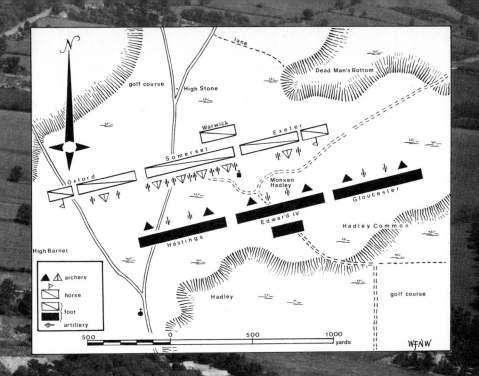

N

golf course · High Stone

lane

Dead Man's Bottom

Warwick

Somerset

Exeter

Oxford

Monken Hadley

Gloucester

High Barnet

Hastings

Edward IV

Hadley Common

archers

horse

foot

artillery

Hadley

golf course

500   0   500   1000

yards

WFNW

Exeter

Monken Hadley Church

Edward IV

Gloucester

Reserve

Tower was soon in Yorkist hands, and on 11 April his sympathizers opened Aldersgate and Edward entered his capital. The Chancellor had not been over-zealous in carrying out his brother's command, and in consequence was imprisoned only for a very short while.

Warwick does not appear to have learned that London was lost until he reached Dunstable on Good Friday 12 April. His progress had been slow, possibly because Edward had detached troops to hold him up, or perhaps because he was waiting for Somerset to join him. His plan to crush Edward against the City walls had failed. What action should he take now? The chroniclers bestow upon him a variety of intentions. The Yorkist author of *The arrivall of Edward IV* says that he hoped to surprise Edward off guard while celebrating the Easter festival in London – which scarcely flatters Warwick's intelligence. More likely are the suggestions that Warwick knew his man and knew that he would not just sit in London waiting to be attacked. Whether he was moving to block Edward's route to the Midlands via Ermine Street or whether Warwick was just waiting for Edward to attack him cannot be told, but we know that he advanced from Dunstable to St Albans on Good Friday, spent the night there and on Easter Saturday moved forward to within half a mile of Barnet, where, on learning that Edward had left London, he took up a position on Hadley Green – then called Gladmore Heath.

Edward needed no prompting to advance upon his enemy; he was never one to shirk a fight and he knew that only by destroying Warwick in open battle could he hope to retain the kingdom. He had been reunited with his wife and had seen his son for the first time on Thursday; Good Friday was spent in religious devotions; and by Saturday he was ready to march. Once more poor Henry was dragged up that northern road to be a helpless spectator of the quarrels that he had started but had long since ceased to influence. It was to be his last adventure.

Again we do not know the numbers that fought at Barnet. One chronicler puts the Lancastrian army alone at 30,000. This is almost certainly an unrealistic figure,* and if we say that Edward

*These high figures are often reached through a series of greatly exaggerated numbers relating to the various private armies that the magnates brought to the battlefield.

moved out of London at the head of 8,000 men to meet about 9 or 10,000 under Warwick we shall probably be nearer the truth.

Warwick had approached from St Albans by the only road existing at that time, which ran through South Mimms to Dancer's Hill and Kitts End; when he arrived at where the High Stone now stands he found himself on the plateau that stretches southward from Hadley Green to Barnet. In the vicinity of the Old Fold golf course's clubhouse the ridge becomes broad enough for him to deploy his army for about 800 yards on either side of the present A 1000 road – although in those days the road ran immediately to the east of the clubhouse – and here he had taken up a position on the afternoon of Saturday 13 April. His right battle was commanded by the Earl of Oxford, who was a very experienced soldier; it seems probable that he had Montagu with him,* for although fitted for independent command Warwick still did not entirely trust him. The centre was commanded by Somerset, and the left nominally by Warwick but with the Duke of Exeter in support. Warwick placed his horse on both flanks, and Somerset had the bulk of the archers in the centre. We get no information about any reserve; this was still not a regular feature of an order of battle, but nearly all the chroniclers make special mention of Edward's reserve. Almost certainly Warwick would not have remained on the left flank during the battle, and he may have been in personal command of a small reserve behind the centre.

Edward arrived at Barnet just as it was getting dark, and he soon cleared the place of Warwick's scouts. In spite of the darkness he wisely decided that his army should not camp in the village, but should take up a position close to the enemy ready for a dawn assault. It is no easy matter to deploy some 8,000 men for battle on unreconnoitred ground in the dark, and it is scarcely surprising that Edward failed to get exactly square to Warwick's line and came rather closer to the enemy than he intended. His right was commanded by his eighteen-year-old brother, Richard Duke of Gloucester; the centre battle he kept for himself, with Clarence under command – probably for the same reason as Warwick had put Montagu under surveillance; and Lord Hastings (who together with Lord Saye and Sele had landed with Edward) took charge of the left. Henry was probably stationed with the reserve, which would have been immediately in the rear of the centre battle.

The darkness of the night and Edward's miscalculation of

*Those who say that Somerset was not present at the battle give Montagu command of the centre.

distance saved his troops from a very unpleasant pommelling, for Warwick, who was superior in artillery – and apparently not short of ammunition – kept up a lively cannonade during the hours of darkness; but the missiles passed harmlessly over Edward's line, and his men were ordered to keep silence and show no fires.

The ground on which the two armies lay that Easter Eve 500 years ago even now holds a good deal of water, and at that time it and the surrounding countryside contained large areas of bog. Warm days and cold nights frequently produce thick mists from such ground, and so it was on the morning of the battle. As the light grew stronger and the darkness rolled away, the cold, stiff soldiers rose from the damp ground, reached for their arms and prepared for battle. In the blanket of fog that surrounded them even outlines could not be discerned, and the closeness of the rival forces was only apparent from the call of the trumpeters and the muffled sounds of armour being donned. At about 5 a.m. the order to advance banners was given, and both armies, high and proud in their bearing, bore down upon each other. This was to be a battle fought mainly on foot; Warwick himself, abandoning his usual custom of leading the first assault on horseback, sent his charger to the rear at the beginning, and throughout fought alongside his men on foot. But one chronicler describes Edward in the battle 'mounted on his white steed'.

The preliminary bombardment of whistling arrows and pounding cannon ball was of short duration, and no sooner had the two hosts, looming out of the murk, become entangled in hand-to-hand combat than it became apparent that Lord Oxford on Warwick's right, and Prince Richard on Edward's, had no enemy to their immediate front. Richard, to get to the Duke of Exeter, had to swing round and ascend a slight slope, but Oxford was on perfectly flat ground and bore down heavily on Lord Hastings's flank. Taken by surprise, Hastings' men seem to have crumbled at the first shock, for we hear nothing of resistance, but only of hasty, disorganized flight. Oxford's men chased them into Barnet and out the other side. So far did these men run that soon they were spreading tidings in London of a Yorkist defeat.

Richard was not able to compensate for the loss of the Yorkist left by an equally impressive victory against Exeter. The Duke's men proved more stubborn, and Richard's task was more difficult. Somehow Exeter got his battle to face the exposed flank, and although sorely battered – he himself was soon to be struck down and left for dead – his troops did not break. In order to give Exeter some support Somerset's battle had to partially conform and both armies now veered round to face almost east and west. This change of front and the continuing mist saved Edward.

Barnet was a battle fought by the individual commanders, for in the fog the overall picture could not have been known to the opposing generals – especially not to Warwick, who we know fought on foot encased in heavy armour. Nevertheless, at this stage victory was in his grasp if only Oxford could return in time to take Edward in the rear. The Yorkist left had fled the field – although Edward may not have known this – the right was hard held by Exeter's men, and even giving ground; and in the centre, after three hours of desperate fighting with bill and halberd, Edward had thrown in his reserve and was still probably outnumbered. Oxford was the key to victory or defeat. The fates decided that it should be defeat.

It was something of a triumph that Oxford managed to rally any of his men, but somehow he rounded up 800; the rest were either lost in the fog or taking their share of plunder for what they had already done. He retraced his steps through Barnet and up the road that led to his old position, but by the time he got back, still groping his way through the thick mist, the two armies had changed position quite considerably. Oxford could hardly be expected to find Edward's column other than by sheer luck, nor could he be blamed, in the general obfuscation that now pervaded the field, for losing Warwick the battle. The first troops with whom his returning men came into contact were those of Somerset; as they came out of the fog some of Somerset's men mistook the de Vere standard of a radiant star for Edward's banner, which carried the device of a sun with rays, and Oxford's troops began to go down under a hail of arrows. The mistake was soon discovered, but worse was to follow. There had been much treachery throughout the Wars, and in this new Lancastrian army there were those whose complete loyalty to Henry had yet to be proved. Someone raised the cry of treason, and panic quickly spread. Soldiers understand defeat, and are often prepared to stand their ground and fight to the last even in a cause which they may not fully comprehend, but betrayal immediately saps morale. Oxford, convinced that the worst had occurred, rode off the field – and not only his men, but many of Somerset's followed him.

It was now around 9 a.m. and Edward's reserve had already been committed; Warwick strove valiantly to shore up his crumbling line, but Edward gave him no respite. Both commanders realized that this was the crisis of the battle, and through the gradually thinning mist the extent of Warwick's disaster was plain to see. Montagu had stood firm, but had been killed – possibly by his own men – in coming to Warwick's assistance; Exeter was reported dead;* and Somerset, like Oxford, had disappeared in a northerly direction. What was left of the Lancastrian army had had enough, they would not rally to Warwick still standing defiant beneath the Bear and Ragged Staff. At last the scales of illusion fell from his eyes; he recognized defeat and turning from the fray lumbered off towards his horse. But he had left it too late. Impeded by his armour, and no doubt exhausted from hours of savage fighting – at forty-two he was not a young man – he never reached his horse, being cut down somewhere in the vicinity of where the High Stone now stands.

During this battle, which lasted between three and four hours, it seems that some 1,500 men were slain – and possibly more perished in the immediate pursuit across ground still called Dead Man's Bottom. As usual the figures given vary widely, but Sir John Paston, who fought with Warwick, is a fairly reliable witness and he admits to the loss of more than 1,000 Lancastrians. Even allowing for the fact that this was a battle in which Edward, angered by the number of men that had abandoned his cause for Warwick, withheld his edict that the common soldier should, as far as possible, be spared, the figure of 4,000 sometimes quoted is too high. Of those killed probably not more than 500 were Yorkists; but the victory was hard won, for Edward lost Lord Saye and Sele, Sir John Lisle, Sir Thomas Parre and no fewer than three members of the Bourchier family: Lord Cromwell, Viscount Bourchier, and Sir Humphrey Bourchier, a son of Lord Berners.

The death of Warwick, however, outweighed every other consideration. The story of this man enshrines all the chivalrous romanticism of the Middle Ages. He was not only immensely popular with the masses, but he made a deeper and more lasting impression on his own century than any other man who was not a prince of the blood. There are those, like King Edward, perhaps on account of the Second Battle of St Albans, ready to decry his military talents, but he was a soldier of considerable capacity and unquestioned courage. In many ways he was unlucky to lose his last battle: in its early stages he was let down by his brother and betrayed by his son-in-law, and later, had he waited only a few days, support coming in from the south would have enabled him to meet Edward with overwhelmingly superior numbers. But a victory for Warwick would have exposed England to further tribulation.

*He did in fact survive the battle.

160

The Battle
of Tewkesbury

4 May 1471

The site of the heaviest fighting is still open country, and indeed has probably not changed very greatly in 500 years. It lies to the west of the A 38(T) road from Gloucester, about half a mile south of Tewkesbury Abbey. There are two principal vantage points: the high ground where the road passes Stonehouse Farm (from where Edward would first have seen the Lancastrian line), and Tewkesbury Park. This latter eminence has only recently become public property, having been bought by Tewkesbury Borough Council for development as a golf course: it offers the best viewpoint, even though from it the battlefield is partially obscured by trees. The left of the Lancastrian line and (in the writer's opinion) the right of the Yorkist is now covered by the densely populated area around Crouch Court and Priors Park. Gupshill Manor, a black and white half-timbered building on the A 38(T) road just south of Tewkesbury, is now a public house; at the time of the battle the road from Cheltenham ran immediately to the west of it, while the one from Gloucester was further again to the west – they joined the present road by Holme Hospital. The museum, in Barton Street, has an interesting model of the battle.

On the very day that Warwick died at Barnet (see p.125 or chapter 10 for a full account) the Queen, whose cause he had so unwisely embraced, landed at Weymouth. She had with her, among others, her son Edward; Lord Wenlock; John Beaufort, Somerset's brother; Sir John Langstrother, Grand Prior of the Order of St John of Jerusalem and a Sir John Fortescue.* From Weymouth the party proceeded to Cerne Abbey, where they learned from the Duke of Somerset the extent of the disaster at Barnet. Momentarily Margaret's great courage deserted her; she declared that she would

---

*If this was the same man as the Lancastrian Lord Chief Justice his presence here must be considered very doubtful. That Sir John Fortescue was attainted after Towton, but later pardoned by Edward IV and retired to Ebrington in Gloucestershire.

return at once to France. But she was dissuaded by the optimism of her advisers and the eagerness of her son.

The Earl of Devon had joined the Queen with a considerable force; Somerset, who had left Barnet for the north with Oxford, but had turned back, had brought some troops with him; the Lancastrians still had a following in the north; Jasper Tudor commanded an army in Wales, and the Bastard of Fauconberg was off the Kent coast and preparing to assault London. With the advantage of hindsight we know that after Barnet and the death of Warwick the Lancastrian cause was adrift on a dark, tempestuous sea, but at the time it did not appear that way even to those who had fought on the losing side. Sir John Paston, who was slightly wounded at Barnet, assured his mother in a letter written only a few days before Tewkesbury that good tidings could soon be expected;* and this was not wishful thinking, but a confidence based upon the number of men that the Lancastrians could eventually gather under the nominal command of their queen and prince.

Edward received news of Margaret's arrival on Tuesday 16 April; this was only two days after Barnet, and as he must have been expecting her to come – for it was known that she was only waiting on a favourable wind – reports that he had already disbanded his whole army may not be absolutely correct, although he would certainly have needed to raise fresh levies. Windsor was chosen as a suitable rallying point, for it was the most strategic place from which to await information as to Margaret's intentions. It was a few days before Edward knew whether the Lancastrians meant to march on London, or in the first instance move northwards and join forces with Jasper Tudor. If she – or more probably the Duke of Somerset, for in the ten years since St Albans Margaret seems to have lost some of her fire – decided on a try for London, Edward at Windsor would bar the way; if she decided to march north then he would have made a start to head them off. Edward arrived at Windsor on 19 April, and by the time the feast of St George had been celebrated the Lancastrian intention had become fairly clear. The King broke camp on 24 April and marched, without undue haste, to Malmesbury, where he arrived on the first day of May.

Somerset, who was in command of the army, and Margaret's other advisers could not have hesitated very long in deciding to march north. Barnet had been lost through impatience; the lesson to be learned was the need to concentrate resources and attack with overwhelmingly superior numbers. The army as at present

*The Paston Letters, Vol. V, p.102.

constituted was sorely in need of money, cannon, powder and other supplies, and even its strength was insufficient for an independent assault upon London. To cross the Severn at Gloucester – a town which held many Lancastrian sympathizers – and join Jasper Tudor would have to be the first objective. If it was to be successfully achieved the minimum of delay was essential. Unfortunately, detours were necessary in order to collect supplies and reinforcements, and this put an intolerable strain on the Queen's army, which was required to march long distances over appalling tracks. From Cerne the army went to Exeter, where Sir John Arundel and Sir Hugh Courteney joined with a strong contingent of troops; after Exeter the route was via Taunton and Glastonbury to Bath. Here the Lancastrians resorted to artifice in sending out patrols and foragers to Salisbury and Yeovil. But Edward was not deceived; by now he had reached Cirencester and was perfectly aware that Margaret was not making for London, although he appears to have been in doubt as to what her immediate intention was.

The south-west had responded well in the matter of manpower, but the Lancastrians were still sadly deficient in artillery and other stores. It was therefore necessary to turn westward and enter the friendly city of Bristol, from where they procured some much needed ordnance, but at a cost in time that was to prove fatal. The Queen's army reached Bristol on 1 May, the same day as Edward arrived at Malmesbury. If he had guessed correctly that her intention was to cross the Severn at Gloucester he was nearer to that city than she was and could have cut her off. But Edward was clearly baffled, and the Lancastrians' next little strategem confused him still further.

The Queen and Somerset had no illusions as to their danger, and spending only one night in Bristol they made all haste for Gloucester, deciding to take the direct road along the plain through Berkeley. The commanders of the rival armies each knew the approximate position of their adversary, and so it was not difficult for the Lancastrians to anticipate Edward's line of march – assuming that his object was to bring them to battle. To gain time was essential; Somerset therefore decided to send his vanguard to take up a position on Sodbury Hill – some ten miles north-east of Bristol – as though to offer battle. The remainder of the army followed, but were ordered to break off to the left and head for Berkeley, leaving the vanguard to withdraw onto the main army, having, it was hoped, delayed the enemy. The ruse became more effective when half a dozen of the King's more eager quartermasters, who had ridden ahead of the army to procure the best billets for their masters, were captured in Chipping Sodbury. Now advancing more cautiously, it was noon on 2 May before the Yorkist army reached Sodbury Hill, only to find the position abandoned and no sign of any enemy.

Edward had been badly served by his scouts, but nevertheless the Lancastrians must be given great credit for a very clever piece of deception, for it is difficult to understand how they managed to vanish so completely, leaving Edward quite mystified as to their whereabouts. There was no choice for the King but to camp that night at Sodbury and await the reports of the patrols which had been sent out in every direction. In these hours of uncertainty only one sensible action illuminates an otherwise sombre picture; it was decided to dispatch messengers mounted on swift animals to warn Sir Richard Beauchamp, Governor of Gloucester, that he was likely to be attacked and that he must hold out until Edward's army could arrive. At last, at about 3 a.m., Edward received definite news that the Queen's army was on the road to Gloucester and already north of Berkeley. Two hours later the army broke camp and Edward led them, now in battle order, along the line of the Cotswolds towards Tewkesbury. The Lancastrians had stolen a march on him, but if Gloucester held they might still be kept from crossing the Severn.

Friday 3 May was a day of strenuous effort for both armies, testing to the uttermost the endurance of man and horse. The Lancastrian army, determined to hold onto their advantage, spent only six hours at Berkeley, being on the march again at midnight. They arrived before Gloucester at 10 a.m. to find the gates firmly closed against them; there was no time for argument with words or guns, because all knew that Edward was close at hand. As they struggled on to Tewkesbury the pace was beginning to tell. Sir Richard Beauchamp led a sortie from Gloucester and some precious artillery, laboriously bumping its way over appalling tracks, was captured. At last, in the late afternoon, the great abbey of Tewkesbury, standing above the little Swilgate brook and shaded by venerable trees, came into sight. Queen Margaret and her men had been on the march for sixteen hours and covered twenty-four miles.

A mile to the south of the abbey the river Severn can be forded at Lower Lode, but the crossing would have taken some time and the men had marched far enough. The decision to stand and fight was dictated more by exhaustion than by confidence in the outcome, but no one can deny that it was the right one. Somerset had the choice of ground and the position he adopted is generally thought to have been one just north of Gupshill Manor, with his left resting on the Swilgate brook and his right stretching to the low ground west of the main road. The writer does not agree that this was his position,

164

and as he is in a minority of two some space must be devoted to an explanation.

The principal authority for this battle is the author of *The arrivall of Edward IV in England* (the *Fleetwood Chronicle*) (see also p.156). The relevant passage runs: '. . . the same nyght they pight them in a fielde, in a close even at the townes ende; the towne, and the abbey, at theyr backs.' Now the Gupshill Manor position is three quarters of a mile from 'the townes ende'; this is certainly not conclusive evidence, for the author in saying 'at the townes ende' may be permitted some inaccuracy, but the position nearer the abbey appears to be a better one. The Lancastrian army is thought to have numbered 6,000 men (the Yorkists had about 3,500 archers and 1,500 cavalrymen) and so they would have required a frontage of around 1,000 yards. In the area between the cemetery and Priors Park the ridge is wide enough for the army to have been deployed without stretching to the brook, and invites a more difficult assault than the Gupshill position; a flank attack was most unlikely, and anyway the brook was no obstacle. But Tewkesbury Park (an area until recently inaccessible to visitors to the battlefield) may hold the key. 'There was a parke, and therein moche wood', near to which Edward sent 200 spearmen, and 'set them in a plomp [such a much nicer word than 'mass'!] nere a qwarter of a myle from the fielde'. This undoubtedly refers to Tewkesbury Park, and the position of these spearmen and their subsequent action seems to indicate that the Lancastrian line just overlapped the present Gloucester–Cheltenham road not very far south of Holme Hospital, and certainly no lower than the Crouch Court–Priors Park area. Neither this position nor the Gupshill one could control or protect the ford at Lower Lode.

Meanwhile, Edward's troops were in no better plight than the Lancastrians. The day was unusually hot for early May, and as the King 'toke his way thrwghe the champain contrye, called Cotteswolde' they could find no food for horses or men, and only one brook near Stroud from which to drink, and that was soon churned to mud by vehicle wheels. At the 'village called Chiltenham', which was reached about 5 p.m., Edward received information that his enemy were preparing to give battle. Pausing only to share out what few iron rations they had with them, the army was on the march again to Tredington; this village was only two miles from the enemy position and near enough to ensure that on the morrow the Lancastrians could not slip away. Edward's army had marched or ridden thirty-five miles in this long day; visitors to Tewkesbury Abbey who have seen the plate armour that was taken from the

165

battlefield by the monks and nailed to the sacristy door will appreciate the immensity of this achievement.

The exact position of the Lancastrian line may be open to argument, but there is no doubt about their order of battle. The Duke of Somerset, who was in overall command, took the 'vaward', as the right-hand column was often called; Lord Wenlock, who had fought for the Lancastrians at St Albans and the Yorkists at Towton and who was finally to be found on the losing side, had command of the main battle, with the young Prince Edward by his side; and the Earl of Devon had the left or rearward wing. There was no reserve, and Queen Margaret had withdrawn either to the town or across the river to await events.

Early in the morning of Saturday 4 May Edward advanced from Tredington to the Cheltenham–Tewkesbury road, which then ran just to the west of Gupshill Manor. When he reached the ground now occupied by Stonehouse Farm the Lancastrian array would have become visible, although possibly not very clearly, for we are told that the ground contained many hedges, deep dykes and foul lanes – 'a ryght evill place to approache'. The King's order of battle must have been reversed at some stage, presumably because Hastings's performance at Barnet scarcely qualified him to oppose the most formidable Lancastrian commander. The chronicler clearly states that Prince Richard commanded the vaward, yet he took up a position on the left of the line with Somerset to his front; the King, who had Clarence with him, commanded the centre, and Lord Hastings had charge of the right wing. The Yorkists also had no reserve, but Edward sent 200 spearmen to protect his flank. These men were placed near to Tewkesbury Park; they may have been mounted, but spearmen are usually taken to mean foot soldiers, and the ground was totally unsuitable for cavalry.

The Yorkists prepared for battle some 350 yards from their enemy and Edward's first move was to bring a fairly heavy concentration of firepower on to Somerset's division. His artillery – in which arm he was considerably superior to the Lancastrians – could have raked the enemy from the battle line, but we are told that the archers formed a part of this preliminary bombardment, and so presumably both arms were somewhat advanced. Somerset had evidently reconnoitred the ground to his immediate front either the previous evening, or that morning before the battle, and when it became apparent that his men had had enough pounding he led most of them (leaving just a deceptive screen) along a partially concealed route to deliver a surprise flank attack. It seems to have been a sound tactical manoeuvre, and was almost certainly part of a coordinated plan whereby as soon as the Yorkist left had been struck Lord Wenlock would deliver a blow at the centre, and no doubt Devon also had orders to advance. It miscarried because the line of approach was slightly at fault, and the attack was completely unsupported.

When Somerset's men came into open ground they found themselves at the junction of the Yorkist left and centre battles; this was an unenviable position to be caught in, for although they undoubtedly took Edward off balance at first, their flank was exposed not only to Gloucester's troops, but to the 200 spearmen as well. This error of direction might have gone unpunished had Wenlock come down and engaged Edward; as it was, after some sharp skirmishing Edward began to roll Somerset's men back from whence they had come. Gloucester's troops do not appear to have played much part until the enemy were in retreat, but the spearmen seeing their opportunity attacked them in the flank. The chronicler indicates that after the initial shock Edward's division, helped by the spearmen, soon had Somerset's men on the run, in which case the spearmen must have been no more than 3–400 yards to the flank – assuming the chronicler was right, and that they were sent to watch the Tewkesbury Park area; they could scarcely have arrived in time had the fight taken place near Gupshill Manor.

Outnumbered and entirely unsupported, Somerset's vaward soon disintegrated and very likely suffered the heaviest casualties of the whole battle. Men fled in all directions, some forward to the safety of the park, others back towards the river, while still others struggled to regain the Lancastrian line. No matter which way they went they were cut down relentlessly. Somerset managed to get back to the ridge where, embittered by the knowledge of defeat, he is said to have dealt somewhat drastically with Lord Wenlock. Seldom if ever in the annals of war has there been a substantiated case of a commander-in-chief cleaving in the skull of a divisional commander for failing to support him, and it is unlikely, even allowing for the ferocity of the times and that Wenlock was a proven turncoat, that this in fact happened. Certainly Wenlock's helmet – if it really was his – which hangs in St Mary's Church, Luton, bears no evidence of such a dastardly act.

Unless Somerset withdrew from his fight before it was truly lost, it is possible that he never even saw Wenlock again, for as soon as

Overleaf: Battle of Tewkesbury with plan inset

R. Severn

Abbey

Holme Hospital

Somerset

Wenlock

LANCASTRIANS

YORKISTS

Gloucester

Edward IV

Gupshill Manor

A38

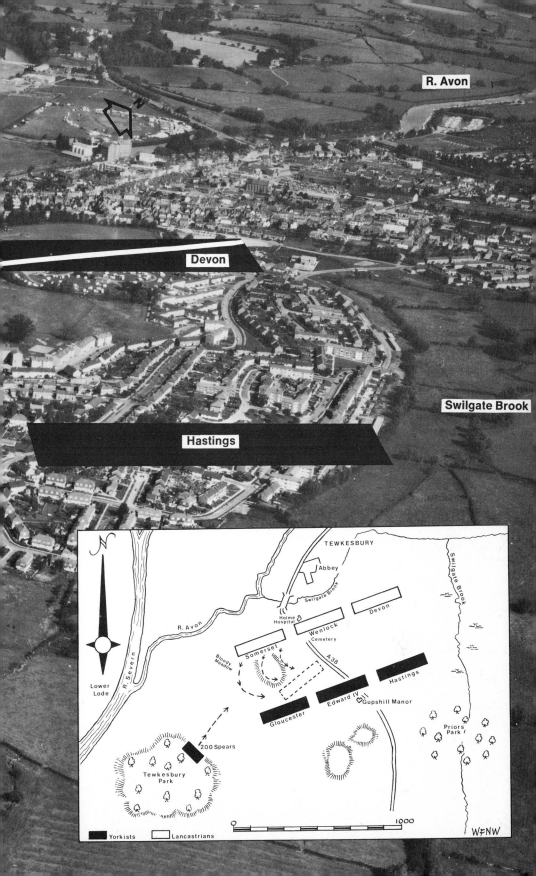

R. Avon

Devon

Swilgate Brook

Hastings

TEWKESBURY

Abbey

Swilgate Brook

R. Avon

Holme
Hospital

Wenlock

Devon

Cemetery

Somerset

A 38

Bloody
Meadow

R. Seven

Hastings

Lower
Lode

Gloucester

Edward IV

Gupshill Manor

Priors
Park

200 Spears

Tewkesbury
Park

Yorkists   Lancastrians

1000

WFNW

the King had got Somerset's battle on the run he seems to have left the pursuit to Gloucester, while he and Lord Hastings advanced their troops up the gentle slope to engage the remainder of the Lancastrian army. We have no details of the short battle that ensued – other than the names of some, including Lord Wenlock, who were killed – but the Lancastrians must have been completely demoralized by the débâcle on their right, for they appear to have offered practically no resistance to an enemy almost certainly inferior in numbers and attacking uphill over difficult ground. Very soon the whole army was in retreat. As the Yorkists advanced, inexorably pressing back their enemy towards the town and the two rivers, they slashed and hacked at all in their path. Many were killed in a field still known (like the one at Towton) as Bloody Meadow, and others were drowned in the Avon or the Severn; a few escaped through the town and others took sanctuary in the abbey.

The chronicler Edward Hall says that 3,000 Lancastrians were slain – which would be about half their total force, and is almost certainly a considerable exaggeration. But perhaps between 1,500 and 2,000 died, for no quarter was given to those caught in these headlong pursuits. The Yorkist losses may have been less than 500. The fate of the Lancastrian principals is of some interest, because after years of ceaseless bloodletting the proud banners of Henry VI, Margaret of Anjou, Edward Prince of Wales, and the powerful Beauforts, so often in the past borne forward in splendid élan, were at Tewkesbury lowered to be seen no more on an English battlefield.

The most important casualty was Prince Edward, for with his death the legitimate descendants of Henry IV were almost extinct – within three weeks they would be. The story of his capture and subsequent murder can be disregarded; undoubtedly he was killed in the fighting, although probably while trying to make his way to the town during the rout. The commanders of the left and centre battles, Lords Devon and Wenlock, were killed (probably before the Lancastrians broke), as were John Beaufort Marquis of Dorset, Sir John and Sir Thomas Seymour and many other knights. What happened in the abbey is uncertain. The Duke of Somerset, Sir John Langstrother, Sir Thomas Tresham and other Lancastrians took sanctuary there, but it is said that the abbey did not possess a franchise as a sanctuary – at any rate not for those guilty of high treason. One story is that Edward and some armed men entered this great church, which even then enshrined centuries of a community's life and faith, and killed many men under its roof; another that Edward was persuaded to offer pardon to those who took sanctuary there. There may be some truth in both stories; but if Somerset, Langstrother, Tresham and other notables were offered pardon, their trial two days later before the Dukes of Gloucester and Norfolk, and subsequent execution, surely violated every canon of good faith.

There remains only to relate the fate of Henry VI and his queen. When Margaret learned of the defeat she and her ladies, among whom was Anne Neville, Prince Edward's wife, made all haste to leave the town. She is credited with having crossed the Severn by the Lower Lode ford and slept that night at Bushley. It seems scarcely possible that she could have done this, for mopping up was going on in Bloody Meadow and along the river bank for most of the day; it is much more likely that she had taken the precaution of crossing the river before the battle, and awaited the result in the house at Bushley known as Paynes Place. She was eventually captured – probably in the priory at Little Malvern – and brought before Edward at Coventry on 12 May. On 21 May this unhappy woman, whose fortunes had suffered so profound a decline and who had sullied and ruined herself in the interests of a weak husband and an untried son, was the object of great abuse and ribaldry as she rode in a litter through the streets of London behind the triumphant Edward. She remained his prisoner for four years until ransomed by King Louis for £50,000 on condition that she surrendered all her father's vast possessions. She died in April 1482.

The news of Edward's crushing victory had a salutary effect upon a people grown weary of war. For many years now the forges had roared almost night and day and the hammers had seldom ceased from fashioning implements of slaughter. It was time to call a halt. There were strong forces still arrayed against the King, but at Coventry he learned from the Earl of Northumberland that those in opposition in the north had laid down their arms, and by the time Edward was before the gates of London the troops that had assailed the city under the Bastard of Fauconberg had already realized the hopelessness of their cause, and had retired back to their Kentish homes.

The last act of the drama was performed amid the stern surroundings of the Tower of London. A few hours after Edward had made his formal entry into London the intelligent, highly sensitive Henry, called to a duty that in spite of many noble gifts he was totally unfitted to perform, passed into the corridors of history. Prince Richard of Gloucester was at hand at the time; what part, if any, he played in the crime will – as on a later occasion in the same place – never be known: but dark deeds sow their crop of dragons' teeth.

CHAPTER 12

Bosworth Field

22 August 1485

The battle was fought about two miles south of Market Bosworth (a small town some nine miles west of Leicester) on and around Ambion Hill, which lies between Sutton Cheney and Shenton. In September 1974 H.R.H. the Duke of Gloucester officially opened the Battle of Bosworth Centre, which the Leicestershire County Council have laid out in Ambion Hill Farm. This centre is open during the summer and autumn months all day at weekends and Bank Holidays, and week-day evenings. In the farmhouse there is an exhibition hall, model room and auditorium. There is a small admission fee to the Battlefield Centre and adjacent car park. There is no charge for visiting the battlefield, and public footpaths now exist enabling the visitor to view the site perfectly. There is a second car park at the dis-used Shenton railway station with an information point, and various picnic sites. One such is called King Richard's Field, stated categor-ically by the Centre as being the place where Richard died – but as the reader will see, the present writer considers this open to doubt.

The Battle of Bosworth has received much attention from histor-ians on account of its important consequences; but the only con-temporary record extant is the *Croyland Chronicle* and it has very little to say about the actual fight. Subsequent writers from the sixteenth century to modern times have had to do their best from this exiguous source, the few relics that have been found on or near the battlefield, and a careful examination of the ground. It is not surprising, therefore, to find a wide divergence of opinion as to exactly what happened. The main outline of the battle can be fairly easily reconstructed; the difficulty comes with details, such as the death of Richard and the positions taken up by the Stanley brothers.

But before recounting the battle it is necessary to examine the events that led up to it. Edward IV died on 9 April 1483, and left his crown and kingdom to his twelve-year-old son Edward, but fully aware of his wife's unpopularity – and more particularly of that of her Woodville relations – he had designated his brother Richard of Gloucester as protector during the young king's minority. When the King died his son was at Ludlow with his uncle Anthony Earl Rivers; Richard was in the north of England, and the Woodville faction had a slender control of the Council in London. Clearly they could not prevent the protectorship, but they hoped to establish a regency council to whom the Protector would be responsible. Towards the end of April the new king, accompanied by his uncle Rivers, his half-brother Sir Richard Grey, his chamberlain Sir Thomas Vaughan, and an escort of some 2,000 Welsh soldiers set out for London. Richard started south from Yorkshire at about the same time.

Richard III was not the wicked monster, distorted in body and mind, that the tendentious writings of Tudor historians would have us believe. It is true that he was below average height, and one shoulder was slightly higher than the other, but there is no reliable record of deformity. The impression of a cunning schemer is also suspect; it would seem that impetuosity, not guile, was the hallmark of his character. He was a sound commander and courageous fighter, who had served his brother loyally under arms in the north; moreover, in his short reign he proved himself to be in many ways an able and intelligent ruler. But he was a cold creature, who kept his own counsel and went his own way; he made some fearful blunders and when he most needed friends he found that friendship, for him, was but a veneer on the harsh canvas of hatred and suspicion.

He was also a typical product of his time in that he was intensely ambitious and, as his behaviour on the road to London shows, sufficiently ruthless to see that any obstacle to his ambition was swiftly removed. Lord Hastings, who at the time of Edward's death was one of Richard's principal supporters, had probably warned him that the Woodvilles had no intention of allowing him unfettered control. He therefore acted promptly in having the unsuspecting Rivers, Grey and Vaughan arrested when they went to meet him at Nottingham, and riding on to Stony Stratford he dismissed his nephew's Welsh escort, and with many protestations of loyalty accompanied the bewildered boy to his capital.

Edward V arrived in London on 4 May; his mother and other members of her family had sought sanctuary in Westminster Abbey on learning what had happened at Nottingham. Richard may not have had designs on the crown at this early stage, but he was determined to resist any opposition to his rule during the minority. To this end he set about securing the loyalty of a number of peers, chief among whom was the Duke of Buckingham, a lineal descendant of Edward III's fifth son and a man scarcely less ambitious than

Richard. Buckingham became the recipient of great riches and rewards, and for a time Protector and Duke worked closely together. Lord Hastings was their first victim. In spite of his intense dislike for many of the Woodvilles, jealousy of Buckingham had driven Hastings into their camp, and he had formed the foolish habit of holding, together with Lord Stanley and John Morton Bishop of Ely, a rival council to the Protector's. At a council meeting at the Tower on 13 June Richard suddenly had these three arrested, and Hastings was summarily executed on Tower Green. This was the Protector's first blunder, for it was one thing to execute Rivers (which he did twelve days later at Pontefract), but another to execute Hastings, who was of the old nobility and whose death would raise powerful antagonisms.

Three days later it became fairly clear that Richard was thinking in terms of the throne. He had probably realized that to rule unchallenged, which was what he intended doing, he would have to be king. He went with the Archbishop of Canterbury, and certain other nobles, to Westminster, where Queen Elizabeth was persuaded (the threat of force was clearly in the background) to surrender her second son, Richard Duke of York, from sanctuary. He joined his brother, who on Buckingham's suggestion had already been 'more comfortably lodged' in the Tower. Both boys were murdered there, probably in the autumn of 1483.

With the Princes safely in the Tower it now became necessary for Richard to justify his intended assumption of kingship. There was no great problem here. The old canard was raked up that Edward's marriage to Elizabeth Woodville was invalidated because he had been precontracted to Lady Eleanor Butler, and that it had been celebrated in an unconsecrated place; therefore Elizabeth's children were bastards. Clarence's offspring were even more easily accounted for, because since Edward had murdered their father in 1478 they could be conveniently excluded from the succession under their father's attainder. This doubtful reasoning did not entirely convince the citizens of London that Richard was therefore the true male Yorkist heir, but Buckingham worked so skilfully for Richard's cause that on 23 June he was able to head a deputation that waited on Richard at his riverside home of Baynard's Castle and swore allegiance to him as King Richard III. The new king was crowned amid the greatest splendour on 6 July.

In October 1483 Richard was faced with what could have been a most serious insurrection had he not got warning of it and struck before the insurgents were fully prepared. Buckingham, like Hastings before him, had suddenly veered over to the Woodvilles.

174

The exact cause of his discontent is uncertain, but it seems that the higher his fortune the higher rose his ambition, and that he thought he could plot a course for himself through devious channels to the throne. It is not his rebellion, nor its failure and his subsequent execution, that is of interest to the student of Bosworth Field, but the third member of the strange alliance.

The Woodvilles, presumably with Buckingham's knowledge and consent, had been in touch with Margaret Beaufort (now married to Lord Stanley) and through her had arranged for her exiled son Henry Tudor to invade England with troops supplied by the Duke of Brittany. On the successful conclusion of the enterprise Henry was to marry Elizabeth of York, and through this union it was hoped that the two great houses of Lancaster and York would be able to live in peace with one another. As is well known, this happy event was deferred for three years, but Henry did make an attempt – if a somewhat belated one – to honour his side of the bargain. He encountered a severe storm, and by the time he was off Poole only two of his fifteen ships were still with him, Buckingham was already dead and the insurrection in the West Country had been suppressed. Henry returned to Brittany; but he had at least shown that he was a force to be reckoned with, and in the months ahead many were comforted – and others disturbed – by the thought of an alternative ruler ready to cross the sea.

Richard was well aware of the insecurity of his position; at home, in spite of all his efforts towards good government, he had many enemies, and across the Channel exiled Lancastrians schemed to place Henry Tudor on the throne. The death of the Prince of Wales in April 1484 was a bitter blow; now without an heir, and with a wife who could bear no more children, he knew that Henry, with his intended bride, would gain many fresh supporters. An attempt that summer to bribe the Duke of Brittany's treasurer to have Henry kidnapped and delivered to Richard almost succeeded, but Henry was warned in time and escaped to Paris. There he was shortly joined by the Earl of Oxford, whose gaoler had obligingly released him from the fortress of Hammes, where he had been imprisoned since his unsuccessful attempt to invade England in 1474.

As 1484 gave way to 1485 King Richard was pursued and haunted by a profound feeling that the very air he breathed was charged with treason. It came almost as a relief to learn that the Lancastrian invasion, so long threatened, was now definitely planned for the summer of 1485. Until the recent treaty of friendship with Scotland, half England had been under arms against possible invasion on two fronts, but now there was something definite against

And at a knyght thenneß wille Begynne

knyght there was a worthy man
a   That fro the tyme that he first Began

Above: Woodcut of The Knight by Richard Pynson, from Chaucer's Canterbury Tales, in the British Museum. Below: 300 years of European helmets

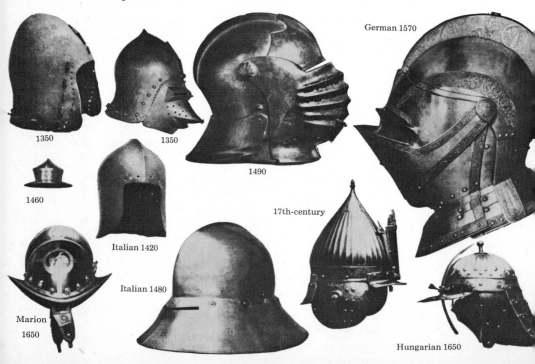

German 1570

1350

1350

1490

1460

17th-century

Italian 1420

Italian 1480

Marion
1650

Hungarian 1650

which to prepare. With the coming of the fighting season garrisons were strengthened and the commissioners of array were ordered to have their musters ready to march at a day's notice. No efforts were spared to portray through proclamations Henry Tudor's bastard descent on both sides of his family, and to remind Englishmen that he would be carried to their shores in French ships crowded with foreign soldiers. Richard took up residence in Nottingham Castle during June, from where he could be kept in constant communication with his lieutenants through his method of posting couriers at twenty-mile intervals along the principal highways.

Henry sailed from Harfleur on 1 August. His small fleet carried nearly 2,000 French mercenaries under Philibert de Chaundé, and with him sailed his uncle Jasper Tudor, Lord Oxford, the Bishop of Ely, Sir Edward Courtenay, Sir Edward Woodville and other knights, both Yorkist and Lancastrian, who had shared his exile. On 7 August the fleet entered Milford Haven and the troops disembarked at Dale. It is sometimes suggested that Henry would never have undertaken so rash an enterprise without first being assured that Lord Stanley, his brother Sir William, and Sir Gilbert Talbot (whose nephew, Lord Shrewsbury, was still a boy) would join him with their followers. In spite of the subsequent behaviour of these three there is no evidence for this, and it is more probable that Henry, although no warrior endowed with personal valour, had sufficient of the adventurer and gambler in his make-up to take his chance without specific guarantees.

Gradually the Welsh gentry rallied to his red dragon standard, the most notable being Rhys ap Thomas. As Henry moved through Cardigan to Montgomery, and from Newton to Welshpool, so his numbers increased – often at the expense of those whom Richard had relied upon to bar his way – and when he reached Shrewsbury Sir Gilbert Talbot joined him with 500 of Lord Shrewsbury's retainers. Neither Sir Walter Herbert in south Wales, nor Sir William Stanley in the north, had made any serious attempt to hinder the invader.

Richard was quickly aware of Henry's arrival, but the ease and rapidity with which the usurper marched through Wales not only angered but clearly also surprised him. In spite of the many preparations that had been going forward throughout the summer, by the time Henry was at Shrewsbury the King had still not mustered all his troops. There is a letter written about this time from the Duke of Norfolk to Sir John Paston desiring him to meet the Duke at Bury St Edmunds with the men he had promised the King, and

some lords from the south were still absent from the royalist camp.*
Lord Stanley had asked permission in July to return to his estates
in Lancashire. This had been granted with the proviso that he
should send his son Lord Strange as a hostage to Stanley's loyalty.
Now he was summoned to return, but made the feeble excuse that
he was suffering from the sweating sickness – there was an outbreak
of this dreaded disease at the time, but anyone who contracted it
usually had little chance to send apologies for absence. At about
the time Richard received Stanley's message Lord Strange was ap-
prehended trying to escape from Nottingham Castle; on being
questioned he implicated his uncle and Sir John Savage, but refused
to admit that his father had traitorous designs.

From Shrewsbury Henry marched to Stafford, where he had a
meeting with Sir William Stanley. Turning south-east from Stafford the rebel army advanced through Lichfield and Tamworth to
Atherstone. At either Lichfield or Tamworth Henry collected some
pieces of ordnance, which put a brake on the rapid progress his
army had been making hitherto. After their meeting at Stafford
Sir William Stanley's retainers had been marching parallel to
Henry's army, while Lord Stanley had been giving the impression
of falling back before the invader and was now south of Leicester.
On 20 August both the Stanleys met Henry at Atherstone, where
Henry probably had to be content with vague assurances from Lord
Stanley who would not at this stage have committed himself, for
his son was in the most unenviable position.

As soon as Richard's scurryers (mounted scouts) brought him
news that Henry was at Lichfield he realized that he could wait at
Nottingham for reinforcements no longer, because the rebels
might decide to take the road for London. Accordingly on 19
August the royalist army, with the King mounted on a great
white courser, left Nottingham for Leicester. Surrounded by
treachery and weighed down by doubts as he must have been,
Richard still held the advantage in numbers. Richard Brooke
cites Baker in his *Chronicles* as putting the King's army at 7,900
men; Norfolk with the vanguard had 1,200 bowmen, flanked with
200 cuirassiers under his son Lord Surrey; the King with the main-
guard had 1,000 billmen and 2,000 pikes, and Sir Thomas Brackenbury (which is wrong, for it was the Earl of Northumberland)
commanded the rearguard of 2,000 billmen with 1,500 horsemen on

*We do not know if Sir John, who was Sheriff of Norfolk, produced
these men on time. But the Pastons were a Lancastrian family, and a
year later Sir John was entrusted by Henry to seize the traitor Lord
Lovell.

the wings.* These figures are probably very near the truth. It is doubtful whether Henry could have mustered more than 5,000 men without the Stanleys.

On 21 August the two armies closed the gap between them. Henry marched east from Atherstone to a place called White Moors, which lies five miles from Atherstone up the Roman road through Fenny Drayton. Richard marched west from Leicester. We do not know the route he took; this would have depended on where he camped the night. The most probable site is the high ground immediately north-west of Sutton Cheney, which is the north-eastern end of a ridge that extends for about a mile in the direction of Shenton. Here the ridge, at 417 feet, reaches its highest point and would have given the King a commanding view over much of the surrounding country. If this was the place of his camp, Richard would have got there along the old road that ran through Kirby Mallory. Thus probably only two miles separated the camps and no doubt the scurryers of both armies reported back the respective positions.

The western end of Ambion Hill, which was a mile from Richard's camp, offers the best battle position in the neighbourhood. We can imagine that both commanders would have been anxious to secure this eminence; but Richard had the comparatively easy approach across a slight saddle and up the very gentle eastern slope of the hill, whereas Henry had at least one bog to circumvent, and a steep climb. The countryside has greatly changed since the time of the battle; what was then uncultivated open ground, with marshy land at the edges of the hill, is now well drained, productive grass and arable fields with a good many trees and hedges, and a large wood immediately to the south of the hill. The site of Richard's Well remains unchanged and is marked by a stone pyramid; it was in fact a spring and as the ground around it is still a little boggy in parts it is reasonable to assume that this, and the nearby Ambion Wood, was the area of marsh spoken of by the early writers. It may have extended to the south-west of the hill in the vicinity of the old railway line. The whole area was drained in the latter part of Elizabeth's reign.

Lead, stone and iron cannon balls of various weight have been dug up from time to time on what is now Glebe Farm; four were uncovered on the west slope of Ambion Hill just below the summit. We can thus be fairly sure that Richard's army did in fact occupy what would seem to be the obvious position stretching from the

*Richard Brooke, *Visits to Fields of Battle in England*, p.164.

crest of the hill back to the area of Ambion Hill Farm. We also get confirmation that Henry must have equipped himself with heavy cannon of the culverin type somewhere en route, for one of the balls weighed $14\frac{3}{4}$ pounds.

The position of the Stanley brothers before and during the battle is much more difficult to assess. After their meeting with Henry at Atherstone Lord Stanley is said to have drawn up his army to the south of the battlefield, the Dadlington area being the most popular among historians, while Sir William Stanley remained to the north at Nether Cotton. There is no evidence at all for either place (for we can discount Hutton's theory of fortified camps), nor for the number of men that the brothers had under command, but it seems probable that they were divided, one each side of the battle ground, and they certainly started the morning as observers and joined in when they saw how matters were going – Lord Stanley, in particular, was a trimmer *par excellence*. No matter where they spent the night of 21 August, they must have drawn close to the field on the 22nd, and perhaps Lord Stanley observed matters from the rising ground of Greenhill Farm – for he could have seen little from Dadlington – and Sir William would have had an excellent view of Ambion Hill from the high ground on the present Bosworth–Shenton road. They probably did not have more than 4,000 men under command between them.

The royalist camp was early astir on the morning of 22 August, and Norfolk set off for Ambion Hill soon after first light. The army probably marched and fought in column of battles, with the King commanding the main battle and marching behind Norfolk, while Northumberland brought up the rear. The men-at-arms would still be mounted during the advance, but on reaching the chosen position they would send their horses to the rear and prepare for battle on foot, clustered around their liege lord. Before he left camp Richard sent a final message to Lord Stanley to join him at once, or else Lord Strange would die; Stanley is said to have replied that he had other sons and that he would not join the King. This may be true, but Lord Strange certainly did not die.

Henry Tudor was not the experienced general that Richard was, and he seems to have underrated the need for speed. His chances of reaching the top of Ambion Hill first were always slender, but he made them no better by dallying in his overnight camp. Richard was almost in position before Henry had encountered his first obstacle – the bog. Considerable confusion has been thrown on the whole battle through the chronicler Hall's statement concerning the effect of the sun on the rival armies. Hall enlarged on the more

180

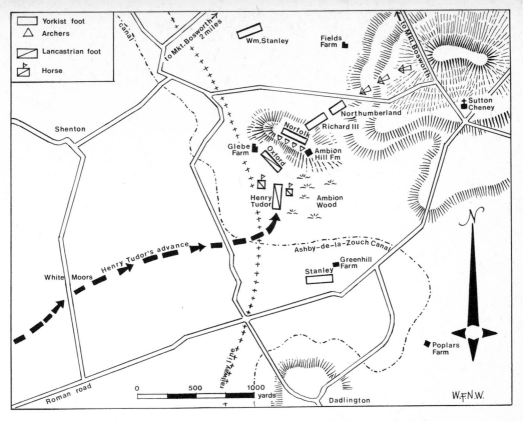

▭	Yorkist foot
△	Archers
▱	Lancastrian foot
⬓	Horse

Battle of Bosworth Field. Note Glebe Farm, below. In this area lead, stone and iron cannonballs have been found from time to time

authentic account of Polydore Vergil and put the sun at one moment in the faces of the royalist army. This was never the case; but the rebel army, which had the sun right in their eyes at the commencement of their march, were temporarily relieved of this handicap when they had to swing north to avoid the marsh at the south and south-western edge of the hill. Henry also sent a message to Lord Stanley before leaving his camp; but the trimmer was still trimming (which makes his reported statement to Richard slightly suspect) and told Henry to make his own dispositions and that he would join him at the appropriate time.

Henry's advance to Ambion Hill would have been, like Richard's, in column of battles with the cavalry on the wings; Lord Oxford commanded the van, and Henry with Lord Pembroke marched at the head of the main battle. Having skirted the marsh, Oxford found himself at the foot of the hill somewhere in the vicinity of where Shenton railway station once stood. A few hundred yards above, the Duke of Norfolk's archers were watching and waiting. It was now that Richard missed what was probably a certain chance of victory. While the main battle of the rebel army was still edging round the marsh, Oxford deployed the vanguard into line with the archers to the front and the billmen close up behind; Sir Gilbert Talbot had command of the Shropshire levies on the right and Sir John Savage with the Welshmen formed up on the left. Oxford also ordered up the artillery. This was a cumbersome manoeuvre to perform with an enemy poised only a few hundred yards away on a hill above, but it was allowed to proceed un-challenged. The battle then commenced with Henry opening up a lively cannonade.

These preliminary bombardments with their accompanying arrow storm never did a great deal of damage, but were sufficiently irritating to encourage the leading ranks to close the gap and indulge in the more acceptable form of slaughter at close quarters. However, on this occasion there was a strange pause with the armies watching each other warily. Oxford, fearful of being encircled if he went forward before the main body had closed up behind him, gave strict orders that no man was to advance more than ten feet from his standard. At first the royalist troops sus-pected some trap in this seemingly unnatural hesitation, and there was a brief interlude before both armies advanced to the attack. The resulting clash must have taken place somewhere in the area of Glebe Farm.

The battle lasted for around two hours. For Richard it was a sorry tale of treachery and tribulation. As Norfolk's and Oxford's men became locked in hand-to-hand combat and the leading ranks were shorn away under the steel flail of sword, pike and bill, they were hastily reinforced by men from the main columns. Henry was not a great warrior and seems to have played little part in directing the battle, but Richard, who lacked patience though not courage, was never far from the fighting, and probably placed his standard on the crest of Ambion Hill. Norfolk, a veteran of many fights, was the first important casualty – some say the victim of a personal confrontation with Oxford – and soon wide gaps began to appear in the array of both armies. After more than an hour the struggle still hung in equipoise, and all depended on two men watching from the sidelines and a third from even closer at hand.

We do not know what promises, if any, were made at Atherstone, but it seems almost certain that Sir William Stanley, a declared traitor who had allowed Henry unchallenged passage through north Wales, had guaranteed his intervention. Lord Stanley would not have committed himself so deeply to his stepson, and Northumberland, who had no desire to go the way of his father and grandfather, both of whom had been killed in earlier battles of this war, was clearly awaiting a lead from Stanley. It was not long in coming, but even before the Stanleys had launched their men against him, the King had been made aware that Northumberland's rearguard would not support him in his hour of need. Now it was all too clear to him how desperate the situation was.

The manner in which King Richard met his death, or the exact spot, will never be known. Only one thing is certain: he scorned every opportunity of safety through flight, and went down fighting in the best traditions of medieval chivalry. Long flowery speeches before the battle, and deeds of exceptional personal valour in the course of the fight, embroider many of the old chronicles. Sixteenth-century historians have woven a tale of combat between the personal adherents of Richard and those of Henry, and almost every succeeding writer has followed this pattern. They may be correct, but Colonel Burne* will have none of it and gives it as his opinion that the King died near the well now called after him, when attempting to ride down Lord Stanley. Such a theory has equal claims on our credence; but let the reader judge for himself.

Those who would have us believe that briefly the two principals met face to face in mortal combat say that at about the time Northumberland's defection became apparent information reached

* *Battlefields of England*, pp.146, 154.

Richard that Henry, although still well in the rear of the fight, had moved from the centre to the more exposed left flank. The King, accompanied only by his personal bodyguard – perhaps eighty men in all – immediately rode down the north-west slope of Ambion Hill and right across the front of Sir William Stanley's men, who were at that moment preparing to ride to Henry's aid. The proud Plantagenet and his few remaining loyal lords bore down upon those protecting the Welsh usurper. In the first few seconds of this conflict of truly majestic splendour Richard cut down Sir William Brandon, Henry's standardbearer, and then unhorsed Sir John Cheyney – a formidable warrior both in courage and poundage. For a few minutes it looked as though this sudden and unexpected onslaught would achieve its object; but just in time Henry's supporters, now supplemented by William Stanley's men, closed around their leader. The Red Dragon of Cadwallader fluttered again and the English king was dragged from his horse and hacked to death. Thus, according to the majority of writers, died the second and last King of England to be killed in battle. Like Harold before him, the victim of a man who had even less claim to the throne than he had.

Colonel Burne holds this account to be totally false. He suggests that on a hot August day the clouds of dust and steam of sweat thrown up by the battle would have made it impossible for Henry's position to be accurately located, and that anyway it would have been too far in the rear for a small body of horsemen to reach unchecked. He suggests that it is more probable that Richard rode round the left flank of his army (the south and south-west of Ambion Hill) in a frenzy of rage to be at the traitor Lord Stanley. Here undoubtedly he would have encountered the bog in which his horse may well have floundered. Hence Shakespeare's line, 'A horse, a horse, my kingdom for a horse', could well have historical fact. No replacement was forthcoming and the King died fighting on foot surrounded by enemies.

Perhaps there is some truth in both accounts. Certainly Henry's standardbearer was killed, and presumably he would never have been far from his lord. On the other hand the marsh and Richard's Well are firmly entrenched in the legend of the battle – and the story that Richard drank from the well before the battle is most unlikely.

With the King dead his followers had no reason, or wish, to prosecute the fight to the very end, and, with the exception of a few who had personal feuds to be settled, most of the royalist army either laid down their arms or abandoned them during flight

184

from the field. They appear to have dispersed in all directions, and the pursuit was a half-hearted affair extending no further than Dadlington to the south. A little way from here, on a hill still known as Crown Hill, Lord Stanley placed the golden circlet worn by Richard in the battle upon the new king's head. It had been found in a thorn bush, presumably hidden there by a looter intent on recovering it.

Most accounts of the battle agree on the casualty figures, and place the royalist army as losing somewhere around 1,000 men, and the victors not more than 200. These figures would indicate that although the pursuit may not have extended very far, at least in places it must have been rather bloody. A number of royalist leaders besides the King fell on this August day, the most important being the Duke of Norfolk, Lord Ferrers of Chartley, Sir Robert Brackenbury, Sir Robert Percy and Sir Richard Radcliffe. Norfolk's son Lord Surrey was captured and sent to the Tower, and Sir William Catesby was one of the few prisoners to be executed. Sir William Brandon was almost the only personage of note to be killed in the rebel army.

King Richard's body was stripped naked, slung over a horse and taken to Leicester in the wake of the victorious army. Here it was exposed to the public view for two days, and after this shameful treatment the last Plantagenet king was buried in the church of the Greyfriars.

The death of the Yorkist Richard and the triumph of the Lancastrian Henry was not the last fight in that sorrowful episode in our history known as the Wars of the Roses. Two years later the impostor Lambert Simnel was made the figurehead of a revolt in which the Earl of Lincoln, whom Richard had nominated as his heir, and Viscount Lovel, one of the late king's most loyal friends, played the principal parts. Henry was obliged to crush them at the Battle of Stoke on 16 June (see p. 190). Bosworth did, however, introduce another great dynasty into a world on the threshold of some of its most magnificent years. In the course of the next century a whole galaxy of dynasties produced some of their brightest luminaries: the Valois in Europe, the Osmanlis in Asia Minor, the Safavids in Persia, and the Mughals in India. The Tudors in England could justly claim their rightful place among these illustrious houses.

Principal Battles of The Wars of the Roses
In Chronological Order

1455: 22 May

First Battle of St Albans. When in March 1454 King Henry VI recovered from the long mental illness that had caused the Duke of York's first protectorate, it was obvious that war could not long be delayed (for the political background see chapter 7). The Duke of Somerset was released from the Tower and reinstated in the King's favour, whereas the Duke of York and his colleagues were dismissed from their offices and sent back to their estates, soon to be in peril of their lives. York summoned his friends to arms, and at the head of 3,000 men and accompanied by Lords Salisbury and Warwick he marched against the King in London. However, Henry left pro-Yorkist London for Leicester and, on learning that York was at Ware, set up his standard at St Albans. The King had with him the Dukes of Somerset and Buckingham, Lords Pembroke, Northumberland and Devon and about 2,000 men.

The Lancastrians attempted to hold the town behind two barriers in Hollywell and St Peter's Streets against Yorkist attacks from the east. Two frontal attacks made no headway, but Warwick infiltrated his troops through an unguarded part of the town's defences and spreading out took both barricades in the flank. The whole action lasted only half an hour and no more than 150 Lancastrians were killed; but the toll among their senior officers was very heavy. Somerset, Northumberland and Clifford were killed; Buckingham's son died of wounds and Buckingham himself was wounded.

1459: 23 September

Blore Heath. After four years of uneasy peace the King presided over a wasting realm. No parliament had been summoned for three years, the country was sadly divided and distressed. The Yorkists were armed, armies were marching across all England. Lord Audley had recently raised a Lancastrian army centred round Market Drayton, and the Queen— through whom the King ruled— sent him orders to intercept Lord Salisbury, who was marching from

Yorkshire to join the Duke of York at Ludlow. The two armies met head on two and a half miles east of Market Drayton at a place called Blore Heath. Salisbury, with 3,000 troops, was outnumbered by more than two to one, but could not avoid giving battle.

Audley took up a position just west of a little stream that crosses the Market Drayton–Newcastle-under-Lyme road, and Salisbury's men were drawn up about 150 yards east of the present Audley Cross, which marks the spot where Lord Audley fell. The Yorkist left rested upon the boggy edge of a wood, but their right was in the air, and Salisbury made a laager of his wagons to protect this flank. Whether Salisbury feigned retreat in order to draw Audley on is not certain, but the Lancastrian commander was definitely the one to attack. Two cavalry charges were repulsed, the first with heavy loss to the Lancastrians, and then they mounted an infantry attack up the hill to the Yorkist position. But this too failed; there was no support from the cavalry, Lord Audley had already fallen and 500 Lancastrians chose this moment to desert to the enemy. Salisbury's victory was complete and in the pursuit, which continued for two miles, the slaughter was very heavy. Possibly 2,000 Lancastrians perished in this battle, but less than 200 Yorkists fell.

1460: 10 July

Northampton. Immediately after Blore Heath the Yorkists were dispersed near Ludlow without a battle, owing to the treachery of a large part of their army. York himself retired to Ireland, Salisbury and Warwick to Calais. The Queen summoned a parliament and Henry gave his assent to a bill of attainder against all the principal Yorkist leaders. At the end of June the Calais exiles made a landing in Kent, seized Sandwich and gathering support entered London on 2 July. Here they were joined by almost all the Yorkist peers and their retainers. An army of some 30,000 was assembled, and leaving a part of it to blockade the Tower—held

by Lancastrians—the remainder under Lord Warwick set out to meet the King. The court had been in Coventry, but on learning of the Yorkist advance the King moved to Northampton, and here on 10 July, entrenched in a meadow just south of the town, Warwick found the Lancastrian army under the Duke of Buckingham.

The Duke had less men than Warwick, but his position was a strong one and his earthworks were lined with artillery The first attack, on a three-battle front, was repulsed; it seemed that the position was too formidable a one for any frontal assault to succeed. Indeed, had it not been for the treachery of Lord Grey of Ruthen, holding the left of the Lancastrian line, Warwick might never have had the victory. But when Grey let in the Earl of March (York's son and later Edward IV) he quickly rolled up the Lancastrian line, allowing Warwick's attack in the centre to succeed. The casualties were not high, but as at St Albans many of the Lancastrian leaders (including Buckingham, Shrewsbury and Egremont) were killed. The King was captured and once more led back to London.

1460: 30 December

Wakefield. In the September after Northampton the Duke of York came to London, and although he failed to win the crown he obtained from Henry the right of succession for himself and his heirs on the King's death. But Queen Margaret, then in north Wales, was not prepared to disinherit her son and soon had a very large army mustering in the north. The Duke of York marched to meet her and with an army of between 5,000 and 6,000 men reached his castle at Sandal (just south of Wakefield) on Christmas Eve. A few days later the much larger Lancastrian host was upon him.

Although details of the Battle of Wakefield are scarce, it appears that York refused to await expected reinforcements and marched out of the castle to give battle. Leaving the castle by the south gate he had to swing round it to meet the Lancastrians, who were assembled between Sandal

England and Wales: Wars of The Roses battlefields

and Wakefield. Heavily outnumbered he found himself between the two arms of a pincer movement and his army was quickly defeated. The Duke himself was killed in the battle, together with many other prominent Yorkists.

1461: 2 February
Mortimer's Cross. Queen Margaret was not present at Wakefield, but she accompanied the Lancastrian army on its destructive march south to St Albans. Warwick arrived in London at the beginning of February. On learning of York's death he appears to have made no effort to get in touch with the Earl of March (now Edward Duke of York) who was then on the Welsh march. But Edward, although only nineteen years old, was already a capable soldier and in a battle at Mortimer's Cross (some four miles south of Wigmore) defeated a Lancastrian force under the Earls of Wiltshire and Pembroke.

We know nothing of the details of this battle, except that in the morning, through some freak atmospheric condition, three suns were said to be visible. Edward took this as a propitious omen and after his victory added the sun to his banner: the device that was to serve him so well at Barnet ten years later (see p. 159). The beaten army was pursued as far as Hereford (some sixteen miles to the south), and although the two commanders escaped ten important prisoners, including Pembroke's father Owen Tudor, were summarily executed in Hereford. Edward then marched to join Warwick, but arrived too late for the second Battle of St Albans.

1461: 17 February
Second Battle of St Albans. The Earl of Warwick left London on 12 February and reached St Albans that evening. He had under command an army variously estimated as between 9,000 and 30,000 men—the former figure being nearer the mark. Margaret had started her march from Yorkshire with some 30,000 men, but many had gone home with their loot; she probably brought 11–12,000 soldiers into the field at St Albans. Warwick covered a long front from St Albans to Nomansland Common with four unconnected defensive positions, and laid out a number of complicated defensive devices.

The Lancastrians opened their attack on Warwick's left position in St Albans itself, and met stiff resistance from his archers positioned round the watch tower and Eleanor Cross. It took them much of the morning before the street fighting was done with, and a swing to their left in order to engage Warwick's position on Bernard's Heath was possible. The main engagement was fought either here or on the high ground

above Sandridge a mile to the north. The wind was blowing a light snowfall into the Yorkists' faces, which greatly hindered their bowmanship; added to this their centre, under Warwick's brother, Lord Montagu, was hopelessly outnumbered and left to fight unaided for many hours. When Warwick eventually brought the right wing to their assistance a pre-arranged desertion by a large contingent of troops from Kent had the most demoralizing effect on the entire Yorkist army, which began to retreat. Although the line was temporarily stabilized by Warwick above Nomansland Common defeat was now inevitable. Warwick, whose generalship on the day had been sadly wanting, at least managed to leave the field at the head of 4,000 disciplined troops. For full details of this battle, see chapter 8.

1461: 29 March
Towton. After St Albans Henry was reunited with his queen, but he refused to let his army advance on London (a costly mistake), and instead the Lancastrians headed north again, plundering as they went. Meanwhile, Warwick acted swiftly and at the beginning of March had Edward proclaimed king in London. Edward fully realized that there could not be two kings in England, and on about 12 March he set out for the north. Lord Fauconberg had marched in advance and Warwick had been despatched to raise troops in the Midlands. Somewhere north of the Trent Edward assembled his large army of about 40,000 soldiers. A slight Yorkist reverse was suffered at Ferrybridge, where Lord Fitzwalter's troops were surprised and their commander killed in an attack led by Lord Clifford; but Clifford's force was soon caught and Clifford himself killed. The Yorkists then proceeded to the higher ground, where the Lancastrians were drawn up between the villages of Towton and Saxton.

The battle that was fought on this windswept plateau lasted for nearly the whole day. Rather more than 80,000 men took part and this time the snowstorm that set in favoured the Yorkists. The advantage seemed to go first to one side then to the other in this fiercely contested battle. About midday the Duke of Norfolk's troops arrived on the field and took position on the Yorkist right flank. With his numbers thus increased Edward was at last able to turn the Lancastrian left and gradually—still fighting desperately—they began to fall back, closely pressed by the Yorkists. Eventually discipline snapped and in the mad rush to cross the Cock Beck and gain the London road thousands of Lancastrians perished. The exact numbers of those who died on the

field of battle, or in the marshy fields of the beck, are not known; but there has been no greater slaughter in any battle fought on British soil. For a full account see chapter 9.

1464: 25 April
Hedgeley Moor. In the years 1462 and 1463 the Lancastrians were continually stirring up trouble in the north of England, with Queen Margaret travelling between Scotland and France attempting to gain assistance (sometimes successfully) for Henry's declining cause. But the Duke of Somerset and Sir Ralph Percy surrendered Bamburgh and Dunstanburgh Castles respectively on Christmas Eve 1462 in return for free pardons, and later Somerset swore allegiance to Edward and was rewarded with high office. Although these castles (and Alnwick as well) were later retaken by the Lancastrians they were soon isolated, and with Henry a wandering fugitive, Margaret driven overseas and the Scots ready to treat with Edward, there were hopes of a permanent peace. However, Margaret was working hard in Lorraine to organize a fresh conspiracy in the north of England, and Somerset quite suddenly betrayed the trust that Edward had shown him and raised the northern counties for Henry. Warwick marched north to subdue the rebellion, and Montagu was sent to the border to escort the Scottish commissioners to York to discuss a renewal of the peace treaty. His journey was not without excitement; on his way to Newcastle with a small escort he narrowly escaped an ambush laid for him by Somerset. A few days later, now with a larger force, he was attacked at Hedgeley Moor, some seven miles south of Wooler, by Somerset and Percy.

It is not likely that either side had many troops in the brief engagement that followed, and the opponents were probably fairly evenly matched, but when Sir Ralph Percy fell leading Somerset's van the Lancastrians appear to have lost heart and fled the field, leaving Montagu to proceed unimpeded.

1464: 15 May
Hexham. The Lancastrian position in the north, where lay their only remaining strength, was fast crumbling. The Scots had agreed to cease sheltering them, and their Northumbrian strongholds could not expect to withstand for long the heavy siege weapons that Edward was hurriedly assembling. But they could still put an army into the field, and Lord Montagu again set out from Newcastle to oppose it. He found Somerset's men drawn up in a meadow called the Linnels some three miles south east of Hexham on the banks of the Devil's Water.

It was a hopeless position from which to fight any sort of battle, the field being almost totally enclosed and too cramped to allow of free manoeuvre. The Lancastrian soldiers seem to have realized this, for many made off at the Yorkist approach without so much as discharging an arrow. It required no great feat of generalship to demolish those that stayed to fight. Montagu practically surrounded the meadow, and then made a frontal attack through the one opening at the east end. Those that were not killed in this attack were pressed across the river into West Dipton Wood and forced to surrender. Battle casualties were not great, but the executions that followed (including that of Somerset) were on a scale unparalleled even in these bloodthirsty times. Henry remained north of the Tyne during the fight and escaped to the Lake District, where he was among predominantly loyal subjects.

1464: June

Bamburgh Castle. After Hexham there remained to the Lancastrians only the three great castles of Bamburgh (opposite the Farne Islands), Dunstanburgh (some twelve miles farther down the coast) and Alnwick. These had already changed hands more than once, and now Warwick and Montagu (created Earl of Northumberland after Hexham), bringing with them Edward's massive siege pieces, set out to smother the last embers of Lancastrian resistance. Alnwick, on 23 June, and Dunstanburgh the next day yielded without resistance, but Bamburgh refused the summons. This castle was held by Sir Ralph Grey and he had been exempted from the general pardon. Soon the debris from the ramparts was being blasted into the sea, and resistance, which never stood a chance of succeeding, quickly collapsed.

The affair is of interest in being the first time that a battering train was used effectively in England. The King's great guns, 'London' and 'Newcastle' (made of iron) and 'Dijon' (a brass cannon), were supported by bombardels, and it was with some ease that they breached the walls, allowing Warwick to lead an assault that completed the work. Grey was seriously wounded, but this did not save him from being dragged before the High Constable, John Tiptoft Earl of Worcester, who had a reputation for recognizing no law but the axe.

1469: 26 July

Edgcote. After Hexham and the surrender of the Northumbrian castles it seemed as though the Lancastrian cause could never recover sufficiently to become a

serious threat to Edward IV. The Beauforts, the Tudor Earl of Pembroke, the Duke of Exeter— in fact almost all the Lancastrian leaders—were in exile, and in July 1465 Henry was caught up on the borders of Yorkshire and Lancashire and sent to the Tower. But the Yorkist strength lay in the twin pillars of the King and Warwick. Between 1465 and 1469 the King, by a series of foolish and underhand acts, estranged Warwick, who from being his most loyal and useful adherent became his most embittered enemy.

The break between Warwick and Edward was the signal for a big revival of Lancastrian activity on both sides of the Channel. Jasper Tudor returned to Wales and here and elsewhere rising broke out; Warwick had crossed to Calais where he was joined by the King's brother Clarence, who married Warwick's daughter there. Warwick, having fermented a serious rebellion in the north of the country, then landed in Kent, where he raised a considerable army with which he marched on London. Edward, who was at Nottingham dealing with the Yorkshire rebellion, found himself between two hostile forces. He had some 15,000 men under arms with him, but the loyalty of many was suspect; however, his newly created Earls of Devon (Stafford) and Pembroke (Herbert) were marching to his assistance with 6,000 and 14,000 archers respectively. Meanwhile the northern rebels, under Sir John Conyers, had carried out a skilful march on Leicester and got between Edward and the Earls. The latter joined forces at Banbury, where Devon and Pembroke quarrelled. As a result, Devon drew off his men, leaving Pembroke with only 14,000 Welsh bowmen to face a vastly superior force under Conyers, and possibly Warwick's army, which was marching towards Towcester On 25 July the two forces were in contact and some skirmishing for position took place round three prominent features near Danes Moor. Danes Moor is situated about five and a half miles north-east of Banbury, some two miles east of Wardington, which is on the Banbury-Chipping Warden (B4036) road. On this day the northerners lost Sir Henry Neville, son of Lord Latimer.

On 26 July Pembroke's men were attacked in force, but through the efforts of their commander and his brother Sir Richard Herbert, held their own for some hours against superior numbers. Eventually, lured down from their hillside position into the valley, and betrayed by the vanguard of the King's army under Sir Geoffrey Gate, who arrived late on the scene and then joined the enemy, the Welshmen broke. One near contemporary

account puts their casualties as high as 4,000, but this is probably a considerable exaggeration. Pembroke and his brother were taken prisoner and summarily executed. The fractious Earl of Devon was captured a few days later and also executed. As a result of the battle Edward became Warwick's prisoner, but after keeping him at his Middleham castle for a while Warwick found it expedient to release him

1470: 12 March

Empingham. In early 1470 there was a rising in Lincolnshire; the rebels were led by Sir Robert Welles, and strongly supported by Warwick and Clarence in spite of their outward display of loyalty to the King. On learning of the rebellion Edward acted with commendable rapidity. Issuing commissions of array he soon had a powerful force with which he marched to Stamford. Sir Robert's father, Lord Welles, and Sir Thomas Dymock, the King's Champion, had been summoned to the King and admitted being implicated in the rebellion. At Stamford, when Sir Robert refused to disperse his men, both his father and Dymock were executed. Edward then proceeded against the rebels.

He found them in a field some five miles north-west of Stamford, just off the present A1 road. There was not even a skirmish; the rebels were so terrified by the few rounds fired by the King's artillery that they fled, hastily casting off their coats with the tell-tale colours of Welles, and giving to the place its name of Losecoat Field. Sir Robert Welles was captured and beheaded, but not before he had made a confession implicating Warwick and Clarence in the rebellion— a fact apparently not previously realized by the King.

1471: 14 April

Barnet. In October 1470 Warwick drove Edward out of England and reinstated Henry as king. Aided by money and ships supplied by his brother-in-law, the Duke of Burgundy, Edward returned in March 1471. Landing in Yorkshire he was soon able to assemble a small army and gather reinforcements and he marched south. Montagu in Yorkshire and Warwick in Coventry were successfully by-passed, while Clarence (unknown to Warwick) was preparing to return to his brother's camp. On 12 April King Edward entered London unopposed. He left again the next day to confront Warwick, who had marched through St Albans with a mixed Lancastrian and Yorkist force of about 9,000 men and taken up a position on Hadley Green, just north of Barnet. Edward, at the head of some 8,000 men, arrived at Barnet on the evening of 13 April, and in spite of the darkness advanced to

189

within a short distance of Warwick.

The battle started early the next morning in a thick ground mist. In the initial stages the Yorkist left (under Lord Hastings) was beaten from the field by the Earl of Oxford's battle, but Prince Richard of Gloucester (the future Richard III) had some success on Edward's right. The fight in the centre was sternly contested. Oxford, returning from the pursuit of Hasting's men, misjudged the position, and in the mist his banners with their star were mistaken for Edward's sun and he was attacked by men from Warwick's centre. Thinking treachery was afoot, Oxford and his followers rode off the field. The battle lasted between three and four hours and ended in a complete victory for Edward. The Earl of Warwick, who had fought on foot, was struck down trying to regain his horse. For full details see chapter 10.

1471: 4 May

Tewkesbury. On that Easter Sunday which saw Warwick's defeat and death at Barnet, Queen Margaret with her young son landed at Weymouth and was soon joined by many Lancastrian leaders with the remnants of their fighting men. The Duke of Somerset took command of the assembled army and, realizing the impossibility of fighting without further reinforcements of men and materials, decided to move towards Wales and join forces with Jasper Tudor, collecting military stores from Bristol on the way. Edward was at Windsor for the feast of St George and as soon as he learned of Somerset's intention he set out —on 24 April—for the West Country. There followed an exciting chase with the Queen's army trying to get across the Severn and Edward desperately anxious to bring her to battle. A little time was wasted in Bristol. Gloucester closed its gates to her and on arrival at Tewkesbury (3 May) the Lancastrians were too tired and too hard pressed to cross the Severn. Somerset decided—wisely, for he had the choice of ground—to stand and fight rather than risk a lengthy crossing with weary troops. He had about 6,000 men, which was rather more than Edward could put against him, and the Yorkists were in no better shape after their gruelling march than their opponents.

The next morning Edward opened the battle with a fairly heavy artillery bombardment, which induced Somerset to lead an attack on the junction of the Yorkist left and centre battles. The situation could have been dangerous for Edward, had Somerset's centre under Lord Wenlock supported him. As it was fighting alone and attacked on two sides, Somerset's men were driven back and the King advanced his battle to the attack. The Lancastrians, demoralized by the débâcle on their right, offered little resistance to Edward and soon the whole line broke. The slaughter during the retreat was heavy: perhaps 2,000 men perished in the battle and on the banks of the Severn. Queen Margaret made good her escape, but her son was killed and Somerset was taken from the sanctuary of the abbey and executed. The battle is fully described in chapter 11.

1485: 22 August

Bosworth. Edward IV died in 1483. His son was only twelve years old and so Edward designated his brother Richard as protector. Richard had Edward's two sons imprisoned in the Tower and himself proclaimed king. He had many enemies both at home and abroad, and on 7 August 1485 Henry Tudor landed near Milford Haven with about 2,000 French mercenaries and a handful of Lancastrian lords and knights. Gathering reinforcements as he advanced through Wales, Henry then marched via Shrewsbury, Stafford and Atherstone. Richard was at Nottingham, and moved from there to Leicester on 19 August, and by 21 August the two armies were in striking distance of each other two or three miles south of Market Bosworth. Richard's army (without the Stanley brothers) was not much short of 8,000 men, while Henry had only about 5,000. However, the loyalty of the Stanleys to Richard was very suspect, and during the battle both of them opted for Henry, bringing with them perhaps a total of 4,000 men.

The battle was fought on and around Ambion Hill, close to Sutton Cheney, and lasted for only two hours. Richard gained the best position, but failed to take advantage of it by attacking Henry's van under Lord Oxford while it was still deploying. In the event Oxford was allowed time to launch his attack and the Duke of Norfolk, commanding Richard's forward battle, was soon killed. For the first hour the fighting was evenly matched, but the battle was lost for Richard through treachery. Both the Stanleys deserted his cause, but even more damaging was the failure of the Earl of Northumberland to bring the rearguard into action when he saw which way the Stanleys were moving. The battle ended with the death of Richard, for his followers had no stomach for continuing the fight after their king had been slain. For a full account see chapter 12.

1487: 16 June

Stoke Field. The early years of Henry VII's reign were by no means carefree; his dynasty was beset by enemies in Britain and at the court of Burgundy; in the spring of 1487 a serious insurrection was launched from Ireland. An imposter called Lambert Simnel, made out to be Clarence's son, Edward Earl of Warwick (who at that time was actually a prisoner in the Tower), was sponsored by an Oxford priest and supported by the Earl of Lincoln, whom Richard had made his heir, and the ardent Yorkist Lord Lovel. Simnel was crowned King of England in Dublin on 24 May 1487, and on 4 June the boy 'king', accompanied by Lincoln and Lovel, landed near Furness in Lancashire and advanced through Yorkshire at the head of 1,500 German mercenaries (kindly supplied by his 'aunt' Margaret, Dowager Duchess of Burgundy). As they marched the rebels gathered reinforcements, although not nearly as many as Lincoln had hoped for. Henry was at Kenilworth, but calling up nearby levies he set off at once for Nottingham. By the time he arrived there (14 June) the rebels were at Southwell, some twelve miles to the north-east. According to the contemporary account of a herald, Henry moved to Radcliffe on 15 June, while the rebel army crossed the Trent by the ford below Fiskerton and took up a position on an open escarpment some 1,500 yards south of East Stoke. Here the King met them on the morning of the 16th as he was marching towards Newark. The rebels held the advantage in numbers (perhaps 9,000 to Henry's 6,000), but apart from the German mercenaries their soldiers were not well armed or trained.

The royalists advanced to the attack in three well spaced out divisions, the van being commanded by Lord Oxford. This division, being somewhat isolated, was severely punished and only saved from complete disaster by the arrival of the King's main battle. As the royalist divisions closed up the rebels were first held and then pushed back off the ridge. The fight lasted for more than three hours and was fiercely contested, the rebel army being well buttressed by the German contingent. Their commander Martin Schwartz and Lincoln were killed in battle; Lovel escaped by swimming the Trent and was never seen alive again, and Simnel was captured and put to work in the royal kitchens. The rebel soldiery were slaughtered by the thousand in a gully at the foot of the ridge and in the marshy riverain fields. They had, however, inflicted very heavy casualties on Henry's army—possibly as many as 2,000 men, most of whom were from the vanguard. By his victory at Stoke Henry secured the safety of the Tudor dynasty.

CHAPTER 13

Scotland and the Tudors

Flodden

9 September 1513

The battlefield of Flodden is one of the few in Great Britain that is still very much the same as it was at the time of the battle. No doubt the fields are better cultivated, the hedges are new and in places scrub woodland has given way to orderly plantations. But apart from a few farm buildings, a slightly enlarged village, a partial drainage of the bog and some new roads the site must have looked very much the same in 1513.

The actual battle took place immediately to the south of Branxton village, which is about three miles south-east of Coldstream and to the south of the main Morpeth–Coldstream road, the A 697, Ordnance Survey one-inch map, sheet 64. The ground over which the battle was fought, and the two Scottish positions prior to the battle, are on private property and can be visited only by permission of the owners. The exception to this is the monument erected on Pipers Hill, which can be reached by a public footpath. However, because of the undulating ground the visitor has no real need to leave the roads to view the field of battle. Just north of the village of Milfield a side road runs north-west to Branxton; about two miles along this road the ground rises steeply and the road cuts across the west end of Flodden Hill. The first Scottish position was on the high ground crossed by this road, from just to the west of it stretching eastwards almost to the main road. The road leads to Branxton Hill (which was the second position of the Scots), and from the top of this hill, near where a track leads to the farm, a good view can be obtained of the battlefield immediately to the north. An even better view of the English position (which was along the ridge where the monument stands) can be had from the fields directly to the north of the farmyard – although, of course, permission from the farmer would be necessary to walk through these.

James IV came to the throne in 1488 after the insurgent lords had defeated his father's troops in battle at Sauchieburn and, in open defiance of the young prince's orders, had murdered their king,

191

who had taken refuge in a nearby mill. The new king was fifteen years old, of an age to be fully aware of the dark deed of shame through which he had ascended the throne. It was to cast a deep shadow across his path, and it is said that in penance for the rest of his life he went girt with an iron chain to which he added a fresh link every year. With the possible exception of Robert I, James IV was the best loved and most forward-looking king to sit on the Scottish throne. In the twenty-five years of his reign he developed the country's commerce, stabilized the currency, improved the navy and efficiently overhauled the administration of justice. These and other achievements more than offset his short-comings and occasional acts of folly.

A contemporary description of James at the time of his death, when he was about forty, tells us that he was of 'middle size and of a strong body and red hair – used to much exercise and of slender diet'. Undoubtedly, he was a man of good physique and pleasing appearance, for his attraction to and admiration for women is well known. Having been deeply in love with Margaret Drummond, whom he would have married had she not been poisoned along with her two sisters at breakfast one morning, he finally consented in 1502 to take Margaret Tudor as his bride. Margaret was an extremely passionate woman, who after her husband's death saw no reason to dissemble her passions. The ten years of their marriage were on the whole happy ones, although even she was unable to satisfy James's carnal lust, and his frequent, and usually fruitful, visits to mistresses were the source of constant complaint.

James's relations with his father-in-law were for the most part cordial. Before his marriage he had made one foolish mistake when he championed the cause of the impostor Perkin Warbeck, but for most of Henry VII's reign James strove, not without some success, to maintain peace in the dangerous and shifting quick-sands of European politics. He had raised Scotland to a position of eminence and often found himself holding the balance of power in the constantly changing alignments of the great European powers. James was always ready to stand by the 'Auld Alliance', but obdurately refused to be drawn into war by England, France, Spain or the papacy.

After Henry VII died in 1509, the English throne was occupied by a man of very different mettle. Henry VIII, with his rich inherit-ance, youthful exuberance and impetuosity, presented the Scottish king with an entirely different proposition from his more careful and cautious father-in-law. Nevertheless, for the first two years of Henry's reign the friendly relationship between England and

*Right: Thomas Howard, Earl of Surrey by Holbein, in Windsor Castle.
Left: James IV, from drawing attributed to Jacques le Bourcq, in the
library at Arras*

Scotland was if anything strengthened. But by 1511 a tight ring
of steel in the form of the Holy League was being drawn around
France by the Papal States, Spain and Venice, and it was not long
before the Emperor Maximilian and Henry VIII decided to join the
League and complete the encirclement. During the next two
years there were many sparks that might have started a con-
flagration between England and Scotland: fierce Border raids for
which both countries could share the blame; semi-official naval
hostilities in which James lost Andrew Barton, one of his best sea
captains, and both countries lost valuable ships; Henry's refusal
to hand over the Bastard John Heron, who had killed Sir Robert
Ker, Warden of the Scottish Middle March; and, most hurtful to
the Scottish queen, her brother's insistence on keeping her legacy
of valuable jewellery. Throughout this time James did all in his
power to avert war; but Henry was determined to invade France,
and his principal concern was that James should not march in his
absence. However, the 'Auld Alliance' was deep-rooted and in
July 1512 James took the decisive step of renewing it.

Even so, when 1513 – the year that was to bring a cataract of misfortune on Scotland – was ushered in England and Scotland were still exchanging civilities. Henry sent Doctor West to Scotland for the second time and James sent Lord Drummond to England; but West was quite unsuccessful in moving Queen Margaret to use her influence in favour of her native country, and as Drummond's offer of reconciliation was conditional upon Henry refraining from war with France it was treated with unconcealed contempt. More successful missions had been carried out by Louis XII's envoy de la Motte. This Frenchman combined in equal measure the talents of soldier, pirate and diplomat: on his way to Edinburgh he was perfectly capable of sinking a few English ships and bringing others captive to Leith. Such high-handed piracy was most satisfactory, but perhaps what endeared him even more to James was a consignment he brought him of wine, gunpowder and other warlike stores.

Meanwhile the French queen added her blandishments. Anne of Brittany begged James to advance as her true knight three feet into English soil and do battle in her honour; and just in case this fervid plea did not strike the chord of chivalrous romanticism in James it was reinforced with 14,000 French crowns and a ring of gold set with a turquoise from off her own finger. This and other legends surround the events leading up to Flodden. We do not know for certain whether Anne sent James her ring, nor do we know what truth there is in the sinister warnings James is said to have received first in the royal chapel at Linlithgow, and then from the market cross in Edinburgh, against undertaking the hazardous enterprise upon which he was then setting out.* What we do know is that by the summer of 1513 the French were in grave peril of destruction; James had agreed to advance into England should Henry invade France, and when in June the English king crossed the Channel at the head of a large army, James made preparations to honour his pledge to King Louis.

On 26 July he sent Lyon herald to Henry, who was encamped outside Thérouanne, with a message to this effect. Henry replied on 12 August in a letter containing a superb piece of Tudor hubris. Having castigated James for constantly breaking the treaty of perpetual peace and dishonourably waiting to attack until Henry was out of the country, he is at pains to show that such perfidious

*Robert Lindesay of Pitscottie in his *The Historie and Cronicles of Scotland*, Vol. I, is the principal source for these and other Flodden legends. Some are undoubtedly not true, but a turquoise ring later preserved in the College of Arms was said to have been removed from James's body after the battle.

behaviour comes as no surprise to him. 'We cannot maruayle, considering the auncient accustomable maners of your progenitours, which neuer kept lenger faythe and promise than pleased them.' He ended by assuring James that he had no intention of desisting from his attack on France.† The die was cast, war was now inevitable. But Henry had had no illusions that it would be otherwise, and before leaving England he had said to the Earl of Surrey, who was appointed Lord Lieutenant of the North, 'My Lord, I trust not the Scots, therefore I pray you be not negligent.'‡ Surrey, son of that Duke of Norfolk who had fought against Henry Tudor at Bosworth Field, was now an old man of seventy, but he was neither negligent, nor negligible, as the Scots were soon to discover.

Supporting the French king actively by an invasion of England was the second big mistake that James made in his relationship with the southern kingdom, and it was to cost him much more dearly than had his support for Perkin Warbeck. He never thought in terms of conquest, but he set himself the task of causing a diversion that he hoped would bring Henry hurrying back from France. James had no illusions as to the dangers and difficulties that lay ahead, and although he is alleged to have said that 'only millers and mass priests' were left in England, this statement is hardly borne out by the size of the army he assembled – or else he had a very healthy respect for 'Christ's Church militant here in earth'. He knew very well that Surrey would march against him with a formidable force; and the events of history should have warned him that Scottish attempts to stir up trouble in England had a nasty habit of rebounding on the Scots.

During the first fortnight of August the bulk of the Scottish army assembled near Edinburgh. It was the largest and best equipped army ever to leave Scotland until modern times, but it was a heterogeneous force, and it is a measure of the King's popularity throughout Scotland that he could command the loyalty and weld into one fighting machine men from the Highlands, Lowlands and Borders, who not so long ago comprised three different races. As usual the numbers have been wildly exaggerated, and modern historians are left to grope their way as best they can through a bewildering number of variations. It seems fairly certain that between crossing the border and the actual Battle of Flodden there was considerable desertion – many who were only there

---

†*Hall's Chronicle*, p.547.
‡ibid, p.555.

for the loot being anxious to get it safely home; it is also generally agreed that there was no great disparity between the strength of the two armies, and that the Scottish army may possibly have been the stronger. It may well be that 40,000 men crossed the border on 22 August, but that rather fewer than 30,000 remained to fight at Flodden. This number would have included a French contingent under Count d'Aussi; the French had what we would now call a military mission in Scotland, which was there partly to strengthen their ally's military effort, but also to teach them modern fighting methods and in particular the use of the continental long-handled pike and the two new pieces of artillery which they had recently given James.

Artillery was still a comparatively new arm, and although useful in siege warfare and for strengthening a defensive position the heavy cannon of those days (culverins, sakers and serpentines) was quite unsuited to any mobile form of warfare, and the Scots needed 400 oxen and twenty-eight packhorses to draw their guns and ammunition. James was very proud of his cannon, and rightly so, for the seventeen pieces of 'great ordnance' that he brought to Flodden Field (and left there) were far superior to anything the English could pit against them. But in the battle, in which artillery played only a minor part, it was the English guns that caused the most alarm.

Lord Home commanded the Borderers, and while the Scottish army was still mustering he opened the campaign with a large-scale mounted raid into Northumberland. It was entirely successful until on 13 August, as the force was returning laden with booty, they were surprised in an ambush near Milfield. Sir William Bulmer's archers took severe toll of the raiders and regained the plunder. This disaster, called by the Scots the Ill-Raid, was an inauspicious beginning, nor were the Borderers destined to redeem this failure in the forthcoming battle.

James crossed the Tweed at Coldstream on 22 August, and having reduced Wark Castle marched downstream to attack Norham. The Bishop of Durham, to whom Norham Castle belonged, considered this great fortress, perched on its inaccessible eyrie many feet above the Tweed, to be impregnable. The visitor today would be inclined to agree with him. But the combination of James's heavy cannon (which certainly proved their worth here) and the castle's inadequately supplied magazine forced the governor to beat the chamade after a siege of only six days. The river Till is a formidable obstacle and in 1513 it was bridged at Twizel, Etal and Ford and then not until Weetwood some ten miles further upstream; it was therefore important for James to take Etal and Ford Castles. Etal was not properly fortified, and the owner of Ford, Sir William Heron, had been taken by the Scots as a hostage for his bastard brother John, who was still at large in England and was soon to join Lord Surrey's army. Lady Heron surrendered the castle in the hope that it would be spared. There are many entertaining stories of James's dalliance at Ford, and how he succumbed to the charms of the chatelaine, who, animated by a desire for vengeance, allowed herself to be seduced so that she could delay the advance of the Scottish army, and inform upon it to Lord Surrey. Alas, most of them are untrue. It is possible that James agreed to her asking Surrey to release two important Scotsmen taken in the Ill-Raid in exchange for her husband; but if so nothing came of it, and after two or three days at the castle James took his leave of Lady Heron and burned her castle down.

Meanwhile, Surrey had been assembling his army first at Newcastle and then at Alnwick, where he arrived on 3 September and where he was joined by his eldest son Thomas Howard, the Lord Admiral, who brought him about 1,000 armed men from off the fleet. England's main army was, of course, in France with Henry, and the one that Surrey had now raised consisted chiefly of a cross-section of northern society. The local lords, gentry, yeomen and peasants formed the backbone of the army. They were not professional soldiers, but they were well accustomed to bear arms, and in the days when archery practice was compulsory they were good bowmen.* Surrey also had his own 500 licensed retainers, who were more akin to professional soldiers, but of these only one was a man-at-arms (heavy cavalryman). The army, which probably totalled about 26,000 in all, was strong in archers and billmen, but weak in artillery and without heavy cavalry – Lord Dacre commanded a force of 'prickers', who were irregular horsemen recruited from the border, and for the approach march most of the infantry would have been mounted.

With the exception of Hastings the Battle of Flodden has evoked more interest and received more attention from historians than any other battle fought on English soil. In consequence we have a large number of accounts, almost all of which differ to a greater or lesser degree as to what were James's and Surrey's intentions before the battle, and as to exactly how the battle was fought. There are a number of contemporary, or near contemporary,

*It is interesting to note that Flodden was the last major battle in which the longbow was used.

sources that can be studied – some of which appear in the biblio-graphy for this chapter – including what is purported to be Admiral Howard's official dispatch.† Other than this, and Lord Dacre's letters to Wolsey and Henry VIII, all accounts are secondhand – even the Bishop of Durham was not present at the actual battle – and much of what they say is slanted towards whichever side they favoured; there are few points upon which they are agreed.

At least one modern writer‡ bases his account on the assumption that James misappreciated Surrey's intention and, thinking he was marching into Scotland, gave the order to retire across the Border but was surprised before he could reach the Tweed. This is not the generally accepted view, and much must depend on what importance can be placed on the interesting – although by no means invariable – custom of those days of challenging one's opponent to battle and even naming the day and time at which the fight was to take place, in much the same way as we would arrange a football match. We tend to forget that warfare in the sixteenth century was a much more dignified – if equally unplea-sant – affair than in modern times, and that the nobility usually set much store on chivalrous conduct.

On 4 September Surrey sent Rouge Croix to James, whose army was still encamped around Ford, to say that as James had invaded the realm, spoilt, burned and raided divers houses, and killed many people, he had come to give battle. Two days later James sent his herald Islay to accept the challenge, and Surrey replied that he would be bounden in £10,000 and good securities 'to gyve the sayde Kynge batayle by frydaye next at the furthest'.* Thomas Howard in his dispatch quotes James as saying 'he would abide him [Surrey] there till Friday at noon'. On arrival at Wooler Surrey was therefore indignant to learn that James had in the meanwhile taken up a very strong defensive position on Flodden Hill. On 7 September he wrote a letter to James reminding him of his agreement to give battle on Friday the 9th in his original position, and expressing surprise that 'it hath pleased you to chaunge your said promyse and putte your self into a grounde more like a fortresse or a campe . . .'. He suggested that James came down on the next day to the plain of Milfield.† James was

†Either Surrey delegated the task to his son, or else his own dispatch is no longer extant.
‡G. F. T. Leather, *New Light on Flodden*.
*Richard Faques, *The Trewe Encountre*.
†State Papers Scotland, Henry VIII, Vol. I, folio 17. P.R.O.

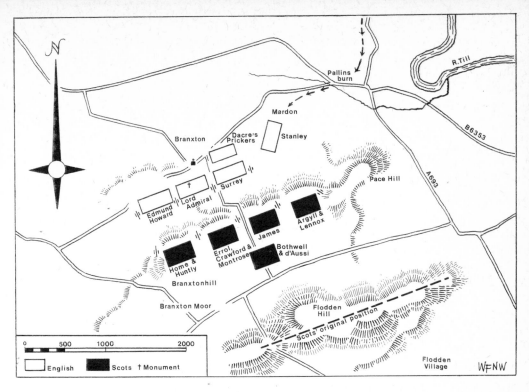

Battle of Flodden. Aerial photograph shows the centre and western sectors of the field, which is virtually unchanged since the time of the battle

most indignant at this suggestion and he had one of his servants tell Surrey 'that it besemed not an erle, after that manner to handle a Kynge' and that he would use no sorcery, 'nor had no trust of any grounde'.‡ This uncharacteristic attitude of the Scots (who usually abandoned a strong position on the slightest pretext) presented Surrey with a grave problem. His offer to fight on what he considered to be fair ground on 8 September had been refused; he clearly couldn't assault James's well-nigh impregnable position; yet his duty was to defeat the Scots, and he almost certainly considered that the original pledge to give battle on 9 September, which had been agreed to by James, still held good. He decided to take a very daring but well calculated risk.

On 18 August 1513 Queen Catherine of Aragon had signed a pardon for the Bastard Heron,** and at around that time he, with a small party of outlaws, had joined Surrey's army. Here was a man who knew the countryside well and could help Surrey with his plan to march round James's flank and tempt him from off his strong position on Flodden Hill. On 8 September the English army crossed to the right bank of the Till by the Weetwood bridge and camped that night in the area just to the north of Barmoor Castle. It appears that, as was so often the case with a Tudor army, the commissariat was breaking down: food was short and the troops were reduced to drinking water. This latter may sound to us no great hardship, but drinking water was much more unpleasant then than it is now – a few years later Thomas Howard, by then Duke of Norfolk, was to lose nineteen men in one day from drinking puddle water.

It is generally agreed that Surrey advanced his army in two main columns, or battles, each with two wings. The column that would be on the right, or vaward, was commanded by the Lord Admiral, with his right wing under his younger brother Edmund Howard, and his left wing under a veteran knight, Sir Marmaduke Constable. Lord Surrey commanded the main battle, or 'rearward' in this advance, with his right wing under Lord Dacre (to whose horsemen had been added a contingent of Northumbrians), and his left wing under Sir Edward Stanley, whose soldiers were men from Cheshire – less a detachment which had been lent to Edmund Howard. Each wing was said to comprise 3,000 men (a suspiciously even number), and *The Trewe Encountre* tells us that Thomas Howard had 9,000 in his main body, while his father had 5,000.

‡*Hall's Chronicle*, p.560.
**Patent Roll 5 Henry VIII, pt.1, m.18, Roll No. 620.

We know that the vaward and the artillery crossed the Till by the Twizel bridge, but where Surrey put the remainder across will never be known. The object of Surrey's daring manoeuvre, in which he marched a half-starved army round the flank of the enemy to put himself and his army between that enemy and home, was principally to deceive James as to his intention in the hope that he would shift from his strong position. There is therefore no real reason why we cannot accept the wording of Howard's dispatch literally: 'The Lord Howard at 11 of the clock the said 9th day passed over the bridge of Twizel with the vaward and artillery and the said Earl [Surrey] following.'* However, most writers have elected to take 'following' as meaning at a later time and not following in Howard's footsteps. Surrey is therefore credited with crossing the Till at almost every bridge or ford between Twizel and Sandyford (about five miles upstream), and Stanley is often thought to have crossed still later and at a third place.

The flank march had probably taken the army through Duddo, and there was no doubt in the minds of Heron and Dacre, who knew the country, that Twizel was the only crossing place for the cannon – Etal was far too close and might have invited another Stirling Bridge. What then was the purpose in dividing the army, for even if it was not done in the face of the enemy it was always a grave risk? There were two possible reasons. The first was speed: for it would have taken a long time to pass 26,000 men and some cannon over the fairly narrow Twizel bridge, and the day was already well advanced. The second was that there was no need for the less heavily encumbered main body to use a bridge, and a shorter march was desirable. But surely a tried and competent commander such as Surrey would never have risked dividing his army widely for the saving of a few miles' marching. It seems probable therefore that if Surrey didn't actually follow his son over Twizel bridge he crossed by the ford at Castle Heaton, a mile downstream. There is also some reason for believing that Stanley's wing acted almost independently and crossed even later than Surrey.

Once across the Till there is further speculation as to the different routes that the columns took to get round behind the Scottish position. This is not a matter of great importance, except to note that when they arrived in the area of the Pallins' burn they

*The dispatch was written in old French and the exact wording is sometimes confusing. Some translations have 'following' as 'after'.

201

would have been confronted by a formidable bog, which was a quarter of a mile broad and stretched in an east–west direction for more than a mile.* There was a narrow bridge, or causeway, across its centre, but the guns had to be taken almost to Sandyford before they could get across. Undoubtedly the Lord Admiral's battle arrived at Branxton village first, but Surrey with the main battle could not have been too far away. To the south of Branxton village the ground rises very slightly, and it was as Thomas Howard was preparing to deploy along this ridge soon after three o'clock on a very unpleasant afternoon, with a southerly wind blowing sheets of rain into the faces of the English, that he observed the entire Scottish army drawn up on Branxton Hill, less than half a mile away.

Meanwhile, what had brought the Scottish host to Branxton Hill? It is not always that design is fulfilled in the planning of a battle, but Surrey's strategem and manoeuvre were soon to be successful. When the English army had headed across the Till for Barmoor, it was quickly lost to view from the Scottish position on Flodden Hill by the lie of the land and the scrub of the sparsely clad slopes; but James was not without information, for his scouts kept a constant vigil. The Scottish king's task was made no easier by the fact that in a loose-knit army such as he commanded it was necessary to make decisions in council. We know very little of these decisions, for most of those who made them never lived to tell the tale. But even if James was convinced that Surrey meant to honour his gage, some of the council were sure that he meant to invade Scotland. The old Earl of Angus (Bell-The-Cat as he was often called), with whom James had never been on the best of terms since they shared a mistress in Janet Kennedy, urged immediate retreat into Scotland, but this James refused, telling Angus he could go home – which the old man did, leaving his two sons to perish in the battle. With this option ruled out by James, he could either go forward into England and call Surrey's bluff, or stay where he was until he was quite sure exactly what the English were doing. He decided on the latter course.

Probably as a precautionary measure he moved part of his force to the eastern slope of Flodden Hill in case Surrey meant to attack him in the flank, and there is some evidence that the cannon were positioned to command the river – although the English army never came within effective range – but it was not until he knew for certain that Surrey was crossing the Till that he gave orders to

*Much of this area is still very boggy, and heavy agricultural machinery has been known to almost disappear in it.

202

move. Branxton Hill, which lay just a mile to the north, offered almost as strong a defensive position as the one he was then occupying, and as soon as Surrey's intention was clear James's obvious course was to deny this hill to the enemy. Accordingly at about midday the Scottish army about-faced (which meant a reversal in the original positions in the line) and marched towards Branxton Hill. The camp followers, in accordance with the Scottish custom, set fire to all the straw and rubbish. No doubt the smoke from this damp dross drifting in the southerly wind added to the murk and gloom of the afternoon, but it certainly could not, as is sometimes alleged, have obscured the Scottish advance – this was effectively done by the valley in between the two hills.

The Scottish army was in five columns, four up and one in reserve, and would have arrived in its new position somewhere around 2 p.m. The left comprised Lord Home and his Borderers, and the Earl of Huntly with his Highlanders; the second column was also divided and the commanders were the Earl of Errol, and the Earls of Crawford and Montrose (jointly); then came the King's column (said to have been the largest) with the Earls of Cassillis and Glencairn and Lords Herries and Maxwell as supporting commanders; the Earl of Bothwell's Lothians were initially in reserve and with them was Count d'Aussi and the French contingent; the extreme right of the line was held by the Highlanders under the Earls of Argyll and Lennox. We are told that a bow shot (probably about 200 yards) divided each column, and allowing room enough in the ranks for the long-handled pikes the line must have stretched for 2,000 yards, which is almost the full extent of the Branxton Hill feature. Robert Borthwick, the Scottish master gunner, had his cannon in position in time to fire a harmless salute to the English as the van crossed the Pallins' burn bog.

Thomas Howard was not a young man at the Battle of Flodden, but this was his first important command on land. He lived to a great age and to fight the Scots and French on many occasions; he was not a brilliant general, although he had his successes, and when later on he was constantly in receipt of armchair advice from Henry VIII in Whitehall he was inclined to grumble. But he can be excused on this occasion for taking the *Agnus Dei* from his neck and sending it with a frantic appeal to his father to close the gap quickly. On reaching the Pipers Hill area he would have been very conscious that his left flank was in the air, for Surrey was still some way behind him, and if James had decided to attack he could have seriously mauled the Lord Admiral and just conceivably defeated the two halves of the English army in detail.

The talisman had the desired effect on Surrey, who hastened to come into line with his two sons. As soon as he saw the Scots drawn up in four forward columns Surrey decided to conform, a manoeuvre that cannot have been too difficult to execute, but one that has never been satisfactorily explained. However, the result was Edmund Howard on the right, possibly with Lord Dacre's Northumbrians attached; the Lord Admiral next to him with Sir Marmaduke Constable; then Surrey, and the left and fourth column would have been Stanley's if in fact he had come up into line at this time, which seems very unlikely. There remain Lord Dacre's 'prickers': these Surrey kept under his own command and used as a mobile reserve. The fact that almost all accounts agree that the battle started with a cannonade is of interest in showing the immense exertions that must have been extorted from the English gun teams, who had to march round the bog and come into line in time to open the battle at about 4 p.m.

Very little damage was done by the artillery of either side in this opening phase, but the English bombardment had some effect on the morale of the Borderers, for there is no doubt that they descended the hill first, and this was probably due to a dislike of being shot at while standing still. With them came Huntly's Highlanders, and the whole column smashed into Edmund Howard's men with undiminished momentum, for the English right flank rested on flat ground. The fight in this sector of the line was very fierce and the Scots had much the best of it. The Cheshire contingent that had been taken from Stanley's command wasted no time in fleeing from the field, leaving dangerous gaps into which the Scots thrust their huge pikes. But the others stood their ground and offered a stubborn resistance. Sir William Fitzwilliam, Sir John Lawrence, Sir Wynchard Harbottle and Sir William Warcop were among the slain, and Sir Henry Grey and Sir Humphrey Lisle were captured. Edmund Howard was unhorsed at least twice, but managed to fight his way to his brother's column. The situation was finally restored when Surrey ordered Dacre's horsemen into action. There is a letter of Lord Dacre's extant in which he records that just as he was moving to Howard's assistance the Scottish cannon opened up and some of his men fled; nevertheless, he broke the back of the attack. Fortunately for the English, Home's Borderers then fell to looting, and neither his men nor Huntly's took any further part in the battle.

What caused James to order the rest of the Scottish army to abandon their strong position and fall upon the enemy we shall never know. Possibly he thought that Lords Home and Huntly, having so badly damaged the right wing of the English, would then turn upon the Lord Admiral's flank – as they should have done – and that now was the chance to roll up the enemy; or possibly once the left wing had gone into action there was no holding the remainder and the King had little choice. This would have been in keeping with Scottish impetuosity, but if so it is strange that the men on the right wing led by Lennox and Argyll kept their position; however, the ground they held is undulating and they might not have seen clearly what was happening on their left. Moreover, if – as seems probable – Stanley's men were not yet in position there would have been no enemy immediately to their front.

In any event the English line had little time to recover from the blow dealt to its right before the two centre columns of the Scottish army, with Lord Bothwell's men in close support of James, advanced upon them. The ground was wet and slippery; the descent from Branxton Hill was fairly steep; a deep ditch (then probably a boggy area) lay at the bottom of the hill, beyond which the ground rose somewhat to the main English position. Not an easy march at the best of times; but for men encased in heavy armour, carrying unwieldy eighteen-foot pikes and being raked by cannon fire, it must have seemed an eternity of time before, trampling over their fallen comrades, they got to grips with the foe. Had Lords Home and Huntly been able to rally their men for further efforts against the English right flank they would certainly have made it a tougher and more dangerous fight for Surrey, but the battle was won and lost in the Pipers Hill–Branxton Church area in the two hours or so in which the whole front joined in close and intensive action. And it was won and lost not so much through the quality of the men engaged – for with few exceptions those on both sides fought valiantly – but through the quality of the weapons.

The English cannon must have done some damage to the advancing Scots, but we are assured that in this main battle their arrows failed for the most part to pierce the Scottish armour. It was the long pike that cost the Scots the battle. This cumbersome weapon was first used by the Swiss as protection against cavalry, which arm they themselves did not possess; with well trained men maintaining the momentum of the heavy phalanx it could be a devastating tool of destruction. But Count d'Aussi had not had sufficient time in which to train the Scots, and anyway by the time they reached the English position the momentum of their attack was already failing. Once forced to fight at a standstill the English bill just chopped the pikes into useless pieces.

What exactly happened on the Scottish right will always remain something of a mystery. Certain facts are known. Argyll's and Lennox's Highlanders did not join in the mêlée on their left front: their battle with Sir Edward Stanley's column was almost a separate engagement; these men, like the clansmen and Borderers of the Scottish left, were not encumbered by heavy armour and were therefore more vulnerable to Stanley's arrows; and, lastly, we gather from most accounts that they did not put up much of a fight. Stanley's column arrived on the battlefield late; whether this was due to his having been purposely delayed as part of a deception plan in the early stages of Surrey's approach march, or to a serious bottleneck at the crossing of the Till, does not greatly matter. When he did arrive Stanley was quick to see where his duty lay – the unbroken Scottish column had to be engaged at once. The eastern end of the Branxton Hill ridge falls fairly steeply just south of Mardon village, before the ground rises again to Pace Hill, and up this slope Stanley's men scrambled – some accounts say the ground was so slippery that the men removed their boots. It seems that Stanley divided his force, keeping a number of men to engage the Highlanders from the front, while the bulk of his troops took them in the flank – if this was so it was one of the earliest examples of fire and movement. At all events the attack, pressed home fiercely, was entirely successful, and soon the Scots were in flight, leaving their gallant commanders and a few staunch supporters to die upon the field.

Stanley then reformed his column and came down the hill to administer the *coup de grace* to the Scottish centre, which had borne the brunt of the afternoon's work. King James, perhaps realizing that he could contribute little by way of generalship, was determined to lead his men in the forefront of the battle. His column was opposed to Surrey's, and he had in close support Bothwell and Count d'Aussi, while on his left the Earls of Crawford and Montrose were hotly engaged with the Lord Admiral's men. But this battle in the centre, and therefore the whole day, had been virtually decided before the effect of Stanley's troops could be felt. Most of the Scottish leaders, including the King, had been slain; daylight was closing in and the carnage of the field was already appalling. For two hours or more the combatants had been locked together in a grim and deadly struggle; in the flail and agony of destruction men had sunk to the ground in tangled heaps, and a proud army had ceased to exist.

That night the English slept on the field they had won. The next morning Lord Home, who had managed to rally some of his Borderers, appeared with them on the skyline, but a few rounds of

206

cannon fire warned them off, and there was little left to stop the half-starved English from enjoying the fruits of the richly provided Scottish camp. All through that day the grisly business of sorting out the dead went on. Many of them were so badly mutilated that they were unrecognizable – indeed only with difficulty could Lord Dacre, who knew him well, and Sir William Scot, his captured secretary, recognize the body of the Scottish king. Among the thousands – probably at least 5,000 – of Scotsmen who were killed were some two dozen earls and barons; James's bastard son by Marion Boyd, the 23-year-old Archbishop of St Andrews; the Bishops of Caithness and the Isles; two abbots and many knights. The chronicles of calamity have few precedents for the extinction in battle of almost a complete generation of a country's nobility. The estimate of English losses made immediately after the battle was as low as 400 men,* but the actual figure was almost certainly higher, and some prisoners were taken when a pursuing force got lost. Only a few men of rank were killed and they were mostly those who fell in the first engagement on the right of the line.

King James has been frequently criticized for losing a battle in which the advantages were all in his favour. He was not an experienced general, but it is difficult to see how he could have done any better, given the Scotsman's inherent desire to be always, and immediately, at the throats of the enemy. He certainly could not have defeated the English army in detail as they were crossing the Till, as is sometimes suggested, because time and space were against him; he might conceivably have done better had he attacked Thomas Howard before Surrey joined him, but his presumed intention of staying on the hill and letting Surrey, who for many reasons had to offer battle quickly, come at him, was a far better proposition. His only mistake, if mistake it can be called, was his failure to hold his men steady on Branxton Hill in the face of alarming, but not too damaging, cannon fire.

As for Surrey, he was an old man but as tough and hard as the sword he held in his hand. He had taken an appalling risk, but fortune had favoured him and he had tumbled and humbled the Scots, who were to cause no further serious trouble for almost thirty years. Howard heads rested lightly upon their shoulders during the Tudor era, the family fortunes rose and fell, but Flodden was definitely a Howard benefit. Edmund was knighted on the field; Thomas would soon become Lord Surrey; and in February 1514 the victor was reinstated in the family title of Duke of Norfolk.

*Letters and Papers of Henry VIII, Vol. I, 444.

CHAPTER 14

The Tudors in Scotland

Pinkie Cleuch

10 September 1547

The site of the battle was most probably in the cultivated ground half a mile south-east of Inveresk church (Ordnance Survey one-inch map, sheet 62), just to the south of the railway line – and perhaps a little to the west of the site marked on the one-inch map. There are two vantage points for viewing the ground. The castle on Fawside (or Falside) Hill was just behind the English position, and with the aid of glasses the visitor can get a good view of the battle area, but the Scottish position is now obscured by buildings. The best impression of their position is obtained from the golf course to the west of the river Esk and just off the B 6415 road. The Scottish centre occupied ground a few yards west of the clubhouse. The Inveresk eminence, which was an important tactical feature at the time of the battle, is now built over, but from it one can get down to the Esk and walk for some way along the bank. This walk gives one a further idea of a part of the Scottish position, but the town of Musselburgh now completely covers the left of their line.

After Surrey's victory at Flodden (see chapter 13) the road to Scotland seemed to lie open. But Henry, who was philandering in France having recently captured two comparatively unimportant towns, allowed the opportunity to pass and decided upon a policy of conciliation rather than one of total conquest. For the rest of his reign Scotland was always an elusive will-o'-the-wisp; no matter how ardently he wooed her – gently or roughly – he was forever chasing and never catching. If he was to succeed he had first to break the 'Auld Alliance' between Scotland and France, and when persuasion failed he resorted to force. His object was union – perhaps even suzerainty – and he hoped to achieve it through a mixture of treachery, marriage and, later, the reformed religion. His approach was often irritatingly arrogant, and for much of his reign the troops he kept on the border were occupied in oppressing a people who seemed to him as stubborn as they were remote.

Apart from the constant border raids, there were at least three more serious engagements during Henry's reign. In November 1542 the Scots invaded the west marches of England and bore down upon Sir Thomas Wharton, who advanced to meet them from Carlisle, with about 15,000 men. On the 24th of the month they suffered a defeat at Solway Moss which was almost as disastrous as Flodden; and although this time their king was not among the slain – indeed James V did not take part in the battle – he was so disheartened by the result that shortly afterwards he took to his bed in Falkirk Palace and died. In July 1543 a ray of sunlight illuminated the otherwise sombre Scottish scene when two treaties were signed at Greenwich, and it seemed as though the union of the two nations would be cemented with the marriage of Edward Tudor and Mary Stewart. But three months later the Regent (the Earl of Arran) was persuaded by that turbulent priest Cardinal Beaton to nullify these treaties. Henry was not the man to be trifled with in this manner, and in the spring of 1544 he sent Lord Hertford at the head of some 35,000 men on a punitive expedition to Edinburgh and Leith. In February 1545 the Scots at last succeeded in turning the tables on their oppressors. At Ancrum Moor they surprised and outmanoeuvred an English force of 3,000 men under Sir Ralph Evers. More than 1,000 Englishmen were taken or slain and among those who perished were Evers, Sir Brian Layton and Lord Ogle. However, it availed the Scots little, for Henry determined on a more terrible vengeance than in 1544 – and in Froude's pithy phrase, 'the heavy hand of Hertford was again laid on Scotland'.

Henry VIII died in January 1547 leaving an uneasy peace with Scotland that rested upon a collateral agreement in the Treaty of Campe with the French, which had been ratified amid much splendour at Hampton Court the previous August. Scotland was included in this treaty so long as she was prepared to honour the terms of the 1543 treaties signed at Greenwich – which, as we have seen, she was not. While Francis I was alive there was little likelihood of trouble from the French – he was old, ill and tired of fighting – but only a week or two after Lord Hertford (by now the Duke of Somerset) had been granted full powers as Protector of the Realm by the young King Edward VI's council Francis died. He was succeeded on 1 April 1547 by Henry II, who was no friend to England, and who was deeply influenced by the Queen Dowager of Scotland's powerful Guise family.

Broadly speaking the Protector attempted to pursue much the same line in foreign affairs as was being taken at the end of Henry's reign. For Scotland, union through the marriage of Mary and Edward was still the linchpin of the English coach of state, although Somerset was determined on a much more liberal policy for the Scots than that of total subjection envisaged by Henry. But the Scots, encouraged by the French king's enthusiasm for their cause (and no doubt unaware of his dangerous designs), made it clear that they had no intention of honouring any treaty that would bind their queen in marriage to the English king.

It is difficult to be certain when Somerset decided that it would be necessary to achieve his purpose by war, but by April 1547 warlike moves were afoot and preparations built up steadily throughout the summer, although Somerset never despaired of getting his way through conciliation. Apart from anything else, in the summer of 1547 a war with Scotland might easily have provoked one with France: Henry II was determined to regain Boulogne before the treaty date of 1554, and Lord Cobham was constantly reporting on the weakness of Calais. Measures to strengthen both these towns had been resented by the French, and although an attack on Calais by Henry might involve him with the Empire, Somerset could not be certain that Charles would stand by his commitment in respect of the 'Old Conquest' – as Calais was called – and a war on two fronts was a possibility. But the union of the two crowns in one empire was the keystone of Somerset's foreign policy, and if the Scots were too stubborn or too stupid to see the advantages that would accrue to them from this 'Godly and honourable a purpose', he considered it his duty to impose it by force. On no account should Henry II and French troops dominate Scotland.

Once having decided upon this policy, it was a pity that Somerset dithered in its execution. Well before June, when warlike activities were temporarily halted – presumably for further peace probes to be made – it must have been obvious that the Catholic, pro-French party had recovered most of the ground lost by the murder, in May 1546, of the Chancellor Cardinal Beaton, and were too far committed to France even to consider Somerset's proposals. At this time St Andrews Castle was still held by the Chancellor's murderers, now known as 'the Castilians'. From the original sixteen who had forced their way into the castle and murdered Beaton their number had grown to 120 – including John Knox – and although they had found the castle well supplied they were glad to be revictualled from time to time by an English ship. Arran had granted them a truce by which they retained the castle until absolution for the killing of Beaton could be received from Rome. This absolution eventually arrived containing the dubious clause *Remittimus irremissibile*, which did not satisfy the Castilians, and

Edward VI, by Holbein, in the Hanover Museum

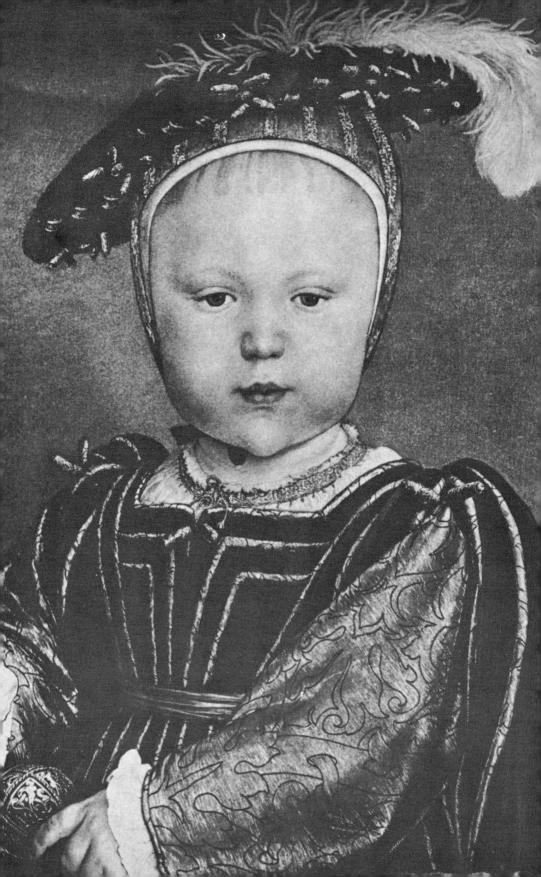

Arran again laid siege to the castle, but with the same irresolution as before – no doubt due to the fact that the Castilians held his son hostage. However, by the end of June the French had taken a hand; a fleet, under the redoubtable captain Leo Strozzi, the Prior of Capua, not only avoided the English ships but bombarded the castle for five days. On the last day of July, having been severely shaken by the naval guns, which had been disembarked and positioned on the abbey and St Salvetor's College, and now cut off by land and sea, the Castilians surrendered to Strozzi.

The key to successful union with Scotland would surely have been the reformed religion, and in apparently making no attempt to relieve St Andrews Somerset blocked the one avenue down which his proselytizing zeal might conceivably have brought him to success; for the capture and removal to France of the Castilians had gravely weakened the Scottish reformers, who if not too enthusiastic over union at least regarded Somerset favourably as a pillar of the Reformation.

Even as late as August the Protector could not bring himself to invade without one more attempt at conciliation. Cuthbert Tunstall, Bishop of Durham, and Sir Robert Bowes met the Scottish commissioners on the border with an offer to waive all outstanding differences between the two countries if the Scots would honour the marriage treaty. When this last attempt at a peaceful settlement failed the massive preparations which had been going forward throughout the summer for a campaign that was calculated to last a month were almost completed. Once more Scotland was to be seared by war, and the wretched inhabitants of that rugged Border country, whose life, based upon a primitive agriculture, was always a constant battle against nature, were yet again to see their homesteads burned about them by those terrible men who wore upon their tunics the fiery cross of St George.

Somerset's army mobilized at Newcastle at the end of August, and marching via Morpeth, Bamburgh and Berwick crossed the border on 1 September. It was not a large force, but it was well balanced. Most accounts put the total around 16,000 – 4,000 of which were cavalry, and there were 1,400 pioneers. A supporting arm of eighty cannon contained fifteen pieces of 'great ordnance', and there were 900 carts and many wagons. One account puts the total transport as high as 12,000 vehicles, but this is almost certainly excessive, for the army was in part supplied by the fleet, which sailed, under Lord Clinton, parallel to the advance. The cavalry arm, which was to play so important a part, and suffer the most casualties, in the forthcoming battle, comprised some 2,000 light horse under the veteran warrior Sir Francis Bryan; 500 horse from Boulogne, brought over by Lord Grey of Wilton, who was given the overall command of the cavalry; 200 mounted Spanish arquebusiers under that experienced mercenary Pedro de Gamboa; an Italian mercenary troop, under their captain Malatesta; and the Gentlemen Pensioners of the Royal Bodyguard.

By 5 September the army had reached Cockburnspath, a small place sixteen miles from the border where a spur of the Lammermuir Hills runs down to the sea. One of Somerset's numerous spies had brought intelligence that the Scots had been preparing defence works here and that the English might be brought to battle. It is a natural position from which to hold up an advancing enemy, and it had the advantage that the high cliffs and surrounding hills offered protection from the guns of the English fleet; but if Somerset's superior artillery could not have blasted the Scots from their hillside positions, their right flank could have been turned. To come so far forward would dangerously have lengthened their line of communication, and in the event of defeat disaster would have been even more total than in fact it was. Some trenches had been dug at Cockburnspath, but Arran had wisely chosen to hold a much stronger position.

Safely through the glen, Somerset indulged himself in his favourite sport of castle-burning. George Douglas's castle at Dunglass, whose small shabbily attired and equipped garrison was commanded by Lord Home's nephew, surrendered; but Lord Home's man at Thornton (Tom Trotter) and the captain of the Hamilton castle at Innerwick were not so obliging. It did not take the English pioneers very long to reduce these two small keeps, and by midday the army was passing Dunbar, whose garrison made an ineffectual hostile demonstration, for which they were not called to task. That night Somerset camped near the much stronger Douglas castle at Tantallon, but he must have decided that too much time would be lost in assaulting that stronghold, for the next day he retraced his steps and after marching through East Linton camped at Longniddry.

From Longniddry the army marched along the seashore and made camp on 8 September in the region of what is now the Prestongrange golf course. A little less than a mile to the south the ground rises steeply to Fawside and Carberry Hills, and Somerset drew the army out of the camp to occupy the forward slopes of these two features. His line would have been well extended, but not dangerously so, for he was not taking up a defensive position. Fawside Castle (which he invested and later burned) was above him and almost in the centre of his line but it was lightly held, and anyway those of his soldiers immediately in front of the castle were in dead ground. Somerset must have known by now that he was hopelessly outnumbered, and the purpose of this extended line may have been to give the Scots a false impression of his strength. There would seem to be little other reason for it, because from this commanding position he could see only too well that the choice before him was a frontal attack or withdrawal – and Somerset was not the man to come so far and turn back without a blow.

Arran had under his command about 25,000 men, and so in numbers he greatly exceeded the English army, but he was much weaker in cavalry (having probably no more than 1,500 lightly armed and mounted troops) and he was also inferior in artillery. Moreover, although the threat to the nation had temporarily closed their ranks, Arran could not be entirely sure of the loyalty of some of his subordinate commanders. He had displayed considerable tactical skill in the choice of his position. His left, under the Earl of Huntly, was protected by the sea, and he had thrown up an earthen wall in an attempt to give protection against the English naval guns; he also stationed the Earl of Argyll and his 3,000 Highland bowmen on this flank. The whole army was behind the Esk, and Huntly's division guarded the only bridge across that river. Arran himself commanded the centre, or main battle, which occupied the ground known as Edmonstone Edge that rose fairly steeply behind the high banks of the river. The Earl of Angus was in command of the vanguard on the right flank, and his southern flank was protected by an almost impassable bog; the cavalry, or what was left of it by the time of the battle, was also positioned on this flank.

When the English army reached Prestonpans the fleet was off Leith, and Somerset ordered Lord Clinton (presumably through a pinnace that kept in touch with the army) to stand his ships off Musselburgh and come ashore himself to confer. Clinton, who had seen the enemy position from behind their lines, was able to give Somerset information of a kind he could not otherwise have obtained. However, although the weather that September was reported to be not too good, it would have been clear enough for Somerset and his lieutenants (the Earl of Warwick, Lord Grey of Wilton and Lord Dacre) to get a detailed view of the enemy's front, for although Edmonstone Edge lay almost two miles from the English lines, the intervening country was flat and open to the river.

At this length of time we cannot be absolutely certain exactly where the Battle of Pinkie was fought, or of some other facts,

because what was then the deep, pastoral peace of partially cultivated fields, dotted with rough patches of gorse and broom, has
now been largely swallowed up by the bricks and mortar and noise
and bustle of busy Musselburgh. But Fawside Hill is much as it
used to be and so (now that most of the trees have been cut down) is
Carberry Hill; from these two vantage points, and from Musselburgh golf course across the river, it is still possible to develop
some sort of topographical sense, and it is not too difficult to put
oneself into Somerset's mind as he stood on Fawside Hill that
September day to confer with his admiral and his army lieutenants.*

Somerset was an experienced general, and more than that he
knew the men he was fighting. They held an impregnable position,
which he had to assault by a frontal attack with a force that was
vastly inferior numerically, although stronger in firepower. He
also knew that the sight of an English army on Scottish soil did re-
markable things to the Scots – he was soon to have further proof of
this – and it must have crossed his mind that given sufficient provo-
cation Arran would find it difficult to restrain his men. But a wise
commander could not count on this, and Somerset had to plan his
assault. On his right front there was a hillock (a now almost in-
distinguishable feature in the town of Inveresk) on which stood –
and indeed its successor still stands – St Michael's Church; this
eminence commanded much of the enemy position and would
afford Somerset excellent opportunities for enfilade fire. Somerset
had to take possession of this hill, and with his inferior numbers he
would want to pack a punch on Arran's left, where even if the
bridge was held the river banks were not so high, and moreover the
fleet would bring cross-fire to bear on the enemy. This then was
the plan. Its execution was made more simple by the impetuosity of
the Scottish cavalry.

On the morning of 9 September the Scottish horsemen crossed the
river and carried out a series of manoeuvres in front of the English
lines, daring their enemy to come off the hillside and attack. At
first Somerset refused to be drawn, but he was prevailed upon by
Lord Grey to allow the heavy cavalry to sweep into action just at
the moment when Lord Home and his men were wheeling around
and therefore off balance. The engagement was short but fierce,

*The present writer, having spent a considerable amount of time
examining the site, studying the map in the Bodleian Library and
reading contemporary accounts of the battle, has drawn his own
conclusions. These do not agree in all respects with what are probably
the two best modern accounts of the battle, written by Sir Charles
Oman and Sir James Fergusson, but he is greatly indebted to these two
authors.

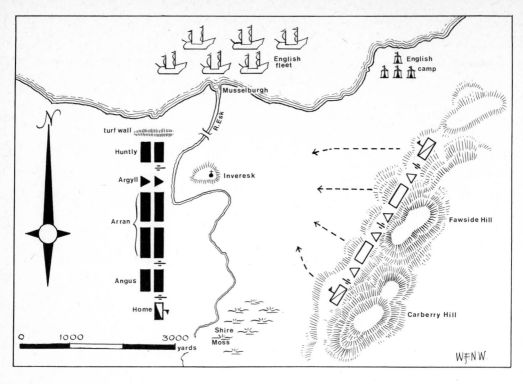

Top: Pinkie Cleuch—8 a.m. Below: Pinkie Cleuch about 10 a.m. The key in the lower plan applies to both illustrations

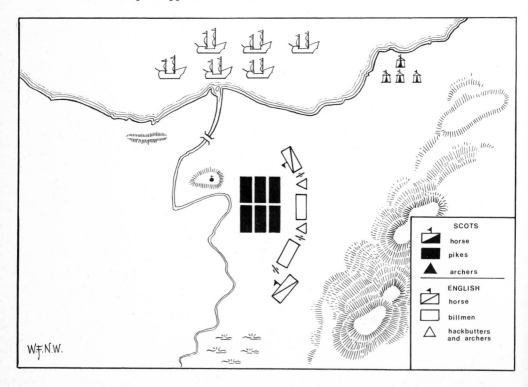

SCOTS		
		horse
		pikes
		archers
ENGLISH		
		horse
		billmen
		hackbutters and archers

and although the Scots, now realizing that they had drawn too great a weight upon themselves, attempted to break off the fight, the English were in no mood to let them go. Before the remnants escaped to their own lines Arran's cavalry had been sadly mauled. Their commander Lord Home was injured when his horse fell during the retreat and his son, with one or two other gentlemen and two priests (Scottish clergy frequently figured in the roll of honour during these border wars), was made prisoner. Through this ill timed and quite pointless performance, Arran's cavalry was no longer a fighting force.

That same afternoon Somerset, now with little risk of being cut off, determined on a forward reconnaissance. Accompanied by his personal staff and a strong escort, he rode over the ground almost as far as the Inveresk hillock. As the party was returning they were startled by the sound of a trumpet behind them, and turning saw a trumpeter and herald, whose tabard bore the royal arms of Scotland. Somerset and Warwick halted to allow these two men to approach. The herald bore a message from Arran – who obviously hoped that Somerset might have been dismayed by the strength of the Scottish position – offering an exchange of prisoners, discussion of peace terms, and a safe conduct for the English to recross the border. Somerset refused the offer, and very properly rejected a challenge from Huntly that in the event of his not agreeing to Arran's terms the matter should be settled personally between Huntly and Somerset with twenty men apiece. Warwick, who did not bear the responsibilities of head of state, was eager to accept this challenge, but Somerset forbade him, and in dismissing the herald commanded him to tell Arran that 'we have been a good season in this country; and am here now but with a sober company, and they a great number: and if they would meet us in field, they shall be satisfied with fighting enough'.*

Another account is that Somerset offered to withdraw if Arran would stand by the terms of the matrimonial treaty, or at least guarantee Mary's continued presence in Scotland for another ten years without contracting her in marriage to a foreigner. This message might well have been sent, but now – as before – it would have been unacceptable to the Scottish leaders, and as such suppressed from the rank and file lest it weaken their resolve to fight.

About eight o'clock on the morning of Saturday 10 September – to be known in Scottish history as 'Black Saturday' – Somerset moved his men forward in the execution of his grand design. His

*E. Arber, *An English Garner: Tudor Tracts*, p.103.

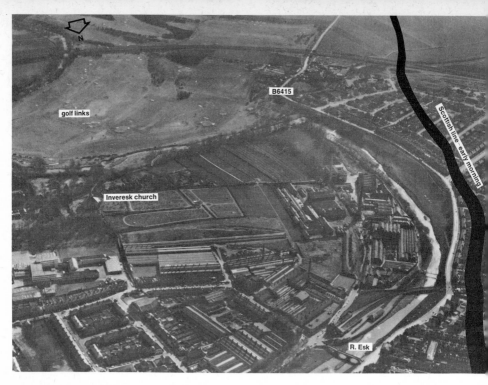

Pinkie Cleuch: Above: Scots' position west of River Esk at about 8 a.m.
Below: Scots' advance from their early morning position to battle line

fifteen heavy pieces of ordnance were probably sakers, whose maximum effective range was about 1,630 paces, and so they would have to be brought for some distance across this open but rough ground, adding further difficulties to an operation that was necessarily somewhat unwieldy. Manoeuvring his force into a position from where it could deliver a strong thrust at Arran's left wing meant having to expose his own left flank, but now that the Scottish cavalry had been almost totally destroyed this was a calculated risk which he was justified in taking. Moreover, it probably had the desired effect of presenting the fiery Scots with a temptation they could not resist.

We should now pause to consider the generally accepted theory that the Scots thought that Somerset was hurrying across their front to make for his fleet and embarkation, and that it was in this belief that they abandoned their strong defensive position in order to defeat the English army before it could be safely embarked. If the relative positions of the opposing forces are marked on the map it is possible to gain the impression that almost the whole English army was sidestepping across the Scottish front; but a careful study on the ground quickly dispels this error. The left flank of the English would certainly have had to turn across Angus's front, but the advance of the remainder towards Inveresk church was

Pinkie Cleuch showing positions at height of battle

almost completely frontal, and only the stupidest Scot in Arran's and Huntly's divisions could have misconstrued this manoeuvre as a retreat on the ships – still less on the camp, which lay almost parallel to the original position on Fawside Hill. And yet it was Argyll's Highlanders who first crossed the Esk.

It seems far more likely that the Scots abandoned their battle-winning position for one of two reasons – probably a combination of both. They could not afford to let the English have possession of the Inveresk hill – hence the early manoeuvre of the Highlanders, who were quickly followed by Huntly's division; and the sight of an English army parading itself on their front may once again have impelled the Scots with a desire to rush with the frenzy of rage at the throat of every English antagonist. Angus was the one leader who could be forgiven for thinking that Somerset was withdrawing his army, but he was the only one who demurred at the order to advance across the river.

Once they had abandoned their position and crossed the river the Scottish army was lost, for it had little with which to match the English cavalry and artillery. Somerset was not slow to adapt his plan of battle to the new, and entirely beneficial, position with which he was now confronted. It was necessary to halt the Scottish advance, which once all the divisions were safely across the Esk had formed itself into a solid phalanx, from rolling him up before he could reorient his centre and right and bring up his artillery; and for this he used his superior cavalry arm. The Scots had adopted their traditional formation of schiltrons, but on this occasion more by accident than design. Once across the river the three wings converged to form one huge mass of pikemen, whose flanks were unprotected, because Argyll's Highlanders had left the battlefield after coming under fairly intensive fire from Clinton's guns while crossing the Esk, and on the other flank what was left of the cavalry remained detached from the battle. However, these sturdy infantrymen, with their leather-quilted jacks, steel helmets and huge pikes, kneeling or standing shoulder to shoulder, were perfectly capable of withstanding cavalry – although, of course, hopelessly vulnerable to artillery.

The fight, which probably took place just south of Pinkie House, where the railway line now crosses arable fields, was hard pounding from start to finish. Most of Somerset's cavalry was on his left wing, and at a time when the Scots, who had advanced from the river at a great pace, had momentarily halted, Lord Grey led his troops against Huntly's division, which was positioned at the north-east of the phalanx. The Scottish ranks were immovable.

The pikemen stood their ground, battered but defiant. When the first charge was thrown back Somerset ordered another, this time against Arran's troops, and once more the horsemen threw themselves upon that bristling wall of steel, only to recoil with their mounts jumping over heaps of corpses and groaning men. Sir Andrew Flammock, who carried the royal standard of England, was nearly taken; however, he emerged from the fray with the standard (less its staff) safely in his keeping. But the enemy had been halted and Somerset had had time to adjust his line and bring his artillery to bear upon the huge and unwieldy mass of Scottish foot. The cavalry had not charged in vain.

Once the guns were in position, the English superiority in this arm was soon to win the day. The sakers had a point-blank range of about 340 paces and the gunners could have asked for no easier or more satisfactory target. As they raked the solid mass of pikemen, the Scots could be seen quivering and writhing under the repeated volleys. Wedged tight, they could only stand and stare as the cannon pulverized the phalanx and cut swathes down which the dead and dying slowly sank to the ground. Now it was also the turn of the Spanish arquebusiers who, riding at full tilt along the flanks of the enemy, poured their fire with devastating effect into the mass of helpless pikemen. At this stage of the battle Somerset decided that the Scots were sufficiently battered for him to advance his infantry, and before their bowstrings could become dampened by the heavy rain that descended over the field his archers had sent a hail of arrows into the rapidly disintegrating Scottish schiltron.

Somerset, with Warwick beside him, had been carefully watching the growing discomfort of the Scots, and when this three-pronged assault of artillery, arquebusiers and archers had thrown the enemy completely off balance he ordered the cavalry to sweep down on them again. In the noise and tumult of this very confused close combat it is difficult to say which division of the Scots broke first. Contemporary accounts agree that Angus was the one commander to keep his head and realize the necessity of an orderly withdrawal out of artillery range, but whether Arran's centre had already broken, or whether seeing Angus's men fall back they lost heart and ran, is uncertain. Visibility had become poor during the rain storm and at one stage Huntly's men mistook Angus's men for English, which only added to the confusion of the hapless Scots. Small wonder, then, that when they saw the whirlwind of English cavalry descend upon them the Scots had had enough. The whole army broke and streamed across the rivers. Some made for Dalkeith, others went back through their camp towards Edinburgh, while yet others raced along the seashore for Leith.

Thus in a matter of hours the entire chivalry of Scotland was beaten. Retreat developed into rout; the English army had by now shaken off the bonds of discipline, and overtaking their ancient foe before they could reach sanctuary scythed them down in thousands. Figures vary, but in the few hours that it took Somerset and his officers to regain control the slaughter had been immense; and no doubt there were many of rank who might have been spared for ransom had they not been dressed like their men. Probably around 10,000 Scots perished on the fields surrounding Pinkie Cleuch that day.* The roll of honour was long and illustrious: Lords Elphinstone, Cathcart and Fleming, Sir James Gordon of Lochinvar, Sir Robert Douglas of Lochleven and many other gentlemen of note. Lord Huntly was unhorsed and soon taken, Lord Home had been wounded the day before and his son captured, Lord Hay of Yester, Sir John Wemyss and the Master of Sempill were also among the prisoners. Angus lay in a furrow and feigned death until the pursuit had passed him, when he found a horse and escaped. The English lost about 500 men, most of whom were from the heavy cavalry, and Edward Shelley, commander of the 'Bulleners' – as the Boulogne horse were called – was England's only important captain killed; Lord Grey had a pike wound in the mouth and many others were wounded, including Sir Thomas Darcy, and Pedro de Gamboa. For the next two days men and women would be searching among the carnage and the debris to remove for decent burial the mortal remains of those they had lost.

The road to Edinburgh, and beyond to Stirling if need be, lay open to the conqueror; but during the next week the English remained comparatively inactive in the area of Leith, which town was burned, as was Kinghorn on the other side of the Forth. It is very difficult to fathom Somerset's thinking at this time. He must have realized that one victory – conclusive as it was – could not by itself achieve its object. He had the Scots at his mercy, and had he acted swiftly he might have seized the young queen before she could be moved to the comparative safety of the island of Inchmahone. Such an action would have enraged the Scots, but Pinkie had done that already, and it would have completely checkmated French designs. Here was a war that probably should never have been started, but once embarked upon should have been pressed to its logical conclusion. As it was, Somerset hoped to control an embittered nation by the retention of a number of strongpoints, and

*Estimates made by Somerset and others present at the battle vary from 7,000 to 14,000, but most accounts fix the figure as around 10,000.

before he left the country – or very shortly afterwards – the English had taken and garrisoned Blackness, the islands of Inchcolm and Inchkeith controlling the Firth of Forth, Broughty Castle at the mouth of the Tay, Dundee, Haddington (whose garrison and defences he later greatly strengthened), and a number of border towns and castles.

At the end of 1547 Somerset had a firm grip on Scotland. Lord Grey had been put in command of the north with his centre on Berwick; he was also Warden of the East Marches, while Lord Wharton remained in charge of the west marches, from which he made frequent sallies into Annandale, doing a considerable amount of damage. Sir Andrew Dudley had command of that exposed and vulnerable outpost Broughty Castle, which the Scots very nearly took back in November, and from it he attempted to hold Dundee. Sir John Luttrell commanded the important island of Inchcolm.

But the year 1548 was one of mixed fortunes for the English cause in the north. Haddington, whose tactical importance was considerable, was to be besieged by a large Franco-Scottish force, and in July the French ambassador met the Scottish Estates in the abbey there – which lay just outside the besieged town – and informed them that Henry II had decided that Mary Queen of Scots should marry the Dauphin. Assent to this match was given 'unanimously', on the understanding that the Scots would retain their freedom, ancient laws and liberties, but there were those among the nobility – and in particular Arran – who thoroughly disliked the strengthening of the French bond. However, the Queen Dowager was now in the ascendant, and by 13 August the Scottish Queen was safely in France, and Somerset must have realized that all hopes of a marriage between her and Edward were gone.

Bibliography

Chapter 1: Norsemen
Chapter 2: Normans
Belloc, Hilaire, *William the Conqueror*,
Peter Davies, 1933.
Bryant, Arthur, *The Story of England*,
Collins, 1953.
Burne, A. H., *Battlefields of England*
(ch. 2 only), Methuen, 1950.
Burne, A. H., *More Battlefields of England*
(ch. 1 only), Methuen, 1952.
Complete Peerage, The, Vol. XII, Pt. I,
St Catherine Press, 1953.
Compton, Piers, *Harold the King*,
Robert Hale, 1961.
Churchill, Winston S., *A History of the*
English Speaking Peoples, Vol. I,
Cassell, 1956.
Douglas, D. C., *William the Conqueror*,
Eyre and Spottiswoode, 1964.
Freeman, E. A., *The Norman Conquest*,
Clarendon Press, 1869.
Fuller, J. F. C., *The Decisive Battles of the*
Western World, Vol. I (ch. 2 only),
Eyre and Spottiswoode, 1954.
George, H. B., *Battles of English History*,
Methuen, 1895.
Lemmon, C. H., *The Field of Hastings*
(ch. 2 only), Budd and Gillatt, 1957.
McGuffie, T. H., 'October 14th, 1066',
History Today, Oct. 1966.
Muntz, Hope, *The Golden Warrior*,
Chatto and Windus, 1948.
Oman, Charles, *A History of the Art of War*
in the Middle Ages, Methuen, 2nd
edition, 1924.
Ramsay, James, *The Foundations of*
England, Vol. II, Swan Sonnenschein,
1898.
Schofield, Guy, 'The Third Battle of 1066',
History Today, Oct. 1966.
Spatz, W., *Die Schlacht von Hastings*, 1896.
Stenton, F. M., *Anglo-Saxon England*,
Clarendon Press, 1943.
Stenton, F. M., *William the Conqueror*
and the Rule of the Normans, Putnam,
1908.

Primary Source
William of Poitiers, *Gesta Willelemi Ducis*
Normannorum et Regis Anglorum,
part translated in *English Historical*
Documents, Vol. 2, Eyre and
Spottiswoode, 1953.

Chapter 3: The Barons' War—Lewes
Chapter 4: The Barons' War—Evesham
Beamish, Tufton, *Battle Royal*, Muller,
1965.
Bémont, Charles, *Simon de Montfort*,
trans. E. F. Jacob, Clarendon Press, 1930.
Blaauw, William Henry, *The Barons' War*,
Baxter, 1844.
Bryant, Arthur, *The Story of England*,
Collins, 1953.
Burne, A. H. *Battlefields of England*
(ch. 4 only), Methuen, 1950.
Burne, A. H., *More Battlefields of England*
(ch. 3 only), Methuen, 1952.
Churchill, Winston S., *A History of the*
English Speaking Peoples, Vol. I,
Cassell, 1956.
Davis, H. W. C., *England under the*
Normans and Angevins, Methuen, 1905.
Denholm-Young, N., *Collected Papers*,
University of Wales Press, 1969.
Knowles, C. H., 'Simon de Montfort
1265–1965', Historical Association
Pamphlet 3409, 1965.
Labarge, Margaret (Mrs Margaret Wade),
Simon de Montfort, Eyre and
Spottiswoode, 1962.
Oman, Charles, *A History of the Art of War*
in the Middle Ages, Methuen, 2nd
edition, 1924.
Powicke, F. M., *King Henry III and the Lord*
Edward, Vols. I and II, Clarendon
Press, 1947.
Powicke, F. M., R. F. Treharne and
C. H. Lemmon, *The Battle of Lewes:*
Essays, Friends of Lewes Society, 1964.
Ramsay, James, *The Dawn of the*
Constitution, 1216–1307, Swan
Sonnenschein, 1908.
Stubbs, William, *Select Charters*, 9th
edition revised by H. W. C. Davis,
Clarendon Press, 1929.
Treharne, R. F., *The Baronial Plan of*
Reform 1258–1263, Manchester University
Press, 1932.
Treharne, R. F., 'The Personal Role of
Simon de Montfort in the Period of
Baronial Reform and Rebellion, 1258–
1265', *Proceedings of the British*
Academy XL, 1954.

Primary Sources
Chronicle by Monk of Lewes, MSS Cott.
Tib. A.X.

224

Chronicle of John de Oxenede, MSS. Cott. Nero, D.II.
Chronicle of Lanercost Abbey, MSS. Harl. 2425.
Chronicle of William of Hemingford, MSS. Cott. Nero, D.II.
Chronicle of William of Knighton, MSS. Cott. Nero, D.II.
De Bellis Lewes et Evesham, MS. Cott. Claudius, D.VI (*Chronicle of William de Rishanger*).
Halliwell, J. O., ed., *Great Chronicles of St Albans*, being the chronicle of Matthew Paris extending to 1259 and William de Rishanger continued to 1322, Rolls Series, Vol. 28, 1863–76.
Holinshed's Chronicle, Vol. II, London, 1807.
Rymer, Thomas, *Foedera*, Vols. I and II, London, 1704–32.

Chapter 5: The Scottish Struggle for Independence—Stirling Bridge and Falkirk
Barrow, G. W. S., *Robert Bruce*, Eyre and Spottiswoode, 1965.
Brown, P. Hume, *History of Scotland*, Vol. I, Cambridge University Press, 1899.
Boutell, Charles, *Arms and Armour*, Reeves and Turner, 1874.
George, H. B., *Battles of English History*, Methuen, 1895.
Grimley, Gordon, *The Book of the Bow*, Putnam, 1958.
Mackenzie, Agnes Mure, *The Kingdom of Scotland*, Chambers, 1940.
Ramsay, James, *The Dawn of the Constitution, 1216–1307*, Swan Sonnenschein, 1908.

Primary Sources
Chronicle of Lanercost Abbey, MSS. Harl. 2425.
Chronicle of Walter of Guisborugh, also referred to as Walter of Hemingford.
Chronicle of William de Rishanger, MS. Cott. Claudius, D.VI.
Stubbs, William, ed. *Vita et Mars Edwardi Secundi*, Chronicles and Memorials of Great Britain and Ireland during the Middle Ages, London, 1883.

Chapter 6: The Scottish Struggle for Independence—Bannockburn
Barrow, G. W. S., *Robert Bruce*, Eyre and Spottiswoode, 1965.
Brown, P. Hume, *History of Scotland*, Vol. I, Cambridge University Press, 1899.
Boutell, Charles, *Arms and Armour*, Reeves and Turner, 1874.
Christison, General Sir Philip, Bt, and Iain Cameron Taylor, *Bannockburn: A Soldier's Appreciation of the Battle*, National Trust for Scotland, 1960.

George, H. B., *Battles of English History*, Methuen, 1895.
Linklater, Eric, *Robert the Bruce*, Peter Davies, 1934.
Mackenzie, Agnes Mure, *The Kingdom of Scotland*, Chambers, 1940.
Mackenzie, W. M., *The Battle of Bannockburn*, James MacLehose, 1913.
Maxwell, Sir Herbert, Bt, *Robert the Bruce*, Putnam, 1897.
Morris, John E., *Bannockburn*, Cambridge University Press, 1914.
Oman, Charles, *A History of the Art of War in the Middle Ages*, Methuen, 2nd edition, 1924.
Ramsay, James, *The Dawn of the Constitution, 1216–1307*, Swan Sonnenschein, 1908.
White, Robert, *A History of the Battle of Bannockburn*, Edinburgh, 1871.

Primary Sources
Barbour, John of Aberdeen, *The Bruce*, ed. J. Pinkerton, London, 1790.
Chronicle of Lanercost Abbey, MSS. Harl. 2425.
Chronicle of Walter of Guisborugh, also referred to as Walter of Hemingford.
Chronicle of William de Rishanger, MS. Cott. Claudius, D.VI.
Gray, Sir Thomas of Heton, *Scalacronica*, ed. J. Stevenson, Maitland Club, 1836.
Holinshed's Chronicle, Vol. II, London, 1807.
Vita et Mod Edwardi Secundi, Chronicles and Memorials of Great Britain and Ireland during the Middle Ages, London, 1883.

Chapter 7: The Wars of the Roses— A General Survey
Ashdown, Charles Henry, *British and Foreign Armies and Armour*, T. C. and E. C. Jack, 1909.
Boutell, Charles, *Arms and Armour*, Reeves and Turner, 1874.
Burne, A. H., *Battlefields of England*, Methuen, 1950.
Churchill, Winston S., *A History of the English Speaking Peoples*, Vol. I, Cassell, 1956.
Harriss, G. L., 'The Struggle for Calais: an Aspect of the Rivalry between Lancaster and York', *English Historical Review*, LXXV, 1960.
Kendall, P. M., *Warwick the Kingmaker*, Allen and Unwin, 1959.
Mowat, R. B., *The Wars of the Roses*, Crosby Lockwood, 1914.
Oman, Charles, *The Political History of England, 1377–1485*, Longmans, 1910.
Oman, Charles, *Warwick the Kingmaker*, Macmillan, 1905.
Ramsay, James, *Lancaster and York: 1399–1485*, Vol. II, Clarendon Press, 1892.

Scofield, Cora L., *The Life and Reign of Edward IV*, Vol. I, Longmans, 1923.
Wolffe, B. P., *Fifteenth Century England: 1399–1509* (the personal rule of Henry VI), Manchester University Press, 1972.
Young, Peter, and John Adair, *Hastings to Culloden*, G. Bell, 1964.

Primary Sources
Bruce, John, ed., *Historie of the arrivall of Edward IV in England*, Camden Society, 1838.
Gairdner, James, ed., *The Historical Collections of a Citizen of London in the Fifteenth Century*, Camden Society, 1876. (William Gregory, Mayor of London 1451–2, was author until 1452.)
Gairdner, James, ed., *The Paston Letters* A.D. *1422–1509*, 6 vols, Chatto and Windus, 1904.
Hall's Chronicle, London, 1809.
Whethamstede, John, *Registrum Abbatiae Johannis, Whethamstede*, 2 vols, ed. Henry T. Riley, Rolls Series, 1872.

Chapter 8: The Second Battle of St Albans

Ashdown, Charles Henry, *The Battles and Battlefields of St Albans*, Gibbs and Bamforth, 1913.
Burne, A. H., *Battlefields of England*, Methuen, 1950.
Kendall, P. M., *Warwick the Kingmaker*, Allen and Unwin, 1959.
Mowatt, R. B., *The Wars of the Roses*, Crosby Lockwood, 1914.
Oman, Charles, *Warwick the Kingmaker*, Macmillan, 1905.
Ramsay, James, *Lancaster and York: 1399–1485*, Vol. II, Clarendon Press, 1892.
Young, Peter, and John Adair, *Hastings to Culloden*, G. Bell, 1964.

Primary Sources
Gairdner, James, ed., *The Historical Collections of a Citizen of London in the Fifteenth Century*, Camden Society, 1876. (William Gregory, Mayor of London 1451–2, was author until 1452.)
Standing, Percy Cross, ed., *Memorials of Old Hertfordshire*, London, 1905.
Stow, John, *Annales*, London, 1615.
Waurin, Jehande, *Anchiennes et Chroniques d'Engleterre*, Vols. II and III, ed. Mlle Dupont, Paris, 1859.
Whethamstede, John, *Registrum Abbatiae Johannis, Whethamstede*, 2 vols, ed. Henry T. Riley, Rolls Series, 1872.

Chapter 9: The Battle of Towton

Burne, A. H., *Battlefields of England*, Methuen, 1950.
Kendall, P. M., *Warwick the Kingmaker*, Allen and Unwin, 1959.
Markham, Sir Clement, 'The Battle of Towton', *Yorkshire Archaeological and Topographical Journal*, X, 1889.
Mowat, R. B., *The Wars of the Roses*, Crosby Lockwood, 1914.
Oman, Charles, *A History of the Art of War in the Middle Ages*, Vol. II, Methuen, 2nd edition, 1924.
Oman, Charles, *Warwick the Kingmaker*, Macmillan, 1905.
Peel, Frank, 'The Battle of Towton', paper read before the Heckmondwike Antiquarian Society in 1884.
Ramsay, James, *Lancaster and York: 1399–1485*, Vol. II, Clarendon Press, 1892.
Ransome, Cyril, 'The Battle of Towton', *English Historical Review*, IV, 1889.
Young, Peter, and John Adair, *Hastings to Culloden*, G. Bell, 1964.

Primary Sources
Ellis, Sir Henry, ed., *Three books of Polydore Vergil's English History, comprising the reigns of Henry VI, Edward IV and Richard III*, Camden Society, 1844.
Gairdner, James, ed., *The Historical Collections of a Citizen of London in the Fifteenth Century*, Camden Society, 1876. (William Gregory, Mayor of London 1451–2, was author until 1452.)
Gairdner, James, ed., *The Paston Letters* A.D. *1422–1509*, 6 vols, Chatto and Windus, 1904.
Hall's Chronicle, London, 1809.
Vergil, Polydore, *Anglicae Historiae*, Camden Society, 1884.
Whethamstede, John, *Registrum Abbatiae Johannis, Whethamstede*, 2 vols, ed. Henry T. Riley, Rolls Series, 1872.

Chapter 10: The Battle of Barnet

Burne, A. H., *Battlefields of England*, Methuen, 1950.
Cass, Frederick Charles, 'The Battle of Barnet', *Transactions of the London and Middlesex Archaeological Society*, 1890.
Honeybourne, M. B., 'Battle of Barnet', Barnet Press, 1971.
Kendall, P. M., *Warwick the Kingmaker*, Allen and Unwin, 1959.
Mowat, R. B., *The Wars of the Roses*, Crosby Lockwood, 1914.
Oman, Charles, *The Political History of England, 1377–1485*, Vol. II, Longmans, 1910.
Oman, Charles, *Warwick the Kingmaker*, Macmillan, 1905.
Ramsay, James, *Lancaster and York: 1399–1485*, Vol. II, Clarendon Press, 1892.

Primary Sources
Bruce, John, ed., *Historie of the arrivall of Edward IV in England*, Camden Society, 1838.

226

Chronicle of the Abbey of Croyland (third continuation), trans. from the Latin by Henry T. Riley, London, 1854.
Gairdner, James, ed., *The Paston Letters* A.D. *1422–1509*, 6 vols, Chatto and Windus, 1904.
Hall's Chronicle, London, 1809.
Holinshed's Chronicle, Vol. III, London, 1808.
Standing, Percy Cross, ed., *Memorials of Old Hertfordshire*, London, 1905.
Stow, John, *Annales*, 1614.

Chapter 11: The Battle of Tewkesbury
Burne, A. H., *Battlefields of England*, Methuen, 1950.
George, H. B., *Battles of English History*, Methuen, 1895.
Hammond, P. W., H. G. Shearring and G. Wheeler, 'The Battle of Tewkesbury', Tewkesbury Festival Committee, 1971.
Oman, Charles, *A History of the Art of War in the Middle Ages*, Vol. II, Methuen, 2nd edition, 1924.
Oman, Charles, *The Political History of England, 1377–1485*, Longmans, 1910.
Ramsay, James, *Lancaster and York: 1399–1485*, Vol. II, Clarendon Press, 1892.
Simons, Eric N., *The Reign of Edward IV*, Muller, 1966.
Young, Peter, and John Adair, *Hastings to Culloden*, G. Bell, 1964.

Primary Sources
Bruce, John, ed., *Historie of the arrivall of Edward IV in England*, Camden Society, 1838.
Gairdner, James, ed., *The Paston Letters* A.D. *1422–1509*, 6 vols, Chatto and Windus, 1904.
Hall's Chronicle, London, 1809.
Holinshed's Chronicle, Vol. III, London, 1808.

Chapter 12: Bosworth Field
Barrett, C. R. B., *Battles and Battlefields in England*, A.D. Innes, 1896.
Brooke, Richard, *Visits to Fields of Battle in England*, John Russell Smith, 1857.
Burne, A. H., *Battlefields of England*, Methuen, 1950.
Cheetham, Anthony, *The Life and Times of Richard III*, Weidenfeld and Nicolson, 1972.
Gairdner, James, 'The Battle of Bosworth', *Archaeologia*, LV, 1896.
Hutton, W., *The Battle of Bosworth Field*, London, 1813.
Markham, Sir Clement, *Richard III: His Life and Character*, Smith, Elder, 1906.
Oman, Charles, *The Political History of England, 1377–1485*, Vol. II, Longmans, 1910.
Ramsay, James, *Lancaster and York: 1399–1485*, Clarendon Press, 1892.

Young, Peter, and John Adair, *Hastings to Culloden*, G. Bell, 1964.

Primary Sources
Chronicle of the Abbey of Croyland (third continuation), trans. from the Latin by Henry T. Riley, London, 1854.
Ellis, Sir Henry, ed., *Three books of Polydore Vergil's English History, comprising the reigns of Henry VI, Edward IV and Richard III*, Camden Society, 1844.
Hall's Chronicle, London, 1809.

Chapter 13: Scotland and the Tudors— Flodden
Barnett, Correlli, *Britain and Her Army, 1509–1970*, Alan Lane, Penguin Press, 1970.
Barrett, C. R. B., *Battles and Battlefields in England*, A. D. Innes, 1896.
Brown, P. Hume, *History of Scotland*, Vol. I, Cambridge University Press, 1899.
Burne, A. H., *Battlefields of England*, Methuen, 1950.
Churchill, Winston S., *A History of the English Speaking Peoples*, Vol. II, Cassell, 1956.
Elliot, Fitzwilliam Elliot Andrew, *The Battle of Flodden and Raids of 1513*, Andrew Elliot, 1911.
George, H. B., *Battles of English History*, Methuen, 1895.
Leather, G. F. T., *New Light on Flodden*, Martins Printing Works, Berwick-upon-Tweed, 1937.
McEwan, Sir John of Marchmont, Bt, *The Battle of Flodden*, privately printed, 1962.
Mackenzie, Agnes Mure, *The Kingdom of Scotland*, Chambers, 1940.
Mackenzie, W. M., *The Secret of Flodden*, Grant and Murray, 1931.
Oman, Charles, *A History of the Art of War in the 16th Century*, Methuen, 1937.
Vickers, Kenneth H., *A History of Northumberland*, Vol. XI, Andrew W. Reid, 1922.

Primary Sources
Articles of Battle, or Gazette of the Battle of Flodden, as published in John Pinkerton, *History of Scotland*, Vol. II, p. 456, London, 1797.
Faques, Richard, 'The Trewe Encountre or Batayle lately don betwene Englande and Scotlande', taken from John Skelton, *A ballade of the Scottysshe Kynge*, London, 1882.
Hall's Chronicle, London, 1809.
Holinshed's Chronicle, Vol. II, London, 1807.
Letters and Papers of Henry VIII, Vol. I, Part II, arranged and catalogued by James Gairdner, H.M.S.O., 1905.

Lindesay, Robert of Pitscottie, *The Historie and Cronicles of Scotland*, Vol. I, ed. A. H. G. MacKay, William Blackwood, 1899.

Chapter 14: The Tudors in Scotland Pinkie Cleuch

Arber, E., *An English Garner: Tudor Tracts*, Constable, 1903.
Barnett, Correlli, *Britain and Her Army, 1509–1970*, Alan Lane, Penguin Press, 1970.
Brown, P. Hume, *Short History of Scotland*, Oliver and Boyd, 1955.
Dalyell, J. G., *Fragments of Scottish History*, 1798.
Fergusson, James, *The White Hind*, Faber, 1963.
Jordan, W. K., *Edward VI: The Young King*, Allen and Unwin, 1970.
Oman, Charles, *A History of the Art of War in the 16th Century*, Methuen, 1937.
Pollard, A. F., *England Under Protector Somerset*, Routledge and Kegan Paul, 1900.

Primary Sources
Hamilton Papers, The, Vol. II, B.M.
Murray, J. H., ed., *The Complaynte of Scotlande*, Early English Text Society, 1872–3.

Lindesay, Robert of Pitscottie, *The Cronicles of Scotland*, Vol. II, ed. J. G. Dalyell, Edinburgh, 1814.

List of books studied in connection with armour, weapons and uniforms

Ashdown, C. H., *British and Foreign Arms and Armour*, T. C. and E. C. Jack, 1909.
Collie, G. F., *Highland Dress*, King Penguin, 1948.
Ffoulkes, Charles, *Armour and Weapons*, Clarendon Press, 1909.
Hunter, Edmund, *Arms and Armour*, Wills and Hepworth, 1971.
Journals of the Society for Army Historical Research, 1921–73.
McClintock, H. F., *Old Irish and Highland Dress*, Dundalgan Press (W. Tempest), 2nd edition, 1950.
Martin, Paul, *Armour and Weapons*, H. Jenkins, 1968.
Norman, Vesey, *Arms and Armour*, Weidenfeld and Nicolson, 1964.
Tappan, E. M., *In Feudal Times*, Harrap, 1931.
Tylden, Major G., *Horses and Saddlery*, J. A. Allen, 1965.
Wilkinson, F., *Arms and Armour*, Ward Lock, 1965.

Index

228